Sturgis

The Story
of the Rally

By Carl Edeburn

✱ Dimensions Press • Brookings, South Dakota

Sturgis: The Story of the Rally

Contents

Acknowledgments

The author is deeply indebted to many individuals who were willing to share their time, inspiration and collections of photographs, rally memorabilia, and memories. Of special note is Pearl Hoel, who provided me with unlimited access to her personal file of pictures and press clippings. At age 97, she also insisted that I stay at her house while doing research in Sturgis — further insisting to prepare breakfast every morning during each stay! Her son, Jack Hoel, also deserves recognition for his assistance in reading and commenting on the manuscript for the early years, providing factual information as well as editorial input. Dick O'Leary, Neil Hultman and Don Vodden comprise a trio of wonderful helpers who provided encouragement, pictures, text, and helpful commentary throughout this process.

The author is also deeply indebted to Dr. John Miller of South Dakota State University for inspiration and encouragement in the initiation of this project. The support of Ken Stewart at the South Dakota State Archives Collection in providing access to the various microfilm files in the state collection was invaluable. The assistance and patience of the staff at the Brookings Public Library was also important. I am also deeply indebted to my son Andrew, who provided his editorial skill and support, and to my wife Cleo, who read all the copy. And, finally, thanks go out to all of those unknown reporters from the *Sturgis Tribune*, *The Rapid City Journal*, *The Black Hills Press*, and the *Rushmore Ads* who covered the rally in the local press.

Additional recognition and gratitude is given to the following: Lowell Amiotte, Everett Brashear, Al Burke, Hal Deckert, Babe DeMay, Dan Deubler, Roxanne and Steve Droste, Kevin Eilbeck, Dave and Kathy Estep, Vern Goodwin, Vicky Goss, Dave Hagen, Bobby and Nancy Hill, Johnny Isaacs, Bobby James, Ken James, Dee Johnson, Denny and Kari Kannenberg, Neil Keen, Gail and Corky Keener, Mike Kidd, Dick Klamfoth, Ann Kniffen, Gary Landeen, Cliff Majhor, Dr. Doug Malo (SDSU), Dick Mann, Bart and Joanne Markel, Bob Moore, Randee Peterson, Barbara Phillips, Terry Poovey, Paul Pressgrove, Peggy Reinhard, Kay Rogerson, Eva Satterlee, Janis Scheets, Charles Seale, Ron Spiegelhoff, Sammy Tanner, Don and Ellie Tindall, Bill Tuman, Keith Ulicki, Kevin Varnes, Don Vodden, Katy Wood (AMA), Kevin Wormstadt, and Ed Youngblood (AMA).

Dedication

This book is dedicated to Pearl Hoel. No one living or dead deserves more credit in relation to initiating, supporting, and maintaining the true spirit of the Sturgis Rally than this wonderful lady. Besides providing emotional support, one has to speculate about the economic and personal demands and the devotion to task Pearl Hoel demonstrated in the support of her husband's dream. How many times did she forgo the purchase of a new pair of shoes, a new dress, a new refrigerator, a new carpet or a new appliance for her kitchen, in the interest of supporting a need of the Gypsies in their weekly meetings, during motorcycle events, and in the massive planning efforts leading up to each year's "Classic"? How many hours of personal time did Pearl Hoel spend doing quiet little public relations moves in the Sturgis community? How many hours did she devote to cooking, typing, serving on committees, entertaining dozens of visitors in her back yard, and planning and delivering the picnic lunch for the Annual Gypsy Tours? How many of her personal efforts were extended during the establishment of the original motorcycle dealership and shop and during those four worrisome years between the demise of Indian and the final solution of associating with Yamaha?

Hats Off To You, Pearl!

Author's Foreword

For many years, beginning in high school, I had been fascinated with the idea of owning a motorcycle but had never had the time or financial resources. I suppose there was also the element of fear concerning the danger of crashing, but the actual decision to purchase one never evolved until I was settled in my career as a professor at South Dakota State University (SDSU) in Brookings, located in the eastern part of the state. One of my graduate students, Ralph, who was also the University Pilot, Director of Transportation and an avid rider, urged me to purchase a bike and join him in his obsession. He had given me riding lessons on his 100cc Honda Trailmaster and after passing my driving test on this little bike, I decided to give it a whirl.

So, in my 40th year, struggling with a bit of mid-life crisis, I purchased an old 250cc Honda Dream from another colleague who worked in the South Dakota Department of Education in Pierre. The price was right, the bike was an ugly cross between blue and purple, and a date was set in late March to ride with the Ralph as a passenger on his 90/6 Beemer the 200 miles to the State Capital to pick up this gem! Another gentleman, Wes, the University's Director of Finance, accompanied Ralph and me to Pierre. This fellow was riding a beautiful Irish Green 1973 600cc BMW, which I later learned was one of two motorcycles that he owned. When the pilot asked Wes why he was taking the old 60/5 instead of his new 90/6 BMW, Wes smiled and said that he wanted to get the winter bugs out of the 600. Little did I know what was going on!

We arrived in Pierre, rode around town and out into the countryside where I was able to take the doggish 250 up to minimal highway speed. After spending the night in a motel, we headed home to Brookings the next morning. On the way home, I realized that my 45 to 55 mph top speed on the Dream was a joke compared to the agility of the two Beemers. About half way home, Wes asked me if I wanted to try riding the 600. I climbed on the 600 and fell in love with it after about two miles. By the time we arrived home, I was quietly informed that he wanted to sell the BMW and asked if I was interested. I agonized for about three days and decided to do it. After selling two of my extra shotguns and wiping out a small savings account I was able to come up with the $1,200 to purchase the 600. On the next weekend we took a road trip into Minnesota and I thought I had died and gone to heaven!

In early May 1977 these two pals convinced me to accompany them on their annual trek to Las Vegas over the University interim break in May. I did and, for the first time ever, lived on a bike for 10 days. I was as ecstatic, addicted and actually hated the last 50 miles coming home — I knew this fabulous adventure was ending. We continued to ride during June and July, limiting our outings to evenings and weekends as my teaching responsibilities for summer school prohibited any longer trips.

When summer school ended on August 1, the next adventure was Sturgis! I knew little or nothing about the Black Hills Motor Classic and had no idea what was going to happen. I was just so happy to get on the road and experience three or four days of riding. It is really difficult to describe my emotions entering Sturgis from the east on Highway 34. By the time we passed the City Park, which was filled with tents and motorcycles, I saw no automobiles — only motorcycles buzzing up and down the stream of traffic. By the time I turned the corner onto Junction Avenue, rode the short block to Main Street and viewed the three blocks of parked motorcycles, my heart was in my throat and the only thought I had was, "What if everyone used motorcycles instead of automobiles for transportation?" In two short miles I had entered a different world.

Needless to say, after four days at the rally, my experience ended early Monday morning when I passed the park now empty and littered with refuse. Where did they all go? As I passed down Main Street, it was filled with cars. The horde of bikers and

The author, 1980.
(Author Photo)

my world of motorcycles had disappeared. My friends had returned to Brookings on Highway 34. I was alone, on my green 60/5, preparing to meet my wife and children at a friend's cabin deep in the Black Hills. As I ate breakfast in Bob's Café, I thought about my first Sturgis experience and reflected on what had happened to me.

I am sure that many of my readers can reflect on similar emotional experiences. As I sat there pondering my hashbrowns, I reflected on a parallel example. One of my best friends at SDSU describes herself as a "Trekkie". This means that she is a Star Trek fan. She does not reveal this fascination to anyone else in her college department, but every year under the auspices of visiting friends or going to a library meeting, she attends a national conference for Star Trek afficionados.

This friend's fascination with Star Trek closely parallels an individual need basic to all human needs — the desire as a member of any minority to belong to a larger circle or society of friends with similar needs and desires. This typical sociological pattern is related to a person's desire to validate his or her personal desire in belonging to the minority group by identifying with a larger and more respectable majority.

Most of the readers who are motorcyclists will quickly understand this phenomenon. Since motorcyclists comprise a minority in the general population, living in this grouping impacts the rider's experiences, resulting in the variety of social and emotional reactions from others that range from outright disdain, scorn and ridicule to actual jealousy, admiration and respect.

Some riders focus on the negative vibes they receive from members of the general population, while others bask in the admiration of those who would dearly love to ride a motorcycle. Some riders are so seriously affected by the disdain and scorn that they, like my librarian friend, hide or apologize for their behavior. Others in responding to such attitudes strike out, flaunting their unique interest in riding by flying in the face of political correctness in their actions and deeds. Most riders, whether they rationalize their minority status, defend the cycling life by searching for others who share their fascination. Evidences of this need at the local level can evolve in phenomena such as the establishment of marque loyalty (generally enhanced by the local Harley Davidson, BMW or Honda dealerships) and/or in local riding clubs. Some band together across the makes and models of bikes or by just hanging out, touring and/or attending motorcycle events. The result of these small group activities results in the evolution of biker bars, restaurants, or other hangouts where the participants can get together, kick tires, compare accessories and show off new trends of motorcycle clothing. Serious riders generally attempt to meet with persons with similar inclinations and motivations at least once a week.

When the first-time rally visitor rides into Sturgis, he or she enters a world where the major means of transport is the motorcycle. The stores and merchants sell only motorcycle related accoutrements and almost everyone you meet rides a motorcycle. This general atmosphere is enhanced by the echoes and odors of hundreds of motorcycle engines alternately assaulting and complementing one's auditory senses. In short, the rider sees, feels, smells, and listens to motorcycles. The Sturgis visitor quickly arrives at the realization and pleasure in imagining how great life would be if everyone lived and acted this way!

At Sturgis this emotion builds from the beginning of bike week on Monday, peaks about mid-week and generally results with pathos, regret, and sorrow in having to return to the reality of an automobile-dominated society on Monday. I was sitting at Bob's over breakfast experiencing this very pathos!

As I stabbed my last piece of toast another reflection emerged in my mind. How in the world did all of this evolve? What had enticed 60,000 motorcycles and an estimated 80,000 persons to come to this sleepy little town for one week in the summer of 1977? How did people know about it? When did it begin? Why did they come to Sturgis instead of dozens of other small towns across America? As a teenager I had seen "The Wild Ones," a movie starring a youthful Marlon Brando in which a motorcycle gang had rioted and taken over a small California town. Why was the Sturgis rally, with sixty thousand participants, not subject to such discord and violence? How did the rally begin? When did it start?

As all of these questions flew around in my mind, I challenged myself to find a book or to look up information concerning the answers to these questions when I returned home to my job at SDSU.

After my return, I went looking for those very answers. Little or nothing could be found. As a professional social scientist, my next step was to visit with my colleagues in the Sociology Department because I felt that my 10 undergraduate credits in sociology had left me with a serious inadequacy in this discipline. I was essentially stonewalled by each of the faculty members I contacted. Either they were unaware, didn't care, or were openly opposed to motorcycling in general. I next turned to a cultural geographer and got the same response.

Finally, I began to visit with older motorcyclists and ask them about Sturgis. During the rally I had heard some mention of "The Races". I also noted that older persons, who recognized me as a rider, would ask if I attended the "Races" in Sturgis. Younger persons would generally react with the question: "Do you go to the Sturgis Rally?" I soon realized that older people in South Dakota still refer to the event as "The Races".

*Main Street
Sturgis, 1979.
(Author Photo)*

With this new knowledge in hand, I sought out Wes, the purveyor of my green 60/
5 BMW and one of my rally companions. On the last day of the rally, Wes had gone to
some "long track" race while Ralph and I had taken a tour to Mt. Rushmore and the
Needles Highway. Since my pack of rally companions had returned to Brookings
without me and I had remained to complete the family vacation, I had not had the
opportunity to talk with Wes about the "The Races".

At this point in my life it seems to be ludicrous that I could spend four days at the
Rally and not know anything about "The Races". In reflection, however, I am sure
that there are many reading this book who actually experienced a similar lack of aware-
ness. The excuse for my ignorance is that by 1977 the rally provided such a variety of
things to do, to see, and to experience that in the four days, racing had not impacted
my visit!

After visiting with Wes I learned that the Long Track was actually a half-mile track
and that the Short Track was a shorter, 1/5 mile racing oval. Wes was ecstatic in describing the thrills and spills he had watched in Sunday's final championship race
program where nationally famous riders were competing. Wes began to fill me in on
his experiences in Sturgis. His first rally was in 1951 and he informed me that in the
early days, the only reason anyone came to Sturgis was to see the races. Wes was not
sure of the actual start of these events, but he was sure that it was sometime prior to
WWII. Since I could not find anything in writing, I was able to discover that 1977 was
the 37th rally and by simple calculation I determined that 1940 would have been the

start date. I later learned of the exclusion of activities during the four years of World War II and determined that the correct year of origin was 1937 or 1938, depending on the interpretation of the different promoters. I was a bit excited about 1937 because that was my birth year.

My next question for Wes was, "How did it start?"

He said "some guy named 'Pappy', who was an Indian Motorcycle Dealer, started it."

"Tell me more!" I begged.

"Don't know," was his answer.

The next year at Sturgis, I spent a good deal of time trying to find old timers in Sturgis who could answer my questions. I now realize I couldn't find anyone except visitors because all the old-timers were all working. Naturally I went to the races to check out that scene and got to see this "Pappy Hoel" guy from a distance. He was working in the pits and was later honored by the PA announcer. The spectators were also informed that Hoel, now characterized as the "The Granddaddy of the Rally", had started the meet with the assistance of a motorcycle club – the Jackpine Gypsies. My initial quest for further information was not fruitful, but I did have a super time at the races.

I returned home, and as the years passed with several more trips to Black Hills Motor Classics, I learned some of the history about the rally's evolution. In 1982, I bought Clarence "Pappy" Hoel's book, *Bits and Pieces*, and learned a little about the early days of the rally. In 1983 I hit upon the idea of personally doing the actual research and writing my own book in a quest to answer my questions.

The author and editor, 1978. (Author Photo)

During the 1984 rally, I approached the people at the *Sturgis Tribune* and asked if I could have access to their file of old newspapers. They essentially blew me off and said they were soon going to write a history of the rally in-house. I tried again to reach the paper in 1988 through a friend who is a businessman in Sturgis. He relayed to me the same degree of non-interest from the local newspaper.

In the early 1990s I discovered that the Black Hills Area newspapers were on file in microfilm at the State Archives in Pierre. Until only recently, I was able to research the early years (1937-1941) and take some notes. I was resolved that, upon retirement, I would pursue my mission full speed.

This effort has finally been realized, and my understanding of how it all happened has been greatly expanded. The historical information in this book was retrieved from those Black Hills area newspaper archives that were accessible, motorcycling magazines like *American Motorcyclist* and *Rider*, AMA archives, and personal interviews with various Sturgis residents, surviving racers, their families and friends. I have worked diligently to retrieve and relate factual information as reported in the limited amount of printed materials available and recalled by the actual participants. I must apologize in advance for any incorrect assertions, including the misspellings of names or places. This book is, therefore, my humble attempt to document the birth, development and evolution of the world's largest motorcycle rally. The effort has fulfilled a personal need for me and hopefully an interesting diorama for you the reader. Enjoy!

Dr. Carl Edeburn
March 2003

Sturgis

The Story of the Rally

Chapter One: Roots

For those readers who are contemplating a first-time trip to the Sturgis Rally or for those who have visited before and want a better understanding of the rally's setting, a general introduction to the Black Hills of South Dakota, the community of Sturgis and the old Fort Meade Cavalry Post (now a Veteran's Administration Hospital) is almost essential. A short description of Bear Butte, a famous Sturgis landmark and sacred rallying point for early Native Americans, is also beneficial.

No history of the Sturgis Rally would be complete without a biographical overview of Clarence "Pappy" Hoel. His active participation in promoting motorcycling in the upper Midwest and especially in the Northern Black Hills is legendary. His initial work in organizing the Sturgis Rally and his continuing support and participation in maintaining its growth would, in themselves, provide for a separate biographical study. His personally-published memoirs, *Life's Bits and Pieces*, (Self Published, 1982) make for interesting reading of his rich and many faceted life.

The old maxim that states "behind every successful man there is a hard working, loving and devoted woman" is truly appropriate in the case of Pearl Hoel, when one comes to understand the efforts of this remarkable woman in the support of her husband's dream. This author met Pearl Hoel during her 96th year. She remains as devoted to the memory of Clarence and supportive of the Black Hills Motor Classic as she was when she participated in the seminal efforts that led to the evolution of this internationally-recognized event.

Don Vodden has been an invaluable resource for understanding both the Jackpine Gypsies and the Black Hills Motor Classic organization. As the last living charter member of the Gypsies, Vodden was able to furnish the author with an eyewitness account of the early struggle to initiate the rally in Sturgis. Don was a high school student when he met with the others to organize the Gypsies in 1936. He went on to become a respected racer at Sturgis and in Colorado. Before choosing a career in the US Army after World War Two, Vodden owned Don's Café, a Sturgis Main Street business known today as Bob's Café. As a local "proprietor" he was permitted to join the original Black Hills Motor Classic group, whose relationship with the Jackpine

Gypsies is explained more fully in ensuing chapters. Vodden, like Pappy Hoel, was highly respected and able to participate in both organizations. As a result, his insights into the early development of the rally are especially important.

Sturgis

The name of a small town nestled in the northwest margins of the Black Hills of South Dakota has become synonymous with motorcycling. This town is Sturgis, and the annual Black Hills Motor Classic held there draws in more visitors than any other motorcycle rally in the world.

Sturgis began as a small village serving the needs of early settlers and Ft. Meade, a cavalry post established east of town in 1878 and named for General George Gordon Meade (1815-1872) who commanded Union troops at Gettysburg in 1863.[1] Sturgis proper was named for either Major Samuel D. Sturgis, the first military commander of Fort Meade, or his son, Lieutenant J.G. Sturgis who died on the Custer battlefield in nearby Southeastern Montana.

Early soldiers identified Sturgis as "Scoop Town" or "Scoop," alluding to the troopers' forays into town where they were fleeced (hence, "scooped") by the rifraff and camp followers who populated this early Dakota Territory settlement. Perhaps the tedious work soldiers performed in cleaning the stables had some meaning in this

Machines of a different kind line Main Street Sturgis in the mid-1880s. (John C. H. Grabill Photo)

characterization as well. Whatever its origin, the name still prevails in that the Sturgis High School athletic teams are characterized as the "Scoopers."[2]

Another element related to the growth of Sturgis proper is its geographical position — nestled on the margin dividing the prairie and the Black Hills themselves. As a result, Sturgis became the Eastern gateway to the Deadwood gold mines. Boulder Canyon Highway (alternate U.S. Highway 14) traces this trail from the west side of Sturgis to nearby Deadwood – the legendary western community of Wild Bill Hickok and Calamity Jane. During rally week this winding route of twisting curves and tricky margins is one of the most often traveled venues as riders are drawn to both the history and the prospect of a good time in Deadwood. Boulder Canyon Highway is also one of the most dangerous routes a first-time Black Hills Motorcycle Classic visitor will ever experience.

The Black Hills

North Dakota has a range of hills called the Turtle Mountains. By contrast, South Dakota and eastern Wyoming are favored with a range of mountains named the "Black Hills." This title is somewhat confusing to first time regional visitors since the "Hills" are actually mountains, and the "mountains" of North Dakota are actually hills.
In 1868, the Fort Laramie Treaty formally established the Hills as the property of the Greater Sioux Nation and forbid white expansion into the area. For Native Americans, the Hills have always been sacred ground and are referred to as "Paha Sapa", which literally means "Hill Black" – an appropriate name for mountains that, when viewed from a distance, appear completely black.*

The subject of Indian Treaty suits since the 1870's, the Black Hills are still vehemently claimed by the Lakota and the Greater Sioux Nation. To the Sioux way of thinking, the "Hills" are still their sacred property. Visitors should be ever mindful of Native American views that the 1868 Treaty is still being violated.

Within the framework of the 1868 Treaty, the Lakota claim has never been disproven but has been largely ignored. This political reality stems from gold discoveries in the early 1870's and a subsequent U.S. Army expedition under the command of General George Custer. Commissioned to explore and protect Indian claims under the 1868 Treaty, the Custer expedition actually validated the presence of gold and publicized

---

* One of the interesting sidelights of this naming/translation process is that present day Lakota speakers suggest that the word Paha or Baha, in actual Lakota pronunciation, alludes to heights. Since the Sioux do not differentiate between hills or mountains, Baha was translated by early missionaries as "hills". These early priests viewed the Black Hills at a distance as low lying hills and then interpreted the meaning of Baha to be hills rather than mountains.[1]

the potential for prospecting. By 1876, the rush was on and the establishment of Deadwood and many other mining camps clearly evidenced the army's inability to prevent treaty violations.

To this day, elements of interest abound to trace both the history of Native American claims and the Black Hills gold rush of 1870s. The mining towns of Deadwood, Central City and Lead still provide fantastic insight to the boom years of over a century ago. Sacred sites of the Sioux and northern Cheyenne include Devils Tower in nearby eastern Wyoming, Crazy Horse Monument north of Custer, and directly adjacent to Sturgis, Bear Butte.

At Bear Butte, situated on the eastern outskirts of Sturgis, hikers and climbers will often encounter an individual Native American performing a sacred fast or pilgrimage at or near the summit. Both locals and motorcycle people visiting the area have generally respected these Native American rites, quietly and respectfully passing Indian spiritual activities without disturbing the participants.

The opportunity to both explore the natural beauty of the Hills and experience historical landmarks has greatly enhanced the evolution of the Black Hills as an extremely desirable touring destination. As characterized by the American Motorcyclist Association guidelines of the 1920s, the Sturgis experience in the Hills can be characterized as the "ultimate Gypsy Tour".[2] Present-day riders visiting the Rally generally cannot hope to see all of the sights during their first trip to Sturgis. As a result, they often return annually in hopes of seeing it all. Further, most riders will say that automobile tourists really have no conception of the beauty of the Black Hills experience unless they have viewed it from the seat of a motorcycle.

Bear Butte in Winter. (Author Photo)

Black Hills Geology 101

For a rally visitor to better understand the unique formation of the Black Hills, one has to imagine a huge, up-thrusting mass of magma, or molten rock, which formed the core of this small mountain range. The hot magma was in the shape of an oval massif extending from Lead and Deadwood in the north to Custer in the south. This chunk of what is now nearly solid granite is roughly fifty miles long north to south and 20 miles wide east to west. Additionally, as the magma thrust upward, it broke through massive layers of sedimentary limestone bedrock, forming a ring of block fault heights that surround the granite oval. These triangularly-shaped limestone hills (called Block Fault Mountains) can be observed to the east of Interstate 90 as visitors travel along the long valley from Rapid City to Sturgis. The hills west of Interstate 90 are the beginning elements of the granite (magma) core and form such heights as Harney Peak, Sylvan Lake, Mt. Rushmore and the Needles.

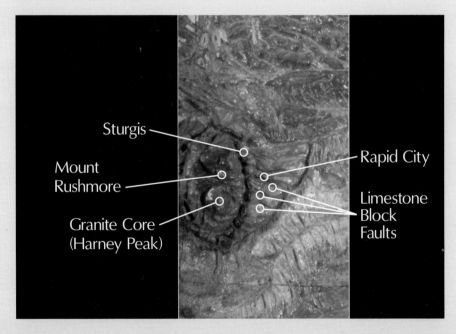

Topographic view of the Black Hills formation. (Courtesy of Dr. Doug Malo, South Dakota State University)

> For better understanding of the Hills' geological phenomena, visitors should visit Bear Butte or Devils Tower in Wyoming. These attractions are actually microcosyms of the larger Black Hills eruption. Devils Tower and Bear Butte were initially the result of an emerging granite core surrounded by limestone crust fractures. At both of these sites, and especially at Devil's Tower, the limestone fractures have eroded away, leaving only the harder granite core intact.

Pappy Hoel

Clarence "Pappy" Hoel, as characterized in the *Sturgis Gazette,* was born and spent all of his life in Sturgis. His father was a part-time freighter and cattleman in the Meade County area, and the Hoel family harvested, stored and delivered ice in the early days prior to refrigeration. Hoel maintained that he was one of the first persons to use a motorcycle to herd cattle and police fence lines.[1]

His life-long love of Indian motorcycles began with his first bike, which was sold to a cavalryman at Ft. Meade who transferred out before Hoel received payment. His second Indian, which had a sidecar, was purchased by Hoel and one of his friends while working in a Black Hills logging camp. The two partners stored the bike in a blacksmith shop somewhere between Rapid City and Sturgis. Hoel stated that he and the friend never returned to pick up this bike.[2]

His third bike was another sidecar-rigged Indian, which he acquired by trading an old smooth bore (worn out) rifle to a Finnish lumberjack. He wrecked this bike on the way to a football game in Spearfish when he rear-ended a Model T Ford while trying to impress some young ladies. He ripped his trousers badly in the crash, but the girls sewed them up so all of them could go to the game.

After spending some time in the Southwest picking fruit, Hoel returned home in 1928, married Pearl Kinney, and decided to get into the motorcycle business. He contacted the Harley dealer in Rapid City to try and set up a branch dealership in Sturgis. While waiting for this deal to materialize, Pappy wrote to the Indian Company and was awarded the Indian franchise for the Black Hills Area. Since he had no money, he talked one of his buddies into buying a new Indian and then used the bike as a demonstrator. He was soon able to sell enough bikes to have the money to locate the dealership in his garage in 1936 — one year before the first Sturgis Rally was held.[3]

Little by little, Hoel developed his Indian dealership into a flourishing operation until World War II broke out in 1941. Gas rationing limited the amount of fuel anyone could buy for automobiles. Ration books were issued for motorcycles limiting them to one gallon per week.[5]

As most motorcyclists know, the Indian Company did quite well in the years after World War II until the early 1950s. In the late 40s, Indian introduced a new line of vertical singles and twins. Pappy Hoel did extremely well in selling these new concept models and was the top dealer in the nation in 1947, selling 44 motorcycles (4.5 bikes/ 1000 population). His success was due in large part to the Indian's lightness and versatility for farm and ranch applications, as readily demonstrated by this enterprising dealer. One of Hoel's impressive efforts took place during a 1949 winter blizzard when train traffic was tied up in the Black Hills for 15 days. Pappy affixed skis to one of the new Indian lightweights and assisted the National Guard in prioritizing which ranches needed food, fuel and forage for cattle.[6]

When the Indian Motorcycle Company folded in 1953, Hoel obtained the dealership for Enfield Indians. These cycles were manufactured in England and were basically Royal Enfields with Indian logos and accessories attached. After the initial foray of these cycles in the U.S. market, problems in distribution and maintenance

Clarence "Pappy" Hoel
(Pearl Hoel Collection)

(parts) became too complicated to support dealer consistency. Although he worked on all brands and continued to repair and service Indians, Pappy Hoel had to abandon the cycle company he loved. He soon secured the dealership franchise for Yamaha, which he maintained until retirement in 1970.[7]

During the years of his Indian dealership, Pappy Hoel was involved in many promotional adventures that established both his persona and the quality of the Indian marquee. With good-natured bantering between Harley Davidson and Indian riders, arguments about cycle quality often led to wagers and ensuing competitions.[8]

One example related in Pappy's memoirs, *Life's Bits and Pieces*, tells the story of using a 27-tooth countershaft sprocket to win a bet. Pappy had a local machinist cut a new sprocket for his 1948 Bonneville Chief. Stock sprockets had fewer teeth to carry the power ratio forward in high gear. Hoel's bet with the crowd of Harley riders was that he could go 90 mph in second gear with his Bonneville. He did so and won the bet. He didn't tell them, however, that the 27-tooth sprocket limited him to 60 mph in third gear.[9]

Hoel's memoirs also relate his experiences with the Army. Since modern warfare essentially eliminated the horse cavalry in the late 1930s and early 40s, Fort Meade was in the process of converting to mechanized transportation in 1940 and 41. One of

Clarence Hoel behind the counter at his motorcyle shop. (Dick O'Leary Collection)

the Army's solutions to the practice of single-horse, single-rider was to place cavalry-men on motorcycles. As can be expected, a large number of these horse loving "hussars" hated the new cycles. According to Hoel, many of these riders sabotaged their machines so they could ride in trucks during convoy maneuvers. Apparently these motorcycle riders not only missed their faithful horses, but felt injury added to insult from the unbearable dust of other vehicles, being much closer to the ground on a bike than on horseback.[10]

At the beginning of the war, Pappy Hoel was hired by the Army to maintain and repair motorcycles at Ft. Meade. After completing (under budget) the rehabilitation of about 200 used Army motorcycles that had been shipped to Ft. Meade, Hoel was shipped to Cheyenne, Wyoming, to repeat this feat. The job at Ft. Meade was carried on during the winter and Pappy had many adventures riding back and forth from Cheyenne to Sturgis on his Indian sidecar rig. Later the family moved to the Cheyenne base, living in a small house trailer "about the size of a travel camper" according to son Jack Hoel.[11]

In the late 1940s, after the war, Pappy Hoel prepared a sidecar to use for hauling his racing bike. This should be interesting to contemporary tourers who use trailers. One wonders if he ever used this sidecar rig to pick up broken down bikes of his customers?[12]

While he was instrumental in organizing the Sturgis Field Meet in 1937 and helping set up the first AMA Sanctioned half-mile race in 1938, Pappy was never too excited about participating in dirt track racing. He preferred the hill climbs, trials and scrambles. He also loved the tricks, performing them at the rally and at county fairs around Western South Dakota and eastern Wyoming. In his autobiography he refers to this practice as "Tricks, Fun and Damned Foolishness". Early motorcycle tricks consisted of such stunts as lifting a side car over stakes and crashing into walls (using dry knotty 1 x 4 boards) and outhouses (constructed of tar paper). This last trick included one rider who took a large pill from the local doctor. He then ran to the outhouse only to have another rider crash through the privy, leaving him in red long johns with a handful of toilet paper. Two other tricks described by Hoel included circling the half-mile track with 12 men on his motorcycle and surfboard races where people rode on boards towed behind the bike (much like water skiers) as the bike circled the oval.[13]

Pappy Hoel's preference for motorcycle events other than track racing did not, however, prevent him from supporting the sport and sponsoring dozens of riders. During his years of involvement with motorcycling, Pappy grew to know and become valued friends of most of the nationally famous racers during the 1940s, 50s, 60s, and 70s.

Pappy always sponsored a rider at Sturgis and his son, Jack, after returning from a successful racing career while serving in the Army in Germany, nearly won the Sportsman Event at Daytona in the early 1960s.[14]

Pearl Hoel

This "most loyal and honorable" supporter of the Jackpine Gypsies Motorcycle Club was born in Cresline, Ohio on November 10, 1905. Her family moved to Rapid City when she was five years old,[1] and Pearl finished high school in Rapid City in 1923.

Because she was an outstanding student and had completed a "teaching class" during high school, the Pennington County Superintendent of Schools encouraged her to take a state exam that would allow her to teach in a rural school. Pearl passed the exam and assumed a teaching vacancy in Mystic, teaching eight children in grades 1-6. Since this was a rural school she ended up doing the custodial work and earned extra money cutting the children's hair and helping their mothers with hair styling.

Pearl Hoel, age 96, at the Sturgis Motorcycle Museum, April 2002. (Photo by Kevin Eilbeck)

After her first year at the Mystic school, Pearl attended Black Hills State Teachers College in Spearfish during the summer of 1924. This work enabled her to earn her First Grade Certificate, allowing her to teach in a graded (town) school. She took a position in Piedmont the next fall teaching third grade. While teaching at Piedmont, Pearl met Clarence (Pappy) Hoel on a blind date to a community dance in Sturgis, and they were married on May 19, 1928 – a union that would last 61 years until Pappy passed away in 1989. Their only child, Jack, was born in 1935.

As a new wife, Pearl gave up her teaching career and began looking for work in Sturgis. When the Hoel's ice business began to wane in 1936 following the arrival of electric refrigeration at Ft. Meade and Sturgis, Pearl supported Pappy's desire to open a motorcycle franchise in the family garage. Hoel's Motorcycle Shop, dealing in Indian Motorcycles, was soon reality. To ensure the success of this new business, Clarence was able to combine his love of riding with organizing a riding club similar to the larger club in Rapid City supported by the Harley Davidson dealer. The Sturgis club provided Hoel an outlet for his passion and was also good advertisement for his business. Pearl recalls that, on one occasion, the club was picnicking on a Sunday outing somewhere in the Black Hills when an automobile tourist stopped and informed the group that they looked like a bunch of Gypsies. Thus, the name Jack Pine Gypsies was born.

During the Great Depression of the 1930s, Pearl worked as an "Investigator" for the WPA to help needy rural families. Using an old car, she would travel around the county, providing these families with food, clothing, social access and, most importantly, hope for the future. Since the price of beef was minimal, WPA officials in Sturgis often purchased hindquarters of beef from the ranchers to deliver to these families. One of Pearl's greatest adventures occurred one night when she was returning to Sturgis after taking possession of a load of fresh meat. On a lonely country road, with the backseat and trunk filled with fresh beef and miles from town, she had a flat tire. After sitting for a short time and hoping someone would come along to help her, she finally decided that she would have to change the tire herself. By the time she had moved a couple of hind quarters out of the trunk to get at the spare tire and the jack, a pack of coyotes, drawn to the scent of the fresh meat, surrounded the car and began howling at her. Although Pearl maintains that she was calm, she admits that this adventure was more exciting then many of the experiences she had riding two-up with Pappy.

When Pearl had completed her work for the WPA, she was hired as deputy to the Meade County Clerk of Courts, Mr. Amos Bovee. Because of her capabilities and enhanced responsibilities when Bovee was not present, Pearl became more important in the eyes of the County Commissioners. As a result, she was appointed Meade County Clerk of Courts when Bovee retired. After serving for several years as Clerk of Courts and providing additional assistance to the county Superintendent of Schools, Pearl decided to run for the office of Register of Deeds. After several years in this position, Pearl was elected County Auditor.

In the lean years of the motorcycle business during World War II and in the 1950s when Pappy experienced the problems of a declining Indian motorcyle franchise, the Hoel family stayed well-fed because, according to Pearl, "we always had groceries because I had a steady job at the Court House!"

This story, and many others like it, are perfect examples of this wonderful woman's desire to support and enhance her husband's career. Pearl's status in Sturgis and Meade County and her ability to be re-elected year after year is a constant reflection of her personality, management skills, and organizational abilities. These talents, along with community respect for her ability to complete hard tasks, her outgoing personality and social skills, were all invaluable assets in promoting the Black Hills Motorcycle Classic.

Her stature in the community alone must have been a major asset that lent definite credibility in winning over the minds of Sturgis power brokers and their wives. One has to consider that if a person as important to the community as Pearl Hoel supported the idea of a motorcycle rally in Sturgis, how could the city fathers individually and collectively not support the idea as a positive one?

There can be little debate that Pearl Hoel is a prime example of the ultimate "good wife". She probably realized that her husband's dream and her own happiness were both fulfilled by her love and support of Pappy's efforts. Without Pearl's dedication and devotion to this dream, the Black Hills Motorcycle Classic might never have survived through its earliest days.

At 97 years of age, Pearl maintained that she always preferred to take a back-seat approach to Pappy's efforts. In this sense, Pearl Hoel is truly the unsung hero in the birth, growth and long-term success of the Black Hills Motor Classic.

Don Vodden

(Don Vodden is the last surviving charter member of the Jackpine Gypsies Motorcycle Club.)

Born and raised in the Sturgis area, Don Vodden became interested in motorcycles in the middle 1930s while in high school. To support his hobby, Vodden held three jobs including pumping gas at a service station, running a delivery service and working in the mess hall at Ft. Meade.

When he was 15 years old, he bought his first motorcycle — a 1918 JD Harley Davidson with a 61 cubic inch engine that had been rigged out for the U.S. Army. He

Don Vodden trains for an upcoming boxing match. (Don Vodden Collection)

soon traded this cycle for a 1927 Indian Scout, which in turn was traded for a 1927 Harley Davidson. His fourth motorcycle, and all-time favorite, was a 1928 Scout. He rode this machine until 1937 when he purchased Roger Satterlee's demo, a 1936 Indian Scout that Satterlee had bought in the hope of starting an Indian Dealership in Sturgis.[1]

One year after becoming a member of the Gypsies in 1936, Vodden's family was in desperate need for money. His father had lost his job, so Don converted a 1927 Buick towncar into a truck, and like the Joads in Steinbeck's *Grapes of Wrath*, the family took off for Oregon and Washington to pick fruit. In October, Don bought a motorcycle and rode home to Sturgis. He stayed with Roger Satterlee for a time and then found work cutting ice for Clarence Hoel.[2]

Because of his association with Hoel and the Gypsies club, Vodden worked hard in the planning of the 1938 rally. Although the downtown merchants had formed their separate and semi-exclusive group, the Black Hills Motor Classic, Vodden and other loyal Gypsies did a great deal of the actual leg-work in making the first AMA-sanctioned races a success. He always helped Pearl Hoel by either driving the pickup truck used to haul the mid-day lunch into the hills for the first Gypsy Tour riders or riding his motorcycle directly to the site and helping the ladies serve the lunch. He also raced in the Saturday and Sunday half-mile races held at the Meade County fairgrounds.

After winning the South Dakota State Golden Gloves Championship at middle-weight in 1939, Vodden turned professional and began boxing in various matches throughout the Black Hills communities. He also traveled into Wyoming, Montana and North Dakota to compete in boxing matches and became known as "Joe Lewis Vodden."

On May 29, 1939, after winning his match at Deadwood, Vodden climbed on the back of George Cobbler's Indian Chief and rode all night to Greeley, Colorado, where he competed in the Island Grove Park Speed Classic. In this single day of racing, Vodden competed against several nationally-rated racers, including "Iron Man" Ed Kretz who had won the first Daytona 200 in 1937, and twice held the AMA National Championship Title. Other racers at this event included Jimmy Kelley, touted as the best half miler in America in 1938, Bruce Pearson, the 1938 Pacific Coast Champion, and J. Braithwaite a Swedish rider and ten-time winner of the Isle of Man Race. Al Nelson, a fellow Gypsy from Sturgis, was Vodden's team mate.

There were a variety of races at this meet. Besides the normal time trials and heat race events, the program included a Trophy Dash, a Novelty Race (two riders), an International Race, an Obstacle Course Race, and Stunts provided by Ed Kretz. The International race included Ed Kretz (American) versus Harrison Reno (German), Jim Kelly (Irish) versus Bruce Pearson (Scotch), and J. Braithwaite (Swedish) versus Richie Takamine, an American-born Japanese rider. This race was probably designed as a crowd pleaser and also to keynote Braithwaite, the European champion.

Since this race had a large purse, Vodden, who won his heat race, the consolation race and did well in the time trials, was awarded $65.00 – a small fortune in those days. He had been holding fourth place in the 25-lap final event till he hit a "marble" (rock) and fell back.[3]

Later in the summer, after competing in the Greeley Speed Classic and the 1938 Black Hills Motor Classic, Vodden ordered a new 1939 Bonneville Scout from Hoel's shop, trading in his 1936 racing bike. The Bonneville turned into a disappointment for everyone, including Clarence Hoel. It did not seem to have proper speed and acceleration. Even though he hoped that the break-in would loosen things up, Vodden did poorly in the 1940 races at Sturgis. After the races were over, he and Hoel tore the engine down and discovered that someone in the Indian Factory had etched the timing marks on the cam gear improperly (two teeth off), thus retarding the valve opening sequence. After adjusting the cam to open properly, the motorcycle performed very well.

By 1940 Vodden had also opened a delivery business in Sturgis and was allowed to join the Black Hills Motor Classic group of merchants. Because of his involvement at

Don Vodden on his new 1939 Bonneville Scout (Don Vodden Collection)

Ft. Meade and interest in a military career, Vodden entered the Army in 1941 and quickly rose to the rank of First Sergeant. For a short time after the war in 1946, he owned Don's cafe (now Bob's Cafe) on Main Street in Sturgis but liked the Army life and re-enlisted. He eventually retired from the U.S. Army in 1962 as a Sergeant Major.[3]

While in the Army, Don had many interesting experiences, including a pep talk given to a young officer languishing in a military hospital in Michigan. The young officer went home to Kansas and eventually became Senator Bob Dole, the Republican presidential candidate in 1996. Vodden also spent time in Germany where he observed and supported Pearl and Pappy's son, Jack Hoel, who was having a spectacular Grass Track career. Vodden said he won a lot of money from his German friends by betting on Jack. As a dirt tracker, Jack Hoel had learned to use his left foot in the corners and was able to beat the European racers who merely leaned in the turns. According to Vodden, in one of the races, Jack Hoel finished two laps ahead of the next rider.[4]

While stateside during his Army career, Vodden always tried to get home to Sturgis for the rally. Now retired, he and his wife spend their winters in Harker Heights,

Texas, and their summers in Eldon, Missouri. At age 85, this last living charter member of the Jackpine Gypsies visits Sturgis every year for the races, the Hall of Fame Breakfast, Pearl Hoel's coffee party and the White Plate Flat Trackers Annual meeting. He is true gentleman and has become a wonderful friend to the author. [5]

Chapter Two:
Inspiration, Birth and the Pre-War Years

In the middle 1930s, motorcycles were fairly common in the Northern Black Hills area, and during 1935 and 1936, a group of local enthusiasts began hanging out, having informal field meets, picnics and "runs." There was a Harley Davidson dealer in Rapid City, 35 miles south of Sturgis, but the constant travel from Sturgis to Rapid City to get parts and support services became tedious. As a result, two men in town recognized the need for a motorcycle shop in Sturgis.

One of these men, a businessman named Clarence "Pappy" Hoel, who was a local rider and owner of a struggling ice business threatened by the evolution of electrical refrigeration, contacted the Harley Davidson people in Milwaukee to try and establish a local dealership. At the same time, a gentleman named Roger Satterlee contacted the Indian Company in Springfield, Massachusetts. Satterlee had purchased a new Indian Scout and was contemplating an application for an Indian dealership in Sturgis. After Hoel received a letter from Harley Davidson refusing a franchise, he immediately contacted Indian with a similar request. Somehow, Hoel was awarded the dealership and began his long career as an Indian motorcycle dealer.

In 1936, the local riders (or "boys") in this post-depression era decided to form a club, and Hoel was able to establish his new motorcycle business leaving Satterlee as a club member. While this may have generated some tension between the two men, the "boys" immediately rallied around Hoel and began ordering new Indians and supporting Hoel's business by purchasing parts, accessories, and mechanical support. Satterlee inevitably sold his Indian Scout to Don Vodden (a fellow club member), and the group officially chartered in late 1936 and selected the name "Jackpine Gypsies Motorcycle Club".

There are several versions of how the "boys" selected the name "Jackpine Gypsies". One person interviewed indicated that the word "gypsy" was taken from the AMA's nationally-sponsored Gypsy Tours of the 1920s. Another suggested that the term "jackpine" was taken from the famous endurance run held yearly in Jackson,

Michigan. Pearl Hoel maintains that one day when both the "boys" and the "girls" were having a motorcycle run and picnic in the Black Hills, they encountered a motorist who asked them who they were. One of the club members responded by saying they were a group of riders from Sturgis, whereupon the motorist blurted out; "you look like a bunch of Gypsies to me!" According to Don Vodden, the last living charter member of the club, at one of the first club meetings, everyone threw a name into a hat and then the proposed club names were read aloud and everyone voted. The winner was Jackpine Gypsies Motorcycle Club, submitted by Nicky Neugebauer, a 22-year old corporal from the Cavalry Troop stationed at Ft. Meade.

Clarence "Pappy" Hoel in front of his Indian motorcycle dealership in Sturgis. (Pearl Hoel Collection)

As chartered, the Gypsies initially comprised 18 local riders. Besides Hoel, they included local businessmen like Archie Campbell, a local service station owner and Harley Davidson rider who had learned to ride in World War I; Roger Satterlee, a young man who owned a pawnshop in Sturgis; and Ray Jeider, a local mortician.

There were also several students in the club. George Cobbler, who was club secretary, was a college student at Black Hills State Teacher's College, while Cecil Gibson, Wayne Milek, Charlie Stephens and Don Vodden were attending the local high school.

Nicky Neugebauer and Gordon Rounds were troopers serving in the Cavalry detachment at Ft. Meade, and the rest of the members were miners from Lead/Deadwood or local fellows who drew a salary. The miners included Carl Hackett, Herby Larson, Ray and Ted Laurenti, and Thomas McLaughlin. Joe Kelley and Charlie Stephens were locals who worked in Sturgis. Eight of these "boys" were married, and the wives, along with girlfriends of the 10 single men, made up the "girls" who were occasionally involved in club activities. Joint outings generally included food provided by the "girls."

In today's busy world of television, movies, and expanded school athletic programs, it is hard to imagine the plethora of lodges, social clubs, veterans groups and other associations that filled the weekday evenings in America's small rural communities of the 1930s. People were very serious about their club memberships and attendance at meetings was deemed extremely important. Today's perception of the serious nature of club activities, which often included arguments about constitutional and by-law amendments, election of officers and explicit secretary-treasurer reports, seems fraught with busy work. In reflection, however, one has to imagine the difficulty in scheduling weekly meeting activities at a time when everyone in rural American was involved with church, choir practice, prayer meetings, 4-H Clubs, VFW, the Mason's Lodge and so on. Their lives were enriched with social activities that are hardly relevant to the contemporary life of Americans today.

The Jackpine Gypsies met weekly to hash out problems, count their money and plan activities. Attendance was encouraged via a nickel raffle where everyone had to toss a nickel in a hat and then at the end of the meeting, one person won the pot. There also seems to have been discussion on collecting dues to support the coffee fund. For instance, the Gypsies' 1938 minutes included a four meeting (four-week) dialogue concerning the purchase of a new coffeepot and tin cups. One member was authorized to purchase 2 dozen tin cups at no more than five cents per cup, and a coffeepot for no more than two dollars. At the next meeting he reported that he had purchased the tin cups for the five cent price but was unable to find a coffeepot for less than $2.98. He asked permission to buy this pot but was refused by vote in that and the next two meetings. Ultimately, there is no record that he ever purchased the coffeepot.

Prior to chartering the Gypsies, several club members had been participating in club activities established by the Rapid City Pioneer Motorcycle Club, or "RPMs". After the Gypsies were chartered, several group rides, picnics and field days were held in conjunction with the RPM group. They even held ice hockey matches during the winter months. These meetings were always characterized by a bit of good-natured rivalry because the RPMs rode mainly Harley Davidsons and the Gypsies, because of Hoel's local Indian dealership, were fans of Indians.

According to Don Vodden the field meets, which comprised various relay races, egg races, suitcase races and slow races, were gradually supplemented by actual dirt track competitions on an old horse track in Rapid City. Early in 1937, the Gypsies decided to pull the weeds out of the old half-mile horse track at the Meade County Fairgrounds in Sturgis, hire a grader to work up the dirt and invite the Rapid City Pioneers to a race in Sturgis. Because the Sturgis track had been converted much earlier for car racing, the corners were banked and everyone enjoyed the extra speed they could make in turning the circuit. As a result, the first dirt track races were held in Sturgis in August 1937, and the participants included mostly Rapid City and Sturgis racers.

The Sturgis merchants were impressed by the number of Black Hills area residents that came to this event, and during the winter of 1937-1938, they formed a separate organization and began planning a weekend of racing as an effort to enhance the local economy. While these merchants viewed themselves as being socially separated from the Gypsies, they were inherently and economically tied to these motorcyclist's assistance in making everything work. This initial two-prong arrangement created an interesting pattern of separation and cooperation in the rally's early years that is still evidenced today.

The pre-war years from 1937 to 1941 are seminal in the establishment of the rally. While the 1937 field-day event drew a tremendous crowd, the 1938 rally was a raging success in contrast, especially in post-Depression rural America. The 1939 rally was even more successful, as were the 1940 and 1941 events.

The Gypsies, formally separated from the merchants promoting the rally, now titled "The Black Hills Motor Classic," created the now famous "Gypsy Tour", held on the Friday just prior to the weekend rally. This organized tour of scenic destinations in the Black Hills was also a major success.

By the end of 1941, however, America was at war and the rally was no longer a viable enterprise because of gasoline rationing and the absence of young riders to participate in the races. Many had been drafted into military service for the duration of the war, and the rally faced its first crossroads. Would "The Black Hills Motor Classic" continue after the war?

August 1, 1937

Contrary to general reports about the Black Hills Motor Classic, the first organized races were held in 1937, rather than 1938. Perhaps this omission is due to a total vacuum of community interaction in organizing the event.

The first rally, actually a "field day", was planned and executed by members of the Jackpine Gypsies in conjunction with motorcycle riding clubs from Lead and Rapid City. Apparently 30 to 35 riders from the Northern Black Hills decided to get together to hold a field day and race at the Meade County Fairgrounds in August. Clarence "Pappy" Hoel was apparently the instigator, organizer and event manager. For some reason (perhaps a slow news week), the *Sturgis Tribune* picked up on the excitement in early July and reported the program in a front page article entitled "Motorcyclists to Hold Field Meet here August 1". According to Hoel, the major emphasis would be on stunts, trick riding (or field events) as well as a few races. The field events and racing were sure to provide the excitement of an accident or two, which might inevitably attract a crowd.[1]

One of the tragedies affecting this first Rally was the death of Edward Borron, a young rider who was the President of the Rapid City Pioneers Motorcycle Club. Borron was riding his motorcycle in the Black Hills on July 20 with two pals, Jack Thomas and James Horner. These three men were out placing posters advertising the Sturgis meet. After they had finished their tasks and were returning to Rapid City, Edward's motorcycle skidded on some loose gravel into a guardrail at Rainbow Cliff in Boulder Canyon west of Sturgis.

All three riders realized that Borron's leg was injured, but he suffered the pain, climbed back on his bike and rode on home to Rapid City. He awoke during the night with intense pain and died at 5:00 a.m. the next morning. Cause of death was not

Motorcycle racers at the field day and races in Sturgis, 1937. (Pearl Hoel Collection)

clearly stated, but was speculated to be from either shock or a blood clot. Boulder Canyon had claimed its first victim.[2]

Racers entered in the 1937 half-mile event included Ferman Schaab and Hoel from the Gypsies, and Dutch Muckler, Angel Hecker, Fritz Coe, Al Nelson, Nooky Scoog and his brother Al from the RPM club in Rapid City. Don Vodden, one of the promising young racers from Sturgis, was in Oregon picking fruit with his family and could not compete.

Interestingly enough, the *Sturgis Tribune* did not print any follow-up of this first rally. Consequently, there is no record of which stunts and tricks were performed or who won the races. There was, however, a very large crowd in attendance – a fact noticed by Sturgis businessmen, who took over management of the Rally in 1938 and 1939, attempting to establish a viable commercial enterprise.

August 12-14, 1938

Based on the apparent success of the first rally and races event in 1937, the town of Sturgis was reasonably excited about planning the 1938 Classic. The success of the 1937 rally was quickly evidenced by the immediate involvement of the Sturgis Commercial Club, which authorized the appointment of "a proper committee" to cover and implement the motorcycle race meet.[1]

The Commercial Club Members, viewing themselves as socially different from the motorcycle club members, established an organization characterized as the Black Hills Motor Classic (BHMC). Confusion on the part of visitors and locals alike continue to persist with regard to this notion. While the "Classic" organizers (the "proper committee") were extremely interested in the rally as a commercial venture, they were hesitant about permitting the young, local riders (the Gypsies) to become members of the BHMC group. As a result, the Commercial Club allowed only members of the local business establishment to join their group. According to Don Vodden, the last surviving Charter Member of the Gypsies, these feelings were duly reciprocated. Members of the Gypsies referred to these merchants as "namby pambies", naïve about motorcycles and racing. According to Vodden, "They had to blond their coffee instead of drinking it black like real men!"[2]

Because Clarence "Pappy" Hoel owned the Indian motorcycle dealership, he was permitted to join the Black Hills Motor Classic group, along with Archie Campbell, who owned a local service station. Each of these Gypsies reported regularly to the motorcycle club concerning the BHMC's decisions and were affectionately known as "spies". Interestingly enough, another Gypsy who served as the local mortician could not join because he merely managed the funeral home for a Rapid City proprietor![3]

Both Campbell and Hoel paid the conservative $2 lifetime membership fee to belong to the BHMC group. This quasi-legitimate relationship continued for many years. Over time, and in the interest of communication, certain Gypsies were allowed to join the "Classic" group thus holding joint membership in both organizations.

Beginning in 1938, the BHMC officially managed the rally and the half-mile races. They were assisted by the Gypsies, who were officially responsible for the Gypsy Tours.*

The transition from the 1937 Jackpine Gypsy Motorcycle Club sponsored happening, where local businessmen and the residents of Sturgis had been spectators, to the economic and social phenomena of a community-supported celebration, was therefore realized in the summer of 1938. To ensure growth and participation, the Commercial Club Committee solicited the support of the Sturgis City Council and the Rapid City Pioneers Motorcycle Club (the RPMs) in addition to the Gypsies. Apparently, the committee members weren't sure if the 1937 event had been a fluke. In any case, additional bikers from the big town (Rapid City) would swell the ranks and bring additional revenues into the community. The committee was excited. After all, Deadwood had their "Days of '76", and Belle Fourche had their rodeo, why not have a community-sponsored moneymaker in Sturgis?

So as not to conflict with either of these local events, the second weekend in August was established as an annual date. This time slot is still honored and supported by the surrounding region. In fact, other entities count on the rally as an asset in planning their own August activities. In 1938, the weekend of August 12-14 was selected. Prize money in the amount of $500 was raised and the committee expected in excess of 200 riders! One of the committee members indicated that, if this event was promoted wisely, they could expect "entries from the whole cockeyed world!"[5]

Committee plans included a parade composed of big bikes (motorcycles), little bikes (children and teens) and business floats. In addition to the Gypsy Tour and the

---

* The Gypsies would later assume the responsibility for new events, like the hill climb, short track and motocross. Because Hoel and selected Gypsies were involved in both organizations, locals and visitors have tended to view them as one and the same. This arrangement continued until 1974 when the BHMC and the Gypsies joined together in managing the half-mile races. This unofficial marriage was due to the downtown group's inability to "work the races" because of the expanding demands in supporting the Main Street elements. The merchant's group continued to supervise city space requirements, vendors and other downtown concerns, funding all operations and retaining all of the profits.[4]

The first nine racers at the first AMA-sanctioned, half-mile race at Sturgis, August 1938.
(Sturgis Museum Collection)

races, a community dance was scheduled and stunts from both Sturgis and Rapid City riders were to be held between races at the fairground grandstand. The plan was to "make this one of the principal sporting events in the entire Northwest"[6] — brave words from the mouths of rural Midwesterners in the final throes of the great depression.

About this time, Pappy Hoel received a letter of support from the American Motorcycle Association (AMA), which inferred that, because of the AMA recognition and publicity for the races, rally planners might expect riders from as far away as Texas and California. Excitement was high throughout the community. This was to be the first AMA-sanctioned half-mile race in the region. By the second week of July, a group of auto racing enthusiasts suggested that auto races be added to the events. The committee was open to this idea and began to plan for additional races, using "hopped" up Model-T Fords. They even hired stunt man "Irish Duggan" to perform "any death-defying stunts," including a head-on collision![7]

By Race Day, the plans had enlarged even further. The prize money had grown to $750, and a street carnival had been contacted to set up in the downtown area. Riders from eight states had registered for the race, including several West Coast riders on their way to attend "The Springfield Mile" event in Illinois. Many indicated that they were going to stop in Sturgis to participate and maybe just hang out.

On race Saturday, a field of nine riders had registered for racing. They included Gale Chandler, Gale Gilkerson, Johnny Spiegelhoff, Fred Ford, Dale Short, Al Nelson, Bill Smith, J.P. Lewen and Don Vodden. All of the racers, except for Spiegelhoff and Smith, were riding Indians. With only nine racers competing, race organizers began to worry about putting on a good show that would include a full afternoon of excitement for Sunday's spectators. The typical approach of holding qualifying heat races to determine placement in the final event was ludicrous. According to Don Vodden it was Johnny Spieglehoff from Milwaukee, Wisconsin who came up with a super solution. In the rider's meeting, Spiegelhoff suggested that they stage a series of challenge races, pairing riders according to their abilities. This arrangement was made, and the crowd loved it![8]

Riding a yellow, 45-cubic inch Harley Davidson, Spiegelhoff won the half-mile championship race. According to the *Sturgis Tribune*, Spiegelhoff "made the 1938 rally his own...although he trailed (Al) Nelson in the three-mile, he won the one-on-one match race (with Nelson), then won the five-mile and took the 10-mile South Dakota Championship Race when Nelson lost control and high sided in the dust".[9]

In his book of memoirs, Hoel indicated that, from a personal standpoint, he was never as interested in speed racing as he was in hill climbs, trials, scrambles, cross country and tricks.[10] In regard to the latter, Hoel performed his burning wall crash at the 1938 rally — a stunt he actually repeated for many ensuing years. It consisted of creating a framework with thin, soft pine boards set aflame just prior to the motorcycle and rider crashing through the burning wall. In later years, a near tragedy occurred when local businessmen, sensing a publicity bonanza, created a wall filled with painted

The Sturgis Tribune, Wednesday, August 17, 1938.

Clarence "Pappy" Hoel performs the "Wall of Fire Crash" at the 1938 rally. (Pearl Hoel Collection)

advertising. The local carpenter who was contracted to build the wall used one-inch tongue and groove lumber. This sturdy wall was then covered with heavy coats of paint and almost led to disaster when Pappy charged it on his Indian 74 Chief. The other events such as hill climb, scrambles, and the short track were to become elements in future rallies.[11]

All in all, 1938 was a signal year for the rally. The transition from a club event to a community-wide project was realized, along with AMA endorsement and a variety of non-motorcycle entertainment. Although the citizens of Sturgis had no idea of what was to come, crucial elements related to community attitudes and perceptions were clearly established and nurtured in 1938.

1938 Champion: Johnny Spiegelhoff

Johnny Spiegelhoff, the half-mile Feature Race Champion at Sturgis in 1938, 1939, 1941 and 1946 was born in Watertown, Wisconsin on April 17,1915. He spent most of his life in the Milwaukee area, living in the communities of Watertown, Sussex and Muskego. He traveled to Mazatlan, Mexico during the winter months in later years to escape the cold weather.[1]

In his youth, Spiegelhoff became famous in eastern Wisconsin and the Chicago area as a speed skater, winning several awards in 1930 and 1931, and his love of speed and competition was probably borne of these early racing experiences. In fact, it's likely that one of his characteristic motorcycle racing moves was forged from this speed skating background.[2] Many fans and racers always commented about Spiegelhoff's ability to look to the rear by peeking under either arm to gauge the proximity of other riders in the pack.[3] This ability was probably learned early in his speed skating days and served him well in racing motorcycles.

His love for motorcycles grew out of living near Milwaukee, the home of the Harley Davidson factory, and living also in close proximity to a Harley dealership, where he hung out, did light mechanic work, and caged rides. He later worked in the Harley Davidson Factory and was assisted in the early years of his racing career by the factory and area Harley Davidson dealers. His racing career began in 1934, riding in club events and area races. He won the Canadian Short Track Championship in 1936. Spiegelhoff became a loyal AMA member early in his career and went on to become an outstanding competitor, winning the ultimate race, the Daytona 200 in 1947.[4]

Beginning with his speed skating days and continuing in his racing career, Spiegelhoff earned the sobriquet "Smiling Johnny." His facial expression in most of his pictures characterizes this nickname, and it is genuinely difficult to identify Spiegelhoff in pictures when he is not smiling.

His four wins at Sturgis began in 1938. According to Al Nelson, who was the hottest "shoe" on the Black Hills area racing scene, he met Johnny at a hill climb in Albert Lea, Minnesota sometime early in the spring of 1938. The two riders became friends on the spot, and Nelson invited

Speigelhoff to come to Sturgis in August and compete in the 1938 half-mile event. Spiegelhoff, loyal to the AMA, refused to come to an "outlaw" event, telling Nelson that should the group seek and be sanctioned by the AMA, he would consider attending. Nelson returned to Sturgis and urged Clarence Hoel to seek AMA status for the first rally — a decision noted in the Jackpine Gypsies Club minutes for 1938. The races were ultimately sanctioned, and Spielgelhoff came.[5]

According to Al Deckert, Spiegelhoff's brother-in-law who also worked at Harley Davidson and served as Johnny's mechanic in 1938, the trip to Sturgis was a combination of business and pleasure. Since Spielgelhoff and his brothers shared a part interest in a wheat farm in North Dakota, Johnny was elected to visit the farm at the time of the harvest in early August to check up on the renter and ascertain their share of the crop. Deckert and Spiegelhoff loaded his yellow 45 cubic inch Harley Davidson

Smiling Johnny Spiegelhoff, 1938 Sturgis Champion (Janis Sheets Collection)

racing bike on a trailer behind Spiegelhoff's Chrysler "Airflow," and with their wives, who were sisters, took off for the wheat farm. After concluding their business, the two women stayed on at the farm, visiting and canning vegetables, while the two men took off for the Black Hills in South Dakota.

Upon arriving at Sturgis, they discovered that only nine qualified riders were in attendance, but more importantly, Johnny recognized that his Harley Davidson was no match for Nelson's highly tuned Indian Scout, which had won the Saturday racing program. Johnny was quite interested in the Indian motorcycle's speed and acceleration, but he was more interested in putting on a good show for the crowd. On Sunday, since there were so few riders, preliminary heat races seemed inappropriate. In the rider meeting prior to Sunday's program of racing, Speigelhoff, a veteran of many of these events, suggested that the riders pair up according to ability and hold a group of paired challenge races. In this way the program was extended to provide the spectators with additional excitement. Everyone agreed, and Johnny ended up paired with Nelson.[6] Ultimately, Nelson and his Indian Scout lost to Spiegelhoff and his Harley on Sunday. The outcome of an Indian winning Saturday and a Harley Davidson winning on Sunday further dramatized the friendly feud between racing fans and probably enhanced annual speculation about races in the ensuing years at Sturgis.

Hal Deckert, Spiegelhoff's mechanic and loyal to Harley Davidson, reported that the two riders were really in cahoots, planning to thrill the crowd by exchanging leads several times during the 10-mile main event. Deckert, who had a 19-year career as a Harley Davidson test rider and had personally clocked over a million miles working for the factory, maintains that Johnny really wanted to win, and therefore timed his lead to coincide with the final lap. Don Vodden, a surviving member of the 1938 half-mile race, tells a different story. He maintains that in those days, prior to calcium chloride applications, the Sturgis track was extremely dusty, and in the final lap, Nelson became confused by the dust in the third turn and high sided his Indian into the hay bales. Spiegelhoff went on to be declared the champion.[7] The *Sturgis Tribune*, loyal to Nelson, ran an appropriate headline the following week: "Spiegelhoff is Very Fast, But Meets His Equal in Rapid City Speed Demon" thus giving credit to the local rider.[8]

The 1938 crowd, composed mainly of persons from Rapid City and the northern Black Hills, were truly entertained. While the majority of the Rapid City motorcycle riders and fans were members of the Pioneers Motorcycle Club (RPM) sponsored by a local Harley Davidson dealership, the Northern Hills group and the Jackpine Gypsies Motorcycle Club members, as well as the Sturgis fans, were loyal to Clarence Hoel and his Indian shop. Both groups were either elated or disappointed on both days. At any rate, these Saturday and Sunday wins initiated coffee shop debates in the area for the next year, undoubtedly adding fuel for promoting the 1939 rally.

After the races, Nelson and Spiegelhoff maintained their friendship, and Nelson actually moved to Milwaukee in the fall and lived with the Spiegelhoff family. One particularly interesting twist of fate occurred in the winter of 1938-39, when Nelson secured a job at the Harley Davidson factory, sold his Indian and began racing Harley Davidsons. Spiegelhoff, on the other hand, lost his Harley Davidson racing support and began riding Indian racing bikes after being approached by Hal Krause, who owned an Indian dealership in Beloit, Wisconsin. Nelson's and Spiegelhoff's friendship continued during the summer of 1939 as they followed the Midwest racing circuit, trailering two bikes: Nelson's Harley and Spiegelhoff's Indian. According to Don Vodden, this was a common arrangement in the early days, and these rider teams often shared both purses and expenses.[9]

Nelson returned to the Black Hills in the fall of 1939, and after the racing at Sturgis, he became heavily involved in his father's' construction business. Speigelhoff went on to continue his racing career.[10]

August 11-13, 1939

With the members of the Black Hills Motor Classic (the Sturgis Commercial Club) at the helm, the 1939 rally was characterized by significant expansion in both attractions and entertainment. The "Speed Classic", as characterized in the *Sturgis Tribune*, initially kicked off with a banquet/planning meeting of over 65 local businessmen and their wives. Apparently, the group was very enthusiastic, and Bruce A. Barnes, the appointed manager of the event, used this forum to generate ideas for a bigger and better show in 1939.[1]

Barnes mentioned that he had already contacted an aerial trapeze act and a trained animal show for the August 12-13 weekend. He also asked for volunteers to construct a 20 x 50 foot stage to be erected in the downtown area. The *Sturgis Tribune* promised to print a 12 page special edition, using colored paper and colored ink. [2]

Special Edition Cover and Rally Poster. The Sturgis Tribune, August 1939.

31

The Model-T races, which had been successful in 1938, were to be expanded, and the parade was to be the biggest and best in Sturgis' history. With regard to motorcycle events, Clarence "Pappy" Hoel was to be in charge. Pappy also indicated that he would lead the Gypsy Tour on Friday prior to the race weekend, and he expected between 400 and 500 riders.[3]

Sticking to an initial tradition established by the Gypsies prior to the 1939 rally, the tour would include lunch at the halfway mark, usually at Mt. Rushmore, and a picnic dinner upon its return to Sturgis. Pearl Hoel and one or two of her friends generally provided or organized both meals for the riders.[4] As for feeding all of the other riders in 1939, the Black Hills Motor Classic committee decided to provide a huge "Dutch lunch and entertainment" at the City Park on Saturday night, August 12.[5]

Discussion of publicity efforts and assistance were also heard during the forum, and many in attendance promised to build floats for the parade. Apparently it had been determined that the existing grandstand at the Meade County Fairgrounds had been inadequate in accommodating race fans at the 1938 rally. Pressure had been focused on the county commissioners earlier in the year to build a new, larger facility ($5,000) in time for the races. This new and "safer" grandstand was built on the straightaway rather than at the end of the track to provide the spectators with the excitement of the higher speeds.[6]

The Black Hills Tour, sponsored by the Gypsies, was planned for Friday, August 11th, one day prior to the weekend of racing and was expected to bring in riders a day early, thus enhancing the entire weekend. This Gypsy Tour would leave Sturgis on Friday morning and visit Mt. Rushmore, the Needles Highway, the State Game Lodge and Sylvan Lake. To keep some of the riders closer to Sturgis, shorter tours to Bear Butte, Spearfish and Deadwood were also planned. Lead and a Homestake Gold Mine Tour was also an option for interested riders.[7]

One of the new events organized for the 1939 rally was a Kiddie Parade and featured four categories, including vehicles, nursery rhymes, pets and miscellaneous. Pearl Hoel and two other women were assigned the task of supervising and judging each of the categories. The first, Vehicles, included decorated tricycles, bikes and wagons; Nursery Rhymes, the second category, included costumes displaying the characters, a Pet Walk including legal animals was the third, and Miscellaneous which, included clowns and tramps, made up the final category. It seems that even local children were learning that the motorcycle races would provide fun and serve as both a positive experience and a highlight of the Sturgis summer.[8]

With regard to motorcycle events, excitement was high. The *Sturgis Tribune* reported rider registration from as far away as Canada and California, and the local

Black Hills Motor Classic (BHMC) committee members and members of the Jackpine Gypsies receiving the AMA Safety Award in 1939. Back row: BHMC members. Front row (Gypsies): Roger Satterlee, Carl Hackett, George Cobbler, Don Vodden, Rex Jeide, Ray Laurenti, Clarence Hoel, Archie Campbell (holding banner). (Eva Satterlee Collection)

Model T racers and riders were prohibited from practicing on the track in anticipation of the August 12-13 races.[9]

Additional attractions included a Saturday night dance at the city auditorium and touted bargains in a variety of summer sales at all of the downtown stores. The Sturgis merchants established the slogan: "Save enough in bargains Saturday to enjoy all of the events of our celebration." The DeWaldo Duo ("Two of America's Leading Slack Wire Performers") was in town to ride their bicycles and unicycles on slack wires while dancing and juggling "in a manner never before seen on the vaudeville stage!" The much-touted animal act consisted of three trick dogs that performed on the large stage erected on main street.[10]

The Jackpine Gypsy Tour held on Friday August 11, included 55 riders with participants from Iowa, Colorado, Illinois, Wisconsin, Minnesota, Eastern South Dakota and the Black Hills area. The award for the greatest distance went to "Speed" Shelby from Ottawa, Illinois. Walter Wicks from Austin, Minnesota took the prize for the Best Dressed Male Rider while Mrs. Cliff Waldron from Huron, South Dakota captured the title of the Best Dressed Female Rider. All three received gifts from the AMA.[11]

On Sunday, Johnny Spieglehoff again emerged as the Black Hills Speed Champion with a time of 10:44.5 on the 10-mile championship race. A highlight of the 1939 races was the entry of two Canadians from Winnipeg, Manitoba, riding large Triumph singles. These riders did very well in the heat races, but they were unable to place in the championship races on Sunday, August 13. The crowd, however, was enchanted by the sound of these huge "one lunger" singles and begged the Canadian riders to return for the 1940 races.[12] Don Vodden, who also ran in this race on his Indian Scout, claims he was not all that enchanted eating their dust.[13]

The 1939 rally established further excitement and interest in the Sturgis community. This bigger and better event, coupled with the larger number of riders and visitors enhanced and improved the local citizens' attitudes toward motorcycles in general. As these social and economic elements were nurtured throughout the community, anticipation for the 1940 rally was apparent. The threat of war emerging in Europe was probably far from the minds of the Sturgis Commercial Club members.

American Motorcyclists Association

One of the most significant elements leading to the growth of the Black Hills Motor Classic is the involvement of the American Motorcyclists Association (AMA). Without the support and organizational efforts provided by this organization, the rally would probably have continued only for as long as Pappy Hoel and his fellow riders had continued to organize and participate in repeats of their 1937 "Field Day". At any point the rally might have gone the way of other community-promotion schemes and would have surely died with the onset of World War II in 1941.

Hoel joined the AMA in 1935, and he probably gained ideas about organizing motorcycle rallies from reading the *Motorcyclist*, a monthly magazine published by this organization. A significant example is his use of the word "Gypsy" in the chartering the Sturgis area rider's club.

The history of the AMA reveals that "Gypsy Tours" were held as early as 1913. The pattern for a Gypsy tour, as spelled out by the AMA, was a small group of riders gathering for organized road riding or for a weekend of fellowship and touring. An actual component of the AMA organizational framework by the end of World War I, Gypsy Tours were held concurrently on a national basis on significant dates, and always on a weekend. The general format was to schedule a ride to a scenic location, have a picnic, and then participate in a variety of competitive events including races, hill climbs, Tours & Trophy (TT) and dirt track events. These "Gypsy" weekends might also include events such as slow races, egg races, stake races and plank rides.[1]

All the elements of the early years of the Black Hills Classic are evidenced in this description. Hoel and his associates almost certainly used the AMA Gypsy model in developing their first Sturgis Rally or "Field Meet" in 1937.

In 1925, 212 AMA-sanctioned clubs reported Gypsy tours on the AMA scheduled weekend of June 20-21. There were probably 50 to 100 more unofficial tours that went unreported. These Gypsy tours, while providing recreational activities for the riders, also created a venue for motorcycle dealers to display their latest machines and give demonstration rides to interested customers. This would have been an ideal opportunity for promotion as most of the motorcycle dealerships in the 1930's were typically small, operating out of a home garage or a gas station.

Pappy Hoel, with his new (1936) Indian Dealership, probably recognized the value of this marketing approach and was able to exploit the possibility of motorcycle sales while still enjoying the riding, the conversation and the fellowship of the riders and their wives.

By 1957, the AMA abandoned the term "Gypsy" for semantic reasons and adopted a new name — AMA Tours.[2] The Gypsy characterization still remains in Sturgis, where Hoel and his riding associates chose the name "Jackpine Gypsies" for their club.

The AMA was actually chartered in 1924 and was made up of two pioneer riding associations: The Federation of American Motorcyclists (FAM), chartered in 1903; and the Motorcycle and Allies Trades Association (M & ATA), chartered in 1916. Since this merger was realized, the AMA has focused on an image of respectability, which includes safety, responsibility, appearance, riding courtesy, and noise.[3]

August 16-18, 1940

According to the July 18, 1940 edition of the *Sturgis Tribune*, advertising for the 1940 rally was underway. Race Manager B. A. Barnes had printed and distributed 5,000 posters in the Black Hills area and had ordered 11 dozen maroon colored shirts with race dates on the back. He expected "all local men to be walking ads wherever they go".[1]

In addition, the *Tribune* reported an increased emphasis on planning for the 1940 rally, which would include a wide spectrum of events, surpassing the impressive efforts made for the previous year's rally. Public acceptance of the event and corresponding races is evidenced most greatly by the fact that free passes to the races were to be available to all Meade County grade school graduates (those who had completed eighth grade).[2] Businessmen in Sturgis were obviously quick to recognize that giving free tickets to 13 and 14-year-old children might induce their parents to come along and spend at least one shopping day in Sturgis rather than going to Rapid City, Spearfish or Lead.

To receive their tickets, students or their parents were to pick up them up at "Motorcycle Headquarters" prior to noon on Saturday, August 17, the day the first races were scheduled. Promotion of this free offer, however, was not limited to the local newspaper coverage. In fact, each local graduate received a letter from the Commercial Club outlining the details along with an invitation to consider attending Sturgis High School in the fall. Commercial Club members went so far as to arrange tours of the high school on Saturday afternoon and had made available information about boarding in town for rural students.[3]

One new twist offered at the 1940 rally was an Endurance Run. This AMA-sanctioned event, later characterized as an Enduro, was organized and planned by the Jack

Pearl Hoel shows one of race manager Bruce Barnes' maroon-colored shirts used in 1940. Barnes expected that "all local men to be walking ads wherever they go." (Author Photo)

Pine Gypsies and was to be held on August 1, 1940, exactly one week prior to the Classic. This was not a speed contest but a rally with timed and estimated speeds between checkpoints on a route that encompassed Sturgis, Deadwood, Hot Springs, Legion Lake, the State Game Park, Mt. Rushmore, Rapid City and then Sturgis. Riders would start with 1000 points and be penalized one point for each minute exceeded or lost. According to *The Sturgis Tribune*, "Merchandise prized amounting to $10 will be rewarded besides the beautiful AMA Trophy, which the winner will receive." Clarence "Pappy" Hoel was to be the race coordinator.[4]

On August 1, 1940, *The Sturgis Tribune* reported that Shorty Cochran of Deadwood had won the 210 mile Endurance Race and the corresponding AMA trophy. The general view among the riders was that Cochran was not necessarily better at calculating his speed, but that he was lucky enough to not get behind groups of gawking Black Hills automobile tourists. (It seems that things really haven't changed much in over 60 years!) The endurance race speeds averaged 34 mph on the out lap (Sturgis to Hot Springs) and 36 mph on the return. Pappy Hoel placed second, and Joe Sisr of Rapid City placed third.[5]

Race Excitement

Race hype started on August 8, nine days prior to Race Day. Manager Bruce Barnes reported that the track was better and faster than ever, and that 30 racers from California to New York State had submitted entry fees. Notables included Henry Stark of Duluth, Minnesota; Leo Hauch of St. Paul; Paul Egeberg of Minneapolis; Johnny Spiegelhoff of Milwaukee and Albert Nelson, a Black Hills area racer. Barnes expressed concern that the two Canadians who were so colorful in the 1939 races with their big Triumph singles were unable to come because of the war in Europe. Barnes also stated that, the "Burning Wall Crash", Pappy Hoel's specialty, would be supplemented by other between-race features. A downtown midway was also planned for weekend.[6]

The Thursday August 15 edition of the *Sturgis Tribune* showed even more excitement for the pending rally. A faster track and "Speed Demons" from Wisconsin, Michigan, Minnesota, Colorado, California and South Dakota all promised a great show. A new feature of the 1940 races would include the use of an electric timer, which was required by the AMA to validate speed records used in totaling points.[7] According to Jack Hoel, the timer used a rubber hose similar to the ones used in the 1950s and 60s at gas stations and by the police in speed trap operations.[8]

Barnes also suggested that, since merchants had reduced their prices, the savings to customers would probably cover a family's expenses for the races and the other

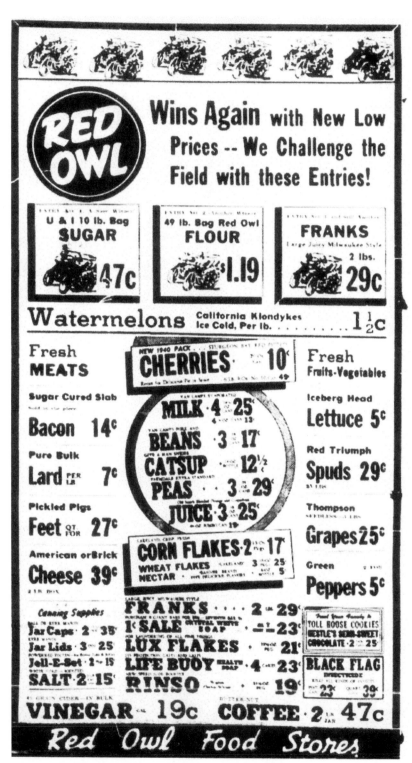

The local Red Owl Food Store shares in rally excitement in this insert to <u>The Sturgis Tribune</u>, August 1940.

attractions. The Gypsy Tour, not to be confused with the Endurance Run of the previous Saturday, would be held on Friday, August 16 and was expected to draw 100 riders. Always designed to entice riders to spend an extra day in the Hills, the 1940 tour would begin in Sturgis and then visit Deadwood, Sylvan Lake, the Needles Highway, Iron Mountain Road and Mt. Rushmore before returning to Sturgis. Ultimately, 62 riders from outside the Black Hills, accompanied by 18 local participants, rode the 1940 tour.[9]

According to Jack Hoel, his father (Pappy) always thought the Gypsy tours had a triple effect on the success of the rally. First, they encouraged the riders to come early and spend money in Sturgis. Second, they treated the visitors to a spectacular ride and

The Gypsy Tour winds out of Mount Rushmore. (Dick O'Leary Collection)

the desire to return with friends in later years, and finally, they served as a reminder to Black Hills residents that it was rally weekend. He said that Pappy estimated that the tour always brought at least 100 additional local residents to Sturgis for the races.[10]

The Gypsy Tour participants, after completing their run, were invited to Bear Butte Lake for a picnic supper sponsored by the Sturgis Chamber of Commerce. Organized by Pearl Hoel and Mrs. Amos Bovey, the picnic included an entertainment program, including tap-dancing – quite a contrast from the dancing programs of present-day rallies. Gypsy tour trophies were awarded to the best-dressed male and female riders as well as to the person coming the farthest distance to the rally.[11]

Race Days

During Saturday's preliminary events, the half-mile time-trials record, which was established by Johnny Spiegelhoff in 1939, was shattered four times. (Spiegelhoff missed the 1940 rally and was unable to defend his half-mile record.) First to topple Spiegelhoff's mark was Robert Searles of Denver who edged out the 31.5-second record with a time of 31.44. He was followed by Fred Ford, also from Denver, who clocked in at 31.25.seconds. The local racer, Al Nelson, then broke Ford's record with a time of 30.8, and finally, Nelson's record was smashed by Henry Stark of Duluth, Minnesota with a time of 30.28 seconds.[12]

On Sunday, August 18, Al Nelson captured the 10-mile championship race before a crowd of more than 2,000 spectators. In this championship final, Nelson got off to a great start, holding a 50-yard lead for the full 20 laps. Henrey Stark of Duluth took second place, and Fred Ford from Denver took third. A Japanese rider from Denver, Roger Takamine, thrilled the spectators on Saturday, but couldn't compete on Sunday because of mechanical problems.

Special attractions on Saturday and Sunday included "Burning Wall Crashes" by Clarence "Pappy" Hoel, a white stallion named "Silver Town", motorcycle stunts by two riders from Denver, and music from the Sturgis High School Band. Race Manager B.A. Barnes praised the contributors and the committees and proclaimed the 1940 rally as the best so far![13]

1940 Champion: Al Nelson

Al Nelson was a local racing hero. An early member of the Jackpine Gypsies Motorcycle Club, Nelson was one of the hot shoes that emerged early on as a skillful dirt-track racer, competing in area "outlaw" races in Rapid City, Deadwood and Sturgis. Born in 1917, Nelson began riding motorcycles in 1933 at the age of 16. A year later, he rode to the Chicago Worlds Fair, picked up his sister and rode on to New York City.

Nelson's racing career began in 1935 when the Rapid City Pioneers Motorcycle Club, locally characterized as "the RPMs", began holding races around the Hills not sanctioned by the AMA. According to Nelson, the track at the Meade County Fairgrounds in Sturgis was the best track

Al Nelson, 1940 Sturgis Champion (Pearl Hoel Collection)

in the area, and club or "outlaw" races drew crowds of spectators. It was recognized early on that the Sturgis track was much faster than the Rapid City track, which probably played some contributing role in the initial 1937 field day event organized by the Jackpine Gypsies.

In early 1938, Nelson became friends with Johnny Spiegelhoff, a rider from Milwaukee, Wisconsin, who ultimately became the 1938 Sturgis champion. Nelson won most of the Saturday races in 1938, but was edged out by his friend Spiegelhoff in Sunday's 10-mile championship final. Caught in a cloud of dust, Nelson got too close to the edge, hit the loose dirt and went down. His engine was clogged with dirt, ending his chance at victory and sealing Spiegelhoff's 1938 win.

In 1939, Nelson moved to Milwaukee and moved in with Spiegelhoff. Nelson rode a few races in the Milwaukee area on his "Daytona" Indian Scout before being contacted by the Harley Davidson people to ride Harley Davidsons. At about the same time, Spiegelhoff switched from Harleys to Indians.

By 1940, Nelson had earned enough points to get his Expert license, and he returned to Sturgis to win the main event on his Harley Davidson. A crowd of 2,000 spectators watched him not only win the 10-mile championship race but also set a track record for the 10-mile that remains unbroken. After winning the Black Hills Motor Classic Championship, Nelson returned home on Monday morning, and at 6:00am, his father handed him plans for a construction project in Wyoming and told him to, "Get to work!" This was, essentially, the end of Nelson's motorcycle racing career.

During the 1939-40 racing season (which preceded his early retirement experience), Nelson had ridden his motorcycle to Langehorne, PA and Daytona Beach, FL to compete in national events. While he and Spiegelhoff had traveled together for some time during the 1939-40 season trailering their bikes, Nelson felt very strongly about riding to each race and suggested that this practice increased his stamina for the distance races.

Nelson sold his Harley Davidson in 1940 and returned to Sturgis for one more series of races in 1941, at which point he was riding a borrowed Triumph. In the Sunday final, he ran into another rider who had gone down, and of course, his old buddy Johnny Spiegelhoff went on to win the race.

In 1941, Nelson moved to Sheridan, Wyoming and worked in his father's construction business. During WW II, he served in the Army Air Corps in Troop Carrier Command in the South Pacific. When he returned from the service, he continued with the family business, supervising bridge construction projects for the rest of his career. He is presently retired and lives with his wife Ellen in Sheridan. Two of his three sons now manage the family construction firm.

Don Vodden and Al Nelson at 1998 White Plate Flat Trackers Association Breakfast. (Don Vodden Collection)

August 1-3, 1941

Clouds of war were clearly looming in Sturgis during the summer of 1941. Although the Fourth Cavalry stationed at Ft. Meade depended heavily on horses, trucks that were formerly used to transport horses were suddenly being used for more general military efforts, such as troop maneuvers. And again, the Canadian riders, who had made such an impact on the crowds in 1939 with their big Triumph singles, wrote saying that they could not come due to wartime restrictions. Both were waiting imminent induction into the military services of the British Commonwealth, which had been at war with Germany since September 1939.[1]

In early July, the *Sturgis Tribune* additionally reported the departure of nine local draftees, bound for Camp Crook, Nebraska and a county-wide canvass for scrap aluminum, which was not to be used for non-defense purposes.[2] Even the farmers were involved in war planning. The Farm Security Act (FSA) of 1941 emphasized that a strong national defense depends on self-sufficient communities, and Meade County was in the process of establishing an FSA Council.

Early plans for the rally included a Patriotic Ceremony which, according to Manager B. A. Barnes, was "...fitting the emergency that we in America are now in."[3] Rider registrations for race participation had been received from a total of 15 states. According to Barnes, this was probably because professional racers who wanted to earn AMA points and set new records for the half mile believed that Sturgis dirt, and hence the dirt track itself, had been recognized as the "world's fastest half-mile dirt track." [4]

By July 24, the Black Hills Motor Classic Planning Committee had anticipated all-around growth in numbers. The Friday Gypsy Tour, which had included 70 riders in 1940, was expected to exceed 100 in 1941. No entry fee was required for this event, which included a picnic lunch provided by Pearl Hoel. When the riders returned to Sturgis, they were, as in 1940, treated to a big evening meal, which included entertainment sponsored by the Commercial Club. In addition, the AMA had sanctioned the 1941 tour and was prepared to award prizes.[5]

Smiling Johnny Spiegelhoff, 1941 Sturgis Champion (Janis Sheets Collection)

A Sioux Falls patrol from the Elk's Lodge indicated that they had purchased new bikes and new uniforms and would send their Motor Wizard Patrol to entertain during the races.[6]

In the midst of all this preparation, the idea of motorcycle sporting events was apparently spreading to other towns in the Northern Hills. On Sunday, July 27, 1941, the Mile High Ramblers Motorcycle Club of Lead held an AMA-sanctioned endurance race. This thirty-mile race over rough terrain demanded that the rider maintain an average speed of 36 miles per hour. Clarence Hoel won this race on his Indian with a nearly perfect score of 999.[7]

Adding to the growing excitement, the *Tribune* reported that Johnny Spiegelhoff, who had won the Classic in both 1938 and 1939, was registered! Since Spiegelhoff had been unable to attend in 1940, local spectators were anxious to see him race again. Beyond the field of Harleys and Indians, the only non-domestic motorcycle racer registered was a Triumph rider from San Diego, California. This bike was described as "English made and can really make noise!" The electric timer, introduced in 1940 to meet AMA regulations, would be used for time trials as well as for the actual races.[8]

On Race Day, Spiegelhoff again won the Championship race but was unable to break Henry Stark's record time of 30.38 seconds in the time trials. The Gypsy Tour failed to meet the goal of 100 riders but did entice twelve additional riders, raising the number of non-resident participants from 70 in 1940 to 82 in 1941. Racer attendance, however, was way up with 22 entrants, seven more than the expected 15.[9]

While only nine draftees departed in early July, the Selective Service Board registered 44 male residents of Meade County for the draft in the last week of July.[10] Change and war alike were coming to America. There would not be a Black Hills Motor Classic in 1942.

Pearl's Room and Board

During the early rallies, Pearl and Clarence Hoel would pitch a circus tent in their back yard to provide a place for visiting riders to meet, visit and sleep. The Hoels also provided coffee and donuts at this site in the evening, after the riders returned from their various daytime excursions and the Gypsy Tours.

Pearl Hoel, with the help of one or two other Gypsy wives, would always provide a mid-day picnic for the Gypsy Tours at some central location in the Black Hills. To plan for the event, Pearl says that she and the other ladies would go downtown on the evening prior to the Gypsy Tour and count the bikes. They would then estimate that about two-thirds of the riders would participate in the tour. The women would then go to the grocery store to purchase the food. The picnic almost always consisted of baked beans, potato salad, wieners, coffee or iced tea and watermelon for dessert. After preparing the food late in the evening, the women would pack it all into Pappy's old pick-up truck, lead the tour out of town, and then head for the State Game Lodge,

Driving the support truck, Pearl leads the first Gypsy Tour out of Sturgis. (Pearl Hoel Collection)

Mount Rushmore, Sylvan Lake Lodge, or a similar centralized destination to set up the noon picnic. To recoup expenses, the price was 65 cents per person, and, according to Pearl, was "all you could eat". The pick-up truck would then follow the riders home to Sturgis and pick up any motorcycles that had broken down along the way.

On one occasion, she offered help to an automobile tourist stalled along the Needles Highway. According to Pearl, "This old Ford car was steaming like Old Faithful," and was parked in the middle of the narrow road, blocking traffic. Since the boiling radiator was in need of water and none was available among these granite crags, Pearl offered the man her remaining iced tea. When she assured the man that the tea did not contain sugar, he went ahead and used it to cool down his car. He later caught up with Pearl's pickup between Deadwood and Lead and thanked her profusely, indicating that it was "the best damn iced tea he had ever had"! Pearl thanked him but had to hurry home and prepare the evening's coffee and donut session.

Pearl had to give up providing the picnic lunch service in the late 1950's when the increasing number of riders simply became unmanageable. At 96 years of age, however, she still hosts a special breakfast during each year's Classic for the Retreads Club and helps prepare the White Plate Flat Trackers Association annual breakfast. When once asked what her favorite downtown rally food was, Pearl replied that she was so busy cooking and providing for her "company" that she didn't have time to visit the Main Street food vendors.

Chapter Three:
The War Years 1942-45

In June 1942, a group of entrepreneurial businessmen originated the idea of "Rooster Days" in Sturgis. Since gas rationing, military service, and other defense efforts had precluded the 1942 motorcycle rally, the Chamber of Commerce committee was determined to make Rooster Day a wartime substitute for the races in 1942.

The gist of Rooster Days was a contest to determine whose rooster was the heaviest or had the longest spurs or the largest comb and so forth. A carnival, parade, entertainment and price reduction sales — all characteristic of previous motorcycle rally weekends in previous years — were to induce the local farming community to Sturgis on Saturday. While the 1942 and 1943 Rooster Days were touted as being successful, the event failed to reappear in 1944 or 1945. In fact, the Sturgis Chamber began sponsoring rodeos in 1943, which were more in line with similar events in nearby Deadwood and Belle Fourche. But the idea of one more rodeo in such close proximity to two established rodeos could never approach the interest inherent in the Black Hills Motor Classic.

While the effects of World War II were being felt around the globe, a stinging fear became more apparent in the minds of local Sturgis residents. Would the rally survive this setback after the war? How would it rebuild local attitudes and rejuvenate spirit and general support from the Sturgis community?

Motorcycle Production

During World War II (WWII), domestic motorcycling was virtually non-existent. While the manufacturers were fabricating motorcycles (largely for military purposes), many were otherwise occupied producing a variety of different war-related parts or components that had no relationship to the motorcycle industry. Harley Davidson produced their 74-cubic inch cycle in military dress and also retooled their assembly line to manufacture the "XA", a copy of the early (1930's) side valve BMW R71. Because of the war, they were able to ignore German patents and produce this BMW clone.

Indian, on the other hand, was less successful than Harley Davidson in fabricating motorcycles for the military and ended up producing parts for other manufacturers. According to Jerry Hatfield, the U.S. Army, for all practical purposes, awarded all of their WWII motorcycle business to Harley Davidson.[1]

The Harley Davidson "XA" model evolved out of a competitive bidding process between Harley Davidson and Indian. The US War De-

The Indian Model 841, dressed for the US Army.

partment issued contracts for the development of prototypes in 1943, and apparently the contract specified a shaft rather than a chain drive cycle. Indian, true to its tradition of innovative research and development, came up with a new prototype. By extending their V-twin to 90 degrees and turning the engine sideways to accommodate the shaft drive configuration, the Indian "Model 841" was born — a motorcycle that closely resembled a contemporary Moto-Guzzi. True to the conservative approach which had borne them safety through the depression years, Harley Davidson took the approach of adapting the proven design developed by BMW. Needless to say, Harley Davidson won the contract and produced several thousand of the "XA" models by war's end. A total of 1,056 Model 841 Indians were produced but never saw military action. Many were surplused out of the Indian Factory in Springfield, Massachusetts for $500 each in 1946.[2]

Choppers

After the war, the military destroyed large numbers of the surplus motorcycles, but on occasion, these cycles were made available to returning servicemen at a nominal price. The author's older brother, a sailor returning to San Francisco after the Japanese surrender, purchased one of these machines for $100. (Since the trains were glutted with returning service men and he was forced to wait eight days for a pass, he planned to ride the motorcycle home to Minnesota and conserve some of his 30-day leave.) After all of the sailors had made their purchases, a transport ship carried the cycles to the center of San Francisco Bay and dumped more than 100 brand new bikes, still in their factory crates, over the side.

A similar incident was related to the author by his brother-in-law, an Army Veteran who had picked up his first post-war job working at Camp Ripley Military Reservation in Central Minnesota. This man had been assigned to a work crew that hand-wheeled about 50 motorcycles to a level pit, where the cycles were laid on their side on the ground. When the work detail had completed this task, a large caterpillar tractor was driven over the motorcycles several times, crushing them into the dirt. The workers then finished their day, using Number 2 shovels to help the dozer cover them up. After leveling the surface, they crew raked the dirt smooth and planted grass seed.

Many military bikes did, however, survive and were available to motorcycle enthusiasts during the late 1940's. Most riders chopped off all the unnecessary military accessories from these bikes, and the term "chopper" entered the motorcyclist's vocabulary.

Chapter 4:
The Post-War Years,
Reconstruction and Rebirth

In 1946, the rally was back on, but the local businessmen planning the first post-war rally were unsure that they would be able to recapture the pre-war excitement. As a result, they informally returned leadership of the rally to Pappy Hoel and the Jackpine Gypsies. By the time the local businessmen realized that it might really work again, it was too late to schedule the carnival and parade, and publicity was limited to summer sales in the local stores. The motorcycle club members, whose efforts were focused mainly on the Gypsy Tour and the half-mile dirt track races at the Fairgrounds, were able to draw an estimated crowd of 4,000 spectators for the two days of racing.

By early 1947, the Commercial Club members, now loosely unified in the new Sturgis Chamber of Commerce and the Black Hills Motor Classic committee, were convinced that investment in the rally was money well spent, and they returned to the level of their pre-war involvement and support. They became more heavily involved in the 1947 Classic, returning the carnival, the parade and a dance. They also mounted a more focused strategy for publicizing the weekend of events.

The1948 rally saw racers and visitors from 28 states, encompassing both the East and West Coasts. Fifty racers were registered for the two days of racing, and the Black Hills Motor Classic was again a viable event.

By 1949, several nationally-recognized racers were entered, and this trend continued throughout the 1950s and 1960s. Apparently the Sturgis half-mile track was really fast, and those riders who were interested in setting new records came to participate. Many riders also commented about their positive experiences regarding the hospitality afforded by local Sturgis residents.

In 1950, a new event, the "Sportsman's" Hill Climb was added to the rally. The focus of this "Sportsman" classification was to entice local riders to participate in the fun.

August 9-11, 1946

The first postwar "Motorcycle Classic" was held on August 9-11, 1946, and while it was touted as one of the "Northwest's Major Events"[1], community involvement failed to generate the high degree of excitement that was present in the final pre-war rally in 1941.

As in 1937 and 1938, Clarence Hoel was again important enough to be designated as the Chairman of Events. While the Commercial Club had assumed the role of management and organization for the 1939 through 1941 "Classics", the onus of being "in charge" was again, at least publicly, relegated to Hoel. The half-mile track was again characterized as one of the fastest in the nation, and the prize money for the nine races was increased to $1,000. Early racer registrations were limited to riders from the nearby states of Wisconsin, Minnesota, Iowa and Colorado. The Jackpine Gypsy Tour was scheduled for Friday August 9, and an evening picnic was planned for Bear Butte Park.[2]

On August 1, the route for the Gypsy Tour was posted. Beginning at Sturgis, the morning route included Rapid City, Mt. Rushmore, Iron Mountain Road, and Coolidge Inn, where a picnic lunch was again provided by Pearl Hoel and her group of motorcycle wives. The return trip included the Needles Highway, Sylvan Lake and Deadwood. All AMA-member participants, as a recruitment award, were to be given a patch for making the Tour. The evening picnic was sponsored by the new Sturgis Chamber of Commerce, which had apparently replaced the pre-war Commercial Club. The official starter was Mr. George Clifford, an officer in the Cedar Rapids, Iowa AMA Club.[3]

By August 8, two days before the rally, only 10 riders had submitted registrations to participate in the race, and only two were farther away than Minnesota, Iowa or Colorado: Peter Freytag from New Jersey and Johnny Spieglehoff from Milwaukee. In addition, the Black Hills Motor Classic committee, sensing that the rally would be successful, had replaced Pappy Hoel as chairman with B. A. Barnes, the successful manager of the 1939-1941 events.[4]

When rally weekend arrived, the total count of admissions showed more than 4,000 spectators. R. B. Williams, Secretary of the Sturgis Chamber of Commerce, served as the public address announcer, and Johnny Spieglehoff walked away with both the five-mile (5.35 minutes) and the ten-mile races with a time of 11.53 minutes. Bill Tuman figured prominently in the class B (Amateur) races, winning both the five and ten mile features on Sunday.[5]

Johnny Spiegelhoff: National Racing Career

After winning the 1939 Expert final at Sturgis, Johnny Spiegelhoff's career in competing at the National Championship level began in earnest. On August 28, 1939 he took a respectable fourth place in the 25-mile championship event at Springfield, Illinois. His next AMA championship attempt was at the same race track a year later on August 25, 1940, where he improved his position to second place, losing in a close race. In 1941, Johnny took his Krause Motors Indian to Daytona where he completed 61 of the required 63 laps before he had to withdraw. Even though he didn't complete the race, he still finished 19th in a field of over 100 riders.[1]

Johnny Spiegelhoff, 1946 Sturgis Champion (Sturgis Museum Collection)

In August 1941, after winning his third championship race at Sturgis, he returned to the "Mile" at Springfield, Illinois, and on August 17 placed third. Apparently a win at Springfield was not to be. On August 31, 1941, he traveled to Langehorne, Pennsylvania, to compete in the last AMA 100 Mile National Championship prior to WWII and ended up in fifth place. When the AMA racing program resumed in 1946, Spiegelhoff again won the championship race at Sturgis and followed up by wining the 100 Mile AMA National Championship at Langehorne. Earning the post position after setting a track record of 40.292 seconds in time trials, Spiegelhoff ended up getting a slow start and had to follow another rider (Billy Huber) for 93 laps before passing him in lap 94. His total time for the 100 miles was 1:13:07:4. The *Indian Motorcycle News* described Johnny as riding "a cool and methodical race, hunched down over the tank as if he were part of that green and orange Indian."[2]

Johnny's next success in 1946 was to win club races at London, Ohio on September 8. His 1946 season was cut short four days later at the Iowa State Fair in Marshalltown. Spiegelhoff was leading the pack in the final event when he and four other riders tangled in the final turn. He suffered a broken arm and was out for the remainder of the season.

By the following February, the arm appeared to be healed because on February 23, 1947, Spiegelhoff went on to win The Daytona 200. He began this race a short distance behind the initial leader, Ed Kretz, who experienced mechanical difficulties between the 11th and 14th lap. Spiegelhoff passed Kretz in lap 15 and maintained the lead for the rest of the race to take the championship. In the final laps he was followed closely by a young, new and exciting Indian racer named Bobby Hill from Columbus, Ohio who spilled on the 57th lap.[3]

In August of 1947, after winning these two top National Championship races back to back, Spiegelhoff returned to Springfield, Illinois for one more stab at the 25 mile championship. He placed fourth in 1947, and in 1948 he ended up fifth. He was never able to capture a first at Springfield.

Johnny Spiegelhoff did not return to compete in Sturgis after the 1946 Black Hills Motor Classic. He indicated that he would retire after the 1948 season, but he held on, racing a few times in 1949. In the early

Johnny Spiegelhoff in retirement. (Janis Sheets Collection)

1950's, Spiegelhoff journeyed to Mexico where he, Ed Kretz and Jack Horn competed in exhibition races.[4]

Soon after, Johnny and his wife Clare opened a dealership, "Spiegelhoff's Motorcycles, Sporting Goods and Bicycles" at 3820 West North Avenue in downtown Milwaukee. Johnny sold the bikes and motorcyles, and Clare kept the books and wrote advertising copy and television spots. According to Hal Deckert, the business closed in 1954 when American-made Indian Motorcycles were no longer available. After his motorcycle shop closed, Spiegelhoff began work as a machine operator in the construction business in the Milwaukee area. When the opportunity to operate equipment in Mexico during the winter months emerged, Johnny Spiegelhoff rode his three-wheeled "Service Car" to Mazatlan, Mexico. This winter employment opportunity continued until 1974, when he contracted hepatitis and died in the hospital at Colima, Mexico. He was 59 years of age.[5]

Johnny Spiegelhoff was important and perhaps even crucial to the development and evolution of the Black Hills Motor Classic in several ways. First, he was instrumental in influencing the Jackpine Gypsies

Motorcycle Club to pursue the process of seeking AMA sanctioning of the Sturgis racing program. This initiated some national publicity and attracted out-of-state riders from California, Colorado and Minnesota as well as Spiegelhoff. Secondly, his idea of providing the challenge races in the initial 1938 program not only was a crowd pleaser, which interested many new Black Hills area racing fans, but also established the friendly rivalry between Harley Davidson and Indian in these same new spectators. Thanks in large part to Spiegelhoff, spectators argued, debated and cheered on their motorcycle preference, preparing them for the ensuing rallies and races at Sturgis. Thirdly, Spiegelhoff provided these rural and inexperienced racing fans with an out-of state "Champion", an Expert racer who returned year after year to win the feature race at Sturgis. This was particularly important in 1946, when many wondered if the rally would survive the war years. Spiegelhoff's return and win in 1946 reassured rally promoters and fans alike that the Black Hills Motor Classic would continue to draw nationally recognized racers.

AMA Competition

By 1925, the AMA was sanctioning 56 race meets and awarding 14 national championships. Each of the 14 championship events were different with regard to race distance and displacement of the participating motorcycle engines. Early displacement rules included only the 500 cc (30.5 cubic inches) and 1000 cc (61 cubic inches) categories. The 750 cc (45 cubic inches) category, which was popular in Europe, was added in 1933.[1]

As automobile fans rallied around the Indianapolis 500, motorcycle supporters selected a 200-mile venue for their premier racing event. The first AMA-sponsored National Championship 200-mile race was held in 1934 at Jacksonville, Florida but was moved to Springfield, Illinois in 1937. After losing the national site to Illinois, Florida promoters established their own 200-mile race, introducing the Daytona 200 in 1937 – one of today's most widely-recognized national motorcycle events.[2] While AMA-sanctioned motorcycle racing was suspended during World War II, it began again with fervor in 1946. Many distance races were added to a new championship program called the "Grand National Series," and the new championships were delegated to different sites. Sturgis, chosen for the National Championship half mile in the flat track category in 1952, was one of these venues. By 1954, Flat Track Grand National Championship dirt track events included the mile, the half-mile, short track and tourist trophy (TT) steeplechase races. Off-road competition grew a great deal in the 1960's with the advent of lighter motorcycles. The motocross category, which grew out of the enthusiasm for scrambles, enduro and desert racing, emerged with AMA-approved rules in 1961. Today, motocross and similar events place third in fan attendance for all kinds of racing in America.[3]

At the outset of the 21st century, over 250,000 motorcyclists make up the membership of the AMA. A major force in government regulations and lobbying, the AMA works constantly to assure and "...coordinate national legal activity against unconstitutional and discriminatory laws against motorcyclists, to serve as a sentinel on federal and state legislation affecting motorcyclists, and to be instrumental as a lobbying force for motorcyclists and motorcycling interests."[4]

An early association with the AMA was essential in the growth and success of the Black Hills Motor Classic. The early pre-war, AMA-sponsored flat track races and Gypsy Tours were crucial to the development and evolution of "Sturgis" as it is exists today.

August 8-10, 1947

According to the *Sturgis Tribune*, the 1947 "Classic" would be held August 8-10. Race Manager Bruce Barnes noted that the fast half-mile track was in good order and was to be subjected to materials that would make it "dust proof". In addition, a new race format was going to be introduced at the 1947 rally. While the crowd had been treated to five and ten mile races in the past, the 1947 program would include an eight mile race.[1] Event planners were anticipating 300-500 cycles, and the August 8 Gypsy Tour was to end with a "Buffalo Feed" Friday night at the City Park. The dance and carnival from pre-war rallies would again take place – the carnival secured by the Chamber of Commerce and the dance sponsored by the VFW.

With regard to the races, the *Tribune* went so far as to remind race spectators that the racing machines were tuned up with powerful engines, had no brakes, and that the riders would be wearing a steel shoe on the left foot. These shoes were sometimes constructed using car bumpers, but some riders purchased custom-made steel shoes from dirt-track "shoemakers". The riders used these shoes on their left foot to stabilize the bikes in the corners.[2]

By Thursday, August 7, over 400 riders had registered for Friday's Gypsy Tour and a Friday night feed sponsored by the Jackpine Gypsies Motorcycle Club. Roselyn Anderson, the very first Miss South Dakota to be sent to the Miss America Pageant in Atlantic City, and Billy Rose, the State Soap Box Derby Champion, were both scheduled to appear during the grandstand show on Sunday between races. Almost 30 racers from as far away as California and Illinois were registered, which was good news. More racers meant more heat races and more thrills for spectators.[3]

The Friday Gypsy Tour experienced one accident when Orville Bogenschuts, a 26-year-old cyclist, lost control of his bike on Strawberry Hill. After receiving first aid, he was transported to St. Joseph's Hospital in Deadwood.

Bill Tuman, #51, in the backstretch at Sturgis in 1947. (Pearl Hoel Collection)

During the Saturday races, a new champion, Bill Tuman, set a new record of 5.17 minutes in the five-mile race. Tuman was able to move from third place to first place in just seven laps. Most important of all to Pappy Hoel, Tuman was able to use his Indian to overcome Floyd Emde, the Pacific Coast Champion, who was riding a Harley Davidson. A total of 25 competitors, including "Novice", "Amateur", and "Expert" racers were involved in the various races. Ed Cruickshank served as the official starter and J.C. "Pappy" Hoel worked the microphone.[4]

Unfortunately, a torrential rainstorm led to the cancellation of the Sunday races. The track had become too muddy for safe racing. According to Bobby James, a novice racer from Pueblo, Colorado and first time visitor to Sturgis in 1947, things got to be a real mess. On Sunday morning, Pappy Hoel asked for volunteers to help dry and pack the track. To do so, they were to drive their cars and trucks around the track to pack it down. According to James, this idea was a bit premature, as the cars could not move in the gumbo, and the trucks were having the same problem unless they were heavily loaded down. Time ran out, and after some discussion in a riders meeting about holding the race on Monday, it was decided to cancel the race because most of the riders and the spectators needed to return to their jobs.

When everyone finally got ready to leave, they discovered that people who left early had depleted the gasoline supply in all of the Sturgis service stations. The Colorado convoy, of which James was a member, had to pool their gas supply from their vehicles as well as their racing fuel before heading out of town. The group was able to eke out their remaining fuel until they reached Newcastle, Wyoming where they found an open gas station and were able to fill their tanks.[5]

1947 Champion: Bill Tuman

Bill Tuman's racing career is a classic example of circumstances or fate. Near the end of World War II, he was working in the Navy Supply Depot in San Francisco, California and contemplating a return to his home state of Illinois. On the way home from work one day, he noticed a sign in the window of Hap Jones Indian Motorcycle Sales stating "Motorcycle Mechanic Wanted." Since Tuman had had some experience working on automobiles, he decided to give it a shot. He told the dealer that he had worked on cars and asked if he could have the job. The man said that he would give him a chance and the next day Tuman showed up for work. "Where are all your tools?" he was asked. "They're being shipped to me from Illinois," was Tuman's response. The dealer said that he would lend him some tools until the shipment arrived. Tuman used the borrowed tools, began to learn the mechanics of Indian motorcycles, and on his first payday, he ran up the street to a hardware store to buy some tools![1]

His skill as a motorcycle mechanic grew rapidly, and in a few months he was promoted to Shop Foreman. One day after work he came home to find that his roommate had taken off with all of his ration books and savings. Tuman had been building up a roll of bills but had stashed a bag of silver dollars under a brick in the fireplace. He jumped on a Greyhound bus and followed the traitor home to Wisconsin where he found

Bill Tuman before coming to Sturgis in 1947. (Sturgis Museum Collection)

the roommate already in jail, arrested for stealing money in his home-town. "He was lucky and I was lucky," said Tuman. "If he had been out of jail I would probably have killed him and then I would have been in jail, too."[2]

Not knowing what to do, Tuman called the abandoned boss in California who urged him to return. Tuman went back to California, built up a racing bike for Mario Stille, a West Coast racer sponsored by Hap Jones, and then traveled as Stille's mechanic to a race at San Raphel. Tuman quickly found himself interested in taking a stab at racing motor-cycles.

He returned to Illinois, built up a racer using an Army Surplus Indian and took second place in his first race at Mendota, Illinois in 1946 be-hind Leo Anthony, an ace Harley Davidson factory racer. Tuman was all of 25 years old.[3]

Later that year, Smitty from Tri-City Indian Sales at Rock Island, Illinois noticed Tuman's natural skill as a dirt track racer and became his spon-sor. With Smitty's help and Indian factory support, Tuman moved quickly through the Novice and Amateur levels and received his Expert license in 1947. The Daytona 200 was his first race as a professional. His win at Sturgis in 1947 was one of Tuman's first victories.[4]

During the 1947-48 racing season Tuman worked hard in the Mid-west fair circuit and took over 130 consecutive first place wins, racing six to seven races each week, but he was unable to win a National until later in his career. He was well liked by his fellow racers and was voted as the Most Popular Rider in the USA in 1950.[5]

A native of Rockford, Illinois Tuman went on to race extensively in the Midwest and on occasion went to the West Coast, where he won the AMA Grand National at San Mateo, California in 1952. Because of fam-ily obligations, he generally raced close to home at Midwest county and state fairs as well as at the Sturgis Classic. The author can even remem-ber watching Tuman race at the Minnesota State Fair in 1951. With few exceptions, Tuman always raced Indian Motorcycles and was a mem-ber of the famous "Indian Wrecking Crew," which included Tuman, Bobby Hill and Ernie Beckman.[6]

In a 2002 interview, both Tuman and his lifelong friend Bobby Hill reflected on their racing days at Sturgis with a great deal of pleasure. While they did not enjoy the zigzag trip they had to make on two lane highways leading to and from Sturgis, they always had a good time. They described Wall Drug on the northern edge of the South Dakota Badlands as an "oasis" where they could finally buy a sandwich and a cup of coffee. They indicated that they enjoyed the family type atmosphere of the rally, the respect and support they received from Pappy Hoel and the rest of the Gypsies, and the clean officiating. They both really liked the Friday night feed and program.[7]

White Plate Flat Trackers Association

Any visitor to Sturgis will discover a monument to all early dirt-track motorcycle racers in the United States. Comprising a large central granite plinth topped with a dirt track bike and rider, the monument lists the history and names of most of the famous dirt-track racers. It was established in the early 1980s by the White Plate Flat Trackers Association (WPFTA).

The WPFTA, conceived and organized by Pappy Hoel and Al Burke in 1979, is dedicated to the memory of early racers. Fearing that early racing legends would be forgotten by contemporary riders, Burke and Hoel organized a reunion for White Plate riders at the 1980 Sturgis Rally. These pioneer riders continue to meet and those who can, ride a lap at the half-mile final on Saturday.[1]

To qualify for membership, a racer has to have earned his white plate, which involves the accumulation of points throughout a racing career. Beginning as a novice with a green number plate, a rider must earn 40 points by winning 1st, 2nd, or 3rd in main events. After 40 points are amassed, the novice can be advanced to the "Junior" or Amateur class and receive a yellow plate with black numbers. White plates with black numerals and letters are awarded to Amateur who can earn 80 points and compete in a minimum of two years of racing with a good safety record. At this point the White Plate includes a letter to designate the region or area of the rider's residence. This letter also differentiates a "Junior" from an "Expert". While the riders in either of these classifications are qualified to ride in "Expert" class AMA races and are the feature race stars and true crowd pleasers on race day, there is yet a higher classification. For those expert riders who place first, second, or third at a National Championship Race, the AMA awards a white plate number from 1 to 99 without the regional (letter) designation. These are the "expert Experts" in that they represent the whole nation rather than a specific area or region. These are the candidates who can be elected to the WPFTA.[2]

Visitors to the rally may observe a gaggle of older riders hanging around the WPFTA monument enjoying each other's company and doing some serious "bench racing." If so moved, one or two of these former racing stars will ride a lap on the famous Sturgis half-mile track, using their old racer in a between-races special event. The sound generated by a vintage Harley Davidson, Indian, BSA, Norton or Triumph four-stroke in this moment is a truly sweet experience in any present-day rally.

White Plate Flat Trackers Monument, Sturgis. (Author Photo)

1947 2nd Place Finish: Floyd Emde

When he arrived in Sturgis on August 12, 1947, Floyd Emde had just set the unofficial world's record for the half-mile track in July at Richmond, Virginia. On Saturday at Sturgis he won both of his heat races but lost in the final lap to Bill Tuman of Rockford, Illinois. The Sturgis Tribune described the race as "not only a race between Emde's Harley Davidson and Tuman's Indian but a race between the East and West's best riders."[1] At the time, Emde was the Pacific Coast Champion, and Tuman had been burning up the tracks in the Midwest. Emde would go on to win the Daytona 200 in 1948 on an Indian. (There is no explanation of why Emde rode a Harley Davidson at Sturgis and an Indian at Daytona.)

Don Emde was born in Seeley, California on March 7, 1919. He grew up in the San Diego area, the son of a California motorcycle patrolman and racer. Emde began dirt track racing in the San Diego area in the late 1930s. He excelled in this area and also in TT Steeplechase. He received his Expert license in 1941 and did well until the war put an end to competition. He came back in 1946, and by 1947, Emde won the Pacific Coast TT Championship at Riverside, California, earning him the title of Pacific Coast Champion. Later in 1947, before his second place finish at Sturgis, Emde had been victorious in the 10-mile National Championship at Milwaukee. In 1948, Emde was one of 153 starters at Daytona, capturing the lead from the outset and never letting go despite an impressive field of competitors that included five former Daytona champions, including Ed Kretz, and Johnny Spiegelhoff. Canadian Billy Mathews, who had won Daytona in 1941 on a Norton Manx, made a run at Emde late in the race. Emde, who had been leading by more than minute at the halfway mark, survived the Matthews assault by only 12 seconds. With his victory at Daytona, Emde established two significant milestones. First, he was the only racer in the history of Daytona to hold the lead for the entire 200 miles, and second, it was the last time an Indian motorcycle was to win at Daytona.[2]

Emde retired from professional racing in the early 1950s to better manage his motorcycle dealership in San Diego. All three of his sons became involved in motorcycling racing, and one of these second generation riders, son Don Emde, won the Daytona 200 in 1972, making the Emde's the only two-win family at this important race. Floyd Emde died on New Year's Eve in 1994.[3]

August 13-15, 1948

Once again, early racer registrations for the 1948 Black Hills Motor Classic indicated that racers were expected from both coasts for the August 13-15 event. Nationally-recognized riders like Bill Tuman (the 1947 Sturgis champion) and Floyd Emde (the Reigning National AMA Champion) were registered by August 12. Race Manager Bruce Barnes indicated that one of the riders from Omaha was planning to fly to the rally. The carnival was booked for the entire week, including the four days prior to the rally, and the local horseback riding association was in charge of the grandstand concessions. This group, new to rally participation, was a further indication of evolving community involvement and endorsement of the rally, joining the traditional support of the Sturgis High School Band and the local Boy Scouts of America troop.[1]

Motorcycles parked at the 1948 half-mile races. (Pearl Hoel Collection)

A minor injury to a young rider — Rolland Nation from Kennebec, South Dakota – couldn't slow down the brewing excitement. Nation had been visiting Sturgis in anticipation of the rally and was injured on the viaduct nine miles south of town.

As a growing tradition, the Gypsy Tour again was received with great success on the Friday before race day with riders representing 28 states.

By race day a record number of 50 racers were entered and competed in front of a capacity crowd. The previous attendance record was easily broken and one of the crowd pleasers, Kelly Meyers from Los Angeles, California, smashed all of the track records on his British-made Triumph. Myers lost the Sunday final, however, and the feature race winner (Expert) was Chuck Basney, also from Los Angeles, who slipped by Myers in the final turn of the 20th lap.[3] Third place was taken by Babe Tancrede., who had won in Daytona in 1940.

The new Indian Arrow and Scout models were demonstrated between races by two women, Joan Vodden of Sturgis and Harriet Anderson of Denver, Colorado.[4] Always with a keen eye to advertising, Pappy Hoel wasn't going to miss a chance to promote his beloved Indian marquee.

Despite the growing numbers of attendees, racers and spectators, community support for the rally and an appreciation for visiting riders remained very positive. According to the *Sturgis Tribune*, Chief of Police Carl Aga indicated that "no trouble was experienced with motorcycle riders or the huge crowd that jammed into Sturgis during the running of the tenth annual motorcycle classics and the gypsy tour." Chief Aga went on, stating that "the department is grateful for the fine behavior during these events. Not a single arrest was made, the department received no telephone calls of disturbance."[5]

1948 Expert Champion: Chuck Basney

Chuck Basney, a native of the Los Angeles area and the 1948 Champion at Sturgis, enjoyed four passions. Three of them had to do with motor sports and speed. Basney enjoyed flying his own airplane and competing in motorcycle racing. He also built high-speed cars to race on dry lake beds in Southern Califonia. The fourth passion was for deep-sea fishing, and during the racing off-season, he journeyed to Baja, California, to pursue this obsession, fishing both in the Sea of Cortez and in the Pacific Ocean.[1]

His motorcycle racing career, an offshoot of his stock car racing competition, began on the very same stock car tracks which were popular in southern California in the post war years of 1946 and 1947. These motorcycle races, commonly called "Speedway Races," were held on the one-fifth mile stock car venues. According to Troy Lee, a former motorcycle racing associate, the one-fifth mile tracks were originally used for cars and motorcycle races. At the time, official short-track motorcycle races were conducted on quarter-mile tracks, and so the term Speedway Race was employed to designate the difference in lap distance. In later years all of the southern California motorcycle short-track venues were designed as 1/5th mile tracks and so the characterization of "Speedway Race" was eventually dropped.(2)

A tile setter by trade, Basney used his extra cash to finance his hobbies. After a recognized career as a Speedway Racer, Basney was approached by a Harley Davidson dealer in Santa Anna and began competing in half-mile dirt track events.[3]

Chuck Basney, 1948 Sturgis Expert Champion. (Pearl Hoel Collection)

Basney came to Sturgis to race in the half mile event in 1948 on an Indian. A virtual unknown in the Midwest, he did poorly in the Saturday preliminary races and complained of engine trouble. Ever the generous race promoter, Clarence Hoel offered Basney the services of his motorcycle shop, and with Hoel's assistance, they tore his engine apart and finished a complete overhaul in the wee hours of Sunday morning. His time trials and heat race places on Sunday were very ordinary, and he was ultimately placed in an outside position in the final event. After a slow start, Basney found himself near the back of the pack, and then surprised everyone in the Sturgis crowd by systematically passing each of the other racers until in the final lap he came out ahead and won the race. Although somewhat disappointing to the Midwestern fans, everyone had to admit that Basney's skill in passing almost everyone in the pack did lend thrills and excitement for the crowd of spectators.[4]

Barbara Phillips, the wife of famous West Coast flat tracker Jimmy Phillips, says that coming from the rear to win was a Basney trademark. She related that he was so good at this crowd-pleasing strategy that he was featured in the early 1950's on the classic television program "You Asked For It," which showed films of his performing this feat in several races. Basney continued racing until 1956 when he was killed tragically in a quarter mile event at Gardena, California.[5]

Indian Motorcycles

The Indian Motorcycle Factory in Springfield, Massachusetts began making bicycles in the late 19th century. These early "Indians" were designed with a large wheel in the front and a small trailing wheel behind. It wasn't until around the turn of the century that Indian began producing bicycles with wheels of the same dimensions.[1]

In 1901, through the creative efforts of a young Swedish engineer named Oscar Hedstrom, an engine was attached to one of these two-wheelers and the first Indian Motorcycle was born. In 1913, the factory produced 32,000 of these early models — an all-time annual production record in the history of Indian Motorcycles.[2]

Guided by Hedstrom, a brilliant inventor and innovator, Indian became a leader in a variety of innovative firsts, including the first foot boards (1912), the first rear suspension system (1913), the first electric starter (1914), and the first twist grip controls (1916). Many of these innovations led to an Indian Motorcycle "Tourist Trophy" win at the International Isle of Man racetrack prior to World War I. [3]

Perhaps one of Indian's most key innovations was an aluminum housing to cover the primary chain linking the engine to the transmission, introduced in the early 1920s. Previous Indian models and competitors alike had always suffered from primary chain failure because of ready access to dust and grit. The new aluminum cover allowed the chain to run in an oil bath making it virtually drip and problem free. By 1922 Hedstrom had perfected a side valve engine, which enclosed the push rods and protected them from the elements. Indian had, in effect, developed the first entirely enclosed motorcycle engine. Enclosing all of the moving parts not only made the Indian more dependable but also led to a significantly quieter engine. Harley Davidson, always conservative in the design and innovation, ultimately copied this enclosed engine design over ten years later in the 1930's.[4]

Indian racing history began with board track racing in the 1910-1912 seasons. In 1911, Indian cycles finished first, second, third, fifth and sixth in the Isle of Man TT. Indian also captured all of the 126 categories established for competition in 1911 by the AMA precursor organization, the Federation of American Motorcyclists (FAM). Indian racers also generally won, in early years, in the so called "Three Flag" endurance races in which riders raced down the west coast from British Columbia to Mexico.[5]

By the 1930's, the motorcycle industry, which had earlier encompassed nearly 75 different manufacturers, was reduced to three American marques: Excelsior/Henderson, Harley Davidson, and Indian. Loyalty to each of these marques typically evolved in riding clubs generally organized around motorcycle dealerships where riders hung out and kicked tires. The Jackpine Gypsies Motorcycle Club in Sturgis was just one of hundreds of similar motorcycle clubs across the United States and Canada.[6]

Government contracts for motorcycles began when police departments in some of the major cities began to see the advantages of replacing horses with this cheaper and more versatile form of transport. This led to similar applications in the military. For some reason, Harley Davidson and Excelsior/Henderson seemed more adept at securing government contracts to produce police bikes. This was clearly evident in city and state law-enforcement agencies and was particularly true during World War II when Indian factory output was almost totally limited to making components for non-motorcycle related defense contractors.

Indian actually made a similar production mistake during World War I. The company managed to win a large share of the US Army's contract for motorcycle production. Indian, however, elected to make a total commitment to the Army for the duration of the war. As a result, the civilian public and Indian dealers were left in a lurch. Without parts or bikes to sell, many Indian dealers took on Harley Davidson franchises. Indian lost the confidence of many dealers, and as a result, never really returned to the level of output they had generated prior to the war.[8]

The history of the Black Hills Motor Classic clearly reveals that Indian Motorcycles were a driving force at the rally, dominating the race outcomes in many of the early Sturgis Rallies until 1953, when the Indian Motorcycle Company ceased production. Early Indian racing heroes included "The Indian Ironman" Ed Kretz and Floyd Emde. Ernie Beckman, Bobby Hill, and Bill Tuman dominated racing circles on Indian bikes in the late 1940s and early 1950s and came to be known as the "Indian Wrecking Crew".[8]

Indians from the 1940s are the most sought-after by collectors. The most common color, bright red, set off by skirted fenders and balloon tires are works of art to motorcycle buffs.

1948 3rd Place Finish: Babe Tancrede

Babe Tancrede, who took third place at Sturgis in 1948, was born on September 15, 1906 in Woonsocket, Rhode Island. Tancrede began riding motorcycles in his teens and soon earned a reputation as an excellent motorcycle polo rider. He won his first major race in the AMA National TT Steeplechase in 1934 and continued to collect numerous victories in TT and hill climbing. In 1936 Tancrede placed second in the Savanna, Georgia 200

In 1940, Tancrede won the Daytona 200. In those days, the 200 was more of an endurance race than it is today. Of the 77 riders at the start, Tancrede was one of the 15 who actually completed the race. At Daytona in 1939, he received the AMA Most Popular Rider Award. Later in 1940, Tancrede won the Laconia, New Hampshire AMA National road race and finished second behind Billy Mathews at the 1941 Daytona 200.[1] After World War II, Tancrede returned to competition with notable second place wins at Laconia in 1948 and 1951.[2]

When he was not racing, Tancrede worked as a motor patrolman for the City of Woonsocket and later established a bulk-heating oil delivery service. A life-long Harley Davidson rider, Tancrede retired from racing in 1952 when Harley Davidson came out with the new hand clutch, foot shifter WR 750 racing bikes. He said that, at age 46, he was too old to master the new configuration.

Tancrede and his wife Stella raised two children. He died in 1995 at 89 years of age.[3]

August 12-14, 1949

The 1949 Black Hills Motor Classic introduced a race weekend "first" that remains a hallmark of the rally to this day. Clarence "Pappy" Hoel, characterized by the *Sturgis Tribune* as "Captain of the Gypsy Tour," negotiated a plan to close Main Street for the grand total of two hours on Friday evening for "contests," following the return of the tour. Apparently, the idea of using downtown rather than the City Park or Bear Butte Park was endorsed by the Chamber of Commerce and the main street merchants.

Prizes for the youngest, oldest, and best dressed male and female riders included Black Hills Gold jewelry. Several merchants indicated that they would sponsor other prizes to enrich this experience and would establish unique contests by rally Friday.[1]

By July 21, reserve seat grandstand ticket requests for the August 13-14 races had been received from out-of-state visitors from as far away as Missouri, Utah, Kansas and Ohio. In the interest of publicizing the Classic locally, the Jackpine Gypsies had been providing motorcycle escorts in other community events throughout the Black Hills area.[2]

Registration for the Gypsy Tour indicated that somewhere between 300 and 500 riders would leave Sturgis on Friday morning, August 12 for the annual trek through the Hills. The continued growth of the Gypsy Tour was clearly becoming an important dimension of the rally, enticing non-race riders to attend and become involved in the Classic. The blocking of Main Street and the introduction of free music events, stunts, and contests seemed to take precedence over the carnival hype of previous years.

Race Manager Bruce Barnes indicated that racer registration requests had been received from over a dozen states and that the Canadian riders, who had wowed the crowd in 1938, were returning. Improved dust proofing techniques in 1948 had led to safer racing and would again be employed. Barnes reassured the readers, however,

Jackpine Gypsies prepare to ride in the Fourth of July parade in Lead, South Dakota. (Neil Hultman Collection)

that although no one had "left the track" in the 1948 races, spectators could still expect some exciting spills and pile-ups.[3]

Touted as the eleventh annual Classic (actually the ninth), riders were greeted at the Gypsy Camp by Hoel's Motorcycle Shop on South Junction Avenue and given free coffee, doughnuts, and rally instructions. The riders were informed of the Gypsy Tour, the races, and the Friday night celebration along with a series of traffic and parking rules. Riders were required to have their cycles parked by 8:00pm so that engine noise would not disturb the Main Street celebration. Besides the prizes for oldest, youngest, and best-dressed riders, additional prizes included longest distance ridden to the rally, the most recently-married couple, the longest-married couple, and the best-dressed motorcycle club. Two additional prizes included the most popular tour rider (elected by the tour participants) and the Queen of the Black Hills Motor Classic. To qualify as "Queen," a woman needed to hold membership in the AMA and reside outside the Black Hills area. The Queen would be selected by a panel of three "impartial" judges. The Jackpine Gypsies would perform a comedy act during the Friday night festivities, but there was no mention of the Friday night feed noted in previous years.[4]

Dick Klamfoth, a 20 year-old rider from Grovesport, Ohio, took the Expert championship for both the five and eight mile races. Klamfoth thrilled more than 5000 spectators in the two days of racing on his Manx Norton. This huge British single was noted for its high torque, distinctive throbbing exhaust, and lightning speed. Having won dozens of races on English, European and East and West coast tracks, the sound of this big Norton single probably reminded old time race spectators of the two Canadians who had first participated in the 1938 and 1939 rallies on their big one-cylinder Triumphs.[5]

The Novice and Amateur race winners saved the day for the Indian and Harley Davidson fans. Dick O'Leary from Jackson, Michigan won the Novice final on an Indian, and Warren Meyer from Minneapolis, Minnesota won the Amateur final on a Harley Davidson. Another Amateur, Joe Holoubek from Omaha, Nebraska broke a half mile track record on Sunday with a time of 29.75 seconds, just under 60mph.[6]

An unfortunate accident on Sunday did, however, result in one casualty. John Kenyen, 21 years old from Sioux Falls, South Dakota, died at the Ft. Meade VA hospital on the following Wednesday as a result of "serious internal injuries." The actual cause of death was a ruptured spleen. Kenyen overturned his machine and was thrown to the ground during a time trial.[7] Jimmy Hayes, a rider from Ogden, Utah had raced in the preliminary events on Saturday, but it was discovered that he had broken an arm. He tried to race on Sunday wearing a cast but was disqualified by the race officials.[8]

In the end, official rally statistics showed a total of 389 AMA members and over 100 non-AMA riders registered for the 1949 classic, but many visitors did not bother to sign up at rally headquarters. Prize winners in the Friday night main street event included: P. K. Tucker of Sioux Falls, the oldest rider; Francis Koller of Edgemont, South Dakota and Matty Shedd best dressed male and female; Mr. and Mrs. Al Stiefel of Tripp, South Dakota took the prize for married most recently; and Mr. and Mrs. Bruce Walters of Peoria, Illinois, as the longest married couple. The long distance rider was from Georgia and Earl Spinner of Sioux Falls was elected as the most popular male rider. Queen of the 1949 Black Hills Classic was Miss Daisy Rundle from Montecello, Iowa.[9]

The Gypsy Tour leaves Mount Rushmore. (Pearl Hoel Collection)

1949 Expert Champion: Dick Klamfoth

Born in Columbus, Ohio on September 10, 1928, Dick Klamfoth grew up on a farm near Groveport, Ohio, was active in 4-H and FFA, and made a history of showing sheep at the county fair during high school.

When he was in the eighth grade, Klamfoth found an old Briggs and Stratton washing machine engine with a large flat pulley and mounted it on his bicycle — his first experience with motorized cycling. At 14, and in his first year in high school, Klamfoth obtained his driver's license and purchased an old 1936 Indian Pony and began riding real motorcycles. He kept this 30.5 cubic inch bike for two years, then traded it in for a 1939 61 cubic inch Harley Davidson and began riding in Enduro competitions. Between his junior and senior year, at age 16, Klamfoth and a buddy decided to take a cross-country trip. After showing his sheep at the Franklin County Fair, the two teenagers jumped on their motorcycles and headed west, two weeks before school started. They headed north, crossed Lake Michigan on the Muskegon Ferry and rode to Milwaukee. They then toured Wisconsin and Minnesota ending up in Sturgis, South Dakota. The two teenagers had joined up with another young rider in Wisconsin and, when they left Sturgis for Denver, the two oldest, who had both finished high school, took off for California. Klamfoth was 16 years old, all alone and had to make his way back to Ohio.

In 1946, after Klamfoth had graduated from high school, a man, who was to become a life-long friend, encouraged him to start dirt-track racing. Klamfoth wasn't very interested and so this friend, "Smitty" invited him along on a trip to Springfield, Illinois to see the "Mile." Klamfoth quickly became enthralled with the idea of dirt track racing.

As fate would have it, a local racer and a friend of Klamfoth's had been injured in a local dirt track race. This rider, named Frank, owned his Indian racing bike in partnership with another rider, Floyd "Nick" Nicodemus. Klamfoth asked if he could use the motorcycle for the rest of the 1947 season. A bargain was struck and Klamfoth entered his first race at a local dirt track. At the starting line, Klamfoth, confused with the different shifter, had the bike in neutral and didn't get going until the rest of the pack was coming out of the second turn. Even though he was a half lap behind at the onset, Klamfoth was still able to take third place in this first dirt track competition.

By the end of the 1947 season, Klamfoth had earned enough points to move up to Amateur status. A Norton dealer from Columbus, Ohio approached him about riding in the Daytona 200 in February of 1948. He went to Florida and took second place as an Amateur. In 1949 as a Rookie Expert, he was asked to ride one of the two Norton Manx machines that were being shipped from England — bikes that had been prepared by Francis Beart, the famous Norton factory racing bike tuner. Beart, who refused to fly, loaded the two bikes in the Queen Mary and sailed to New York. Klamfoth met Beart at Daytona, started practicing on this brand new bike, and won the 200 in his first race as an Expert. After winning in Daytona at only 20 years of age, Klamfoth came to compete and win in Sturgis. He would win Daytona again in 1951 and 1952.

Dick Klamfoth, 1949 Expert Champion, taking the checkered flag. (Sturgis Museum Collection)

Klamfoth's Sturgis career was quite successful, always placing in the final events. He took first place in 1949 and again in 1959. During his first years he rode Nortons, and in later years he took to racing BSAs.

One of his fondest memories of Sturgis included winning in 1949 as a Rookie and receiving a Black Hills Gold pheasant tiepin from Clarence Hoel. He still uses this pin exclusively when he puts on a tie. Another memory, from his second year at Sturgis in 1950, had to do with a horse. As Klamfoth was moving into the third turn of his time trial, he noticed a horse on the track. It seems that the Meade County Sheriff wanted to get into the infield and rode his horse across the track between the third and fourth turn, just as Klamfoth was completing his lap. He was able to dodge the horse and still do an acceptable time. Klamfoth says he had experienced rabbits and dogs on the race track but never a horse. He says he knew he was "really in the Wild West when I saw that horse!"

His third fond memory of Sturgis happened in 1975. Klamfoth had retired from racing in 1962 and started a Honda dealership in his hometown, just north of Columbus, Ohio. This business grew rapidly, and for several years, Dick Klamfoth had the largest Honda dealership in the world. Because of the time-consuming work in running this business, Klamfoth had really lost touch with the motorcycle-racing scene. He had taken a week off in 1975 for a family outing, but primarily to take his daughter to Cody, Wyoming and then on to Tulsa, Oklahoma where she was attending college.

When they stopped in Sturgis, they noticed that the rally was on, so they decided to go to the races. When they were walking up into the Grandstand, the public address announcer stated that Mike Kidd had just broken Dick Klamfoth's record. His children were notably impressed. Klamfoth then saw Pappy Hoel standing up and staring at him. After a while, Hoel came over and said, "You're Dick Klamfoth! I haven't seen you in 10 years!" After a short visit, Pappy took him down to the podium where he was introduced to the crowd.

Now officially retired, Klamfoth returns to Sturgis almost every year to visit Pearl Hoel and attend the White Plate Flat Trackers annual meeting. He also hosts a weekend event at his home in Ohio for the "Over the Hill Gang," which includes about 200 retired racers. This gathering often falls on the weekend before the Sturgis rally, and Klamfoth then hops on his bike early Monday morning for the ride to South Dakota. He generally gets to Sturgis on Wednesday morning and stays to see the races. Dick Klamfoth is also actively involved in activities at Daytona, where he has almost single-handedly developed a large park and monument honoring the early "200" winners. He lives with his lovely wife Beverly in Groveport, Ohio.

Dick Klamfoth, 1949 Sturgis Expert Champion (Dick O'Leary Collection)

Manx Norton

The Manx Norton was developed from the Norton International, which was the "quintessential British road-racer of the 1930s." This motorcycle was, essentially, designed for the famous Isle of Man TT, hence the name Manx. Like the earlier International, the Manx had a reputation for speed and maneuverability because of its overhead camshaft engine and frame. As a racing motorcycle, the Manx was unsurpassed in the UK and Europe, but it did not arrive in America until the late 1940's.

An Ohio motorcycle dealer anxious to promote the marque furnished three tuned Manx machines to Klamfoth and two other promising riders for the 1949 Daytona. The Manx featured a 495 cc double overhead camshaft (DOHC), making it even faster than the International's single overhead camshaft (SOHC) engine. With the speed generated by the double overhead camshaft configuration, coupled with the high torque from the long stroke, a Norton racer was easily able to overcome the performance of the side valve Harley Davidson and Indian

The 495cc Norton Manx.

bikes. This DOHC design was, in fact, later used as an excuse to limit these cycles in AMA sponsored events. Although light and skittish in the sand, the Manx's speed on the paved straightaway made the difference at Daytona, according to Klamfoth.[1] All three Nortons were honored on the podium at the 1949 Daytona with Klamfoth in first place and the other two riders, Billie Mathews and Tex Luse, placing second and third.[2] This win undoubtedly re-awakened American motorcycle aficionados and racers to the potential of British cycles.

1949 Amateur Champion: Dick O'Leary

One of the most beloved racers at Sturgis during the late 1940s and early 1950s was Dick O'Leary, who was born in Kalamazoo, Michigan on January 2, 1927. He grew up in Kalamazoo, and after losing an eye aboard ship in 1945, was discharged from the US Navy. He bought a surplus 45 cubic inch Harley Davidson and did some traveling.

O'Leary soon became fascinated with motorcycles and purchased an old Indian Scout to try his hand at dirt track racing in 1946. After competing unsuccessfully as a Novice in about 10 races in Michigan, Indiana, and Ohio, he was approached by Chuck Sweeney from Jackson, Michigan who offered to tune his racing bike. The first time O'Leary rode this bike, he finished in the money and continued to make a living racing until his retirement in 1953.

By 1948 O'Leary had heard good reports about the track and racing at Sturgis. He came to the rally for the first time in 1948 with Frank Weimer, another of Chuck Sweeney's racers. Weimer was originally from Sturgis and later rode racing motorcycles for Pappy Hoel. The two racers drove to Sturgis in a pickup truck, sleeping outdoors and even once in a haystack along the way. One of O'Leary's adventures at this 1948 rally was meeting Rochester, the batman and chauffeur in the

Jack Benny radio and TV series. Benny was playing in Rapid City and Rochester, an avid motorcycle racing fan, had driven up to Sturgis for the races. After a lot of kidding around, Rochester offered to race with O'Leary using Benny's famous Maxwell motorcar if Dick would come to Hollywood.

In 1949, O'Leary returned to Sturgis for the races, sponsored by Art Hofer, a different Indian motorcycle tuner from Ohio. O'Leary was looking forward to a good time after the kind treatment he had received in 1948. He won the Amateur final in 1949 and because of good time trial was asked to move up and compete in the Expert Final.

O'Leary returned to Sturgis in 1950 alone. In his initial time trials on Sunday, O'Leary broke the track record of 29.75 seconds, posting a

Dick O'Leary takes the championship "flag" lap after winning the 1949 Amateur Final. (Dick O'Leary Collection)

time of 29.06. Because of heavy rains on Saturday, the 1950 races were moved up to a Sunday-Monday format. In the warm-ups on Monday, O'Leary suffered a broken foot. He recalled, "I came to Sturgis feeling very good about the town, the track and the people. Pappy Hoel was a great guy and a very good friend. I was very proud that I broke the track record and I think I could have taken the final race. We were taking the allotted lap before line-up and they had watered the track between time trials. I went into the third turn and it was wet...down I went. The bike bounced up and the peg came down on my left foot and broke all the bones in the foot. That was it for that day!"

O'Leary was treated at the Ft. Meade Hospital and returned to the track in time to see Chet Dykgraaf win the final. To demonstrate the

Dick O'Leary sports both the track record and a broken foot, 1950. (Dick O'Leary Collection)

concern Hoel and the other Gypsies had for this rider, they scrounged up enough money to fly O'Leary home to Michigan to recover. While at the hospital in Michigan, O'Leary received several telegrams and letters from Pappy Hoel. His love and respect for his Sturgis friends was, without question, one of the most sincerely demonstrated elements in the history of the rally's early years.

In 1951, Dick O'Leary returned to Sturgis. By this time, he was so well liked and familiar with the local people that he was asked to perform in the Friday night program. In the Sunday Final he led the race until the last turn, saw the checkered flag and was feeling the elation of a win and victory lap when he suddenly was passed by his good friend Bill Tuman who "beat him by a wheel." According to O'Leary, Tuman was the only "one I would like to have been beaten by."

In 1952 O'Leary was run off the track on Saturday in practice. His engine was clogged with sand and incapacitated. He worked all night trying to fix it but had to use his back-up motor, which was not fast enough to win. This was to be his last race at Sturgis.

After the 1950 accident in Sturgis, O'Leary kept the cast on for four weeks before he and Bobby Hill finished the season on the East Coast. They had several wins, O'Leary racing as an Amateur and Hill as an Expert. To earn money over the winter, O'Leary raced throughout Florida, competing in Tampa, Davis and Pompano Beach. These were "outlaw" races (non-AMA sanctioned) and O'Leary learned a lesson about competing in "outlaw" racing. After winning the Tri-State Championship, a 15-mile feature race at Pompano Beach, he and the other riders discovered that the race promoters had taken off with all of the gate receipts. "That was the end of my outlaw career," said O'Leary. After this debacle, he raced in the 1951 Daytona 200, but blew an engine in the middle of the race.

In 1952, Dick O'Leary had a super year, taking second place behind the famous Ernie Beckman in the Michigan State Championship. He traveled all over the country during the season, winning many races. After repairing the engine damaged at Sturgis at Jim Tagaris' shop in Denver, he went on to win at Dodge City, Kansas. He was scheduled to race at

Dick O'Leary, 1949 Sturgis Amateur Champion (Dick O'Leary Collection)

Sedalia, Missouri, the mile at Springfield, and the Championship race at Milwaukee when he got appendicitis and had his appendix removed in the Boonesville, Missouri Hospital. Because he had to spend 10 days in this hospital, he missed all of these big races.

O'Leary spent the rest of the winter racing in Tennessee, Alabama Georgia, and Florida. By the time he got to Daytona his engines were shelled, and he could not compete.

In the Spring of 1953 at a race in Mishawaka, Indiana, O'Leary was involved in a serious accident. He was leading the race when another racer went down and then slid into his bike. His motorcycle hit the fence and stopped, but O'Leary went airborne and cleared the fence. He hit a service road outside of the track and suffered a mangled leg and a broken back. The doctor at the Indiana Hospital wanted to amputate the broken leg, but O'Leary's wife Diane called the family doctor in Michigan, who met his ambulance at the St. Joseph, Michigan hospital. This doctor saved his leg using a 12-inch plate and 12 screws. He was in a body cast for four months and had to wear a leg brace for an additional three months. This accident effectively terminated O'Leary's career as a racer.

O'Leary established a battery business and eked out a living until 1959, when he went to work for a printing company in Grand Rapids. In 1972, he started a glass business with his sons and was quite successful. He retired in 1980, moved to Florida and lives in a mobile home park, where he works as the sales manager. O'Leary is still an avid dirt track racing fan, attends as many races as he can and remains excited by vicariously experiencing the thrill of racing.

Dick O'Leary was inducted into White Plate Flat Trackers Association as a charter member in 1982 and Pappy Hoel asked him to serve on the initial WPFTA Board of Directors. He was honored to do so and served well in this capacity. At 75 years of age, Dick O'Leary is alert, involved, and excited by life. He treasures his years as a motorcycle racer and enjoys involvement with all of his old racing friends who he meets at Daytona and at the "Over the Hill Gang' weekends at Dick Klamfoth's home in Ohio. He returns to Sturgis whenever he can .

August 11-13, 1950

The 1950 rally was to see the expansion of motorcycle-related events and include a hill climb in the foothills of Bear Butte.[1] This was not a typical hill climb event but actually a "Trials" type activity initiated by the Jackpine Gypsies Motorcycle Club and scheduled for July 16, 1950. Bruce Barnes, manager of the Classic, was optimistic about the "hill climb" as a precursor of the 1950 rally, and a "good number" of entries were expected to participate.[2] Unfortunately, after much planning and publicity, the event was rained out and had to be rescheduled for September 17. This was apparently the first and last attempt at scheduling this particular event, which ended up as an informal "Field Day Event" involving local riders.

The Friday August 11 Black Hills Gypsy Tour and Program was, for the first time, to be escorted by two South Dakota State Highway Patrol and a second Fort Meade nurse. Only one nurse had accompanied the 1947-1949 tours. According to Jack Hoel,

The Gypsy Tour at Mount Rushmore, 1950. (Pearl Hoel Collection)

the assistance of the State Troopers in escorting the tour was invaluable, especially when it came to facilitating traffic at Mt. Rushmore and in clearing intersections in Deadwood, Rapid City and Hot Springs. Their radios provided access in case of emergencies, and their presence contributed to the conduct of the riders and automobile tourists. The South Dakota State Patrol, along with every Governor since 1950, have been supportive of the Black Hills Motor Classic. Their efforts have also constituted a good deal of public relations in regard to their own image.[3]

The main street program, which was first tried in 1949, did not work well because there were too many spectators, and the City Park provided a wider area for the audience, which by now included large numbers of townspeople in addition to the motorcyclists.[4] The Friday evening meal was "on your own", but the program of events beginning at 8:00 pm, had moved back to the Gypsy Camp at Bear Butte Park.[5]

Program sponsors included the Don Crosby School of Dance, the Fort Meade Veterans Association, the Sturgis High School Band, and the downtown merchants. Events included a band concert, tap dancing, a vocal trio, juggling, and recognition of the oldest and youngest riders, the best dressed male and female riders and the best-

The Big Board, 1950. (Dick O'Leary Collection)

Bill Tuman, Dick Klamfoth and Kelly Meyers at Sturgis, 1950. (Neil Hultman Collection)

dressed club. During the Friday night program, Joan Loberg of Minneapolis was crowned queen and another Minnesotan, Don Schueller from Sauk Rapids was named king.[6]

August 12 and 13 were race days. After a successful 157-mile Gypsy Tour on Friday and a successful program held in the City Auditorium, the races were to begin at 1:30pm on Saturday. The fast Sturgis half-mile track was drawing more and more nationally-recognized riders who were anxious to win points and to set new half-mile records. The total purse had grown to $2100.[7]

The Saturday race schedule was canceled due to rain and the Board of Directors decided to continue the event on Monday, August 14. Between 5,000 and 7,000 spectators attended the Sunday races, and a small crowd was present on Monday to watch 60 racers compete for the prize money. Joe Holoubek's time trial record of 29.25 seconds was broken by Dick O'Leary from Jackson, Michigan with a time of 29.06.[8] On Sunday, the first day of racing, the Novice race was won by Don Gerjevic of Omaha, Nebraska. Dick McDougal of Albuquerque, New Mexico was the winner at the Amateur level. Dick Klamfoth (1949 champion) edged out Chet Dykgraaf. Third place was taken by Bill Tuman, the 1947 champion.[9]

On Monday, the Novice winner was Tex Wright of Lennon, Michigan, and James Snyder from Columbus, Ohio took the Amateur championship. In the Expert final, Klamfoth did not repeat his Saturday victory, losing to Chet Dykgraaf. Kelley Meyers of Riverside, California took second, and Klamfoth ended up in third. Dykgraaf, like Klamfoth and Tuman, was recognized as an AMA Grand National Winner.[10] It was becoming clear that some of the best racers in the United States and Canada were making it to Sturgis every year.

1950 Expert Champion: Chet Dykgraaf

Chester "Chet" Dykgraaf, a contemporary of early Classic Champion Johnny Speigelhoff, began his professional career in 1938. When he started racing in the county and state fair circuit before World War II, Dykgraaf noted that purse winnings were as low as three dollars for a first place finish! As the sport began to gain popularity, Dykgraaf indicated that in good summers, he could average about $300 per week — a super salary in the post-depression years.

Chet Dykgraaf was born in Holland, Michigan in 1914. In his childhood, his parents bought a hotel in Grand Rapids, which was close to a motorcycle shop. Young Chester became interested in riding. He purchased a basket case Harley Davidson, put it together and began riding the back roads around Grand Rapids. He earned his Expert license in 1939 and went to Daytona to compete in the 200 in 1940. He took 6th place, his best finish at Daytona.[1]

In 1942 Dykgraaf took on a racing arrangement with a Norton dealer who supplied him with a racing bike and limited support. After a short time, British parts and support efforts were cut off by the war, and Dykgraaf began riding Harley Davidsons.[2] After the war, he went back to Nortons and became one of the top racers during the post war years.

In September 1946, Dykgraaf won the Springfield Mile and was declared the National Champion. In 1948 he placed second at Langhorne, Pennsylvania and the Springfield Mile with a third place at the Milwaukee Mile. In 1950, after taking the championship race at Sturgis, he was severely injured in a race at South Carolina's Darlington Speedway. In this crash, Dykgraaf broke both legs and was informed by the doctor that he would probably never walk again. He hired an ambulance to take him home to Michigan where a doctor used bone grafts to save his legs. He

Chet Dykgraaf, 1950 Expert Champion at Sturgis, waits in the practice lane. (Dick O'Leary Collection)

was back on the circuit by 1952 and continued racing until 1953. He sold his last motorcycle in 1976 at the age of 79.[3]

In an interview with the AMA's Bill Andrews, Dykgraaf reminisced about his early wins and suggested that his win at Springfield, taken by less than a bike length from fellow Hall of Famer Kenny Eggers, was due to his pre-race inspection of Egger's bike. After realizing that Eggers speed was due to a sprocket ratio, Dykgraaf used a different sprocket and won the race. Dykgraaf never liked to be too far ahead of the pack and was accused by one rider of backing off the throttle on the straights!

Dykgraaf was inducted into the White Plate Flat Trackers as a Charter Member. He was also inducted into the National Motorcycle Hall of Fame in 1990 and as a Charter Member of the AMA Hall of Fame in 1998.[4]

During his racing career, his father had purchased a berry farm and Dykgraaf, at 39, decided to retire from racing and help his father. He ran the farm until the early 1960's when a brother-in-law brought him into a soft drink company. He later owned and operated this business until 1982 when he retired and moved to Florida. Dykgraaf and his wife, Jane, now live in St. Augustine, Florida.[5]

Early Racers

Early racers were a dedicated breed. In the days before company sponsorship, motorcycle racing was tough and demanding: a labor of love with a devotion to the sport, the machines, and the excitement of riding. Dirt track racers had to suffer their own expenses and spend sleepless nights driving from one county fair or rally dirt track venue to be ready for the next race.

According to Pappy Hoel, there was a real brotherhood among the clan. Starting with the first race of each year, a rider would have to look forward to spending the summer sleeping in a van, a pickup truck, or an old car. In some cases, a rider would back his bike out of a trailer to provide a night's sleeping space. One of the reasons riders liked to come to Sturgis was the dedication and support from Hoel and other members of the Jackpine Gypsies Club in finding sleeping space, meals, and a place to work on their bikes. Some of the riders developed friendships with homeowners in the Black Hills area and were guaranteed a place to stay, often in a scenic locale. These racers would then return year after year.

One time, Pappy made some space for late evening arrivals in his ice house. Finding nowhere to sleep, this group had approached Hoel, who put them up sleeping on damp canvas tarps covering a thin layer of sawdust covering the many layers of ice in his icehouse. Hoel had a hard time the next morning explaining to these shivering riders that they had just spent the night sleeping on top of 1,000 tons of ice.[1]

Breakdowns were also a problem for riders. When a racing bike had a breakdown, riders would often find themselves miles from the nearest dealer. This required that racers carry a supply of the most common repair components in their van or trailer. Their active support of each other was clearly evidenced in their willingness to share with one another. If a part was lacking, even those riders in direct competition with each other and riding the same brand of bike were generally willing to help out. According to Pappy's son, Jack, brand loyalty, however, was fierce. No Indian racer ever helped a Harley rider and vice-versa.[2]

Another reason racers loved Pappy Hoel and Sturgis was probably due to the support he rendered in lending his tools, workspace, and parts. The brotherhood of traveling together, sometimes sharing haystacks for sleeping or parts for broken-down bikes always ended when the competition began, only to resume when the race was over.[3]

According to Neil Hultmann, Pappy was always concerned about racers who did not win any money at Sturgis and generally gave them enough to buy food and gas to get to the next racing event. He also wrote to the top Indian Motorcycle racers, encouraging them to come to the races. Those who won on an Indian could expect a little cash bonus from Pappy on their way out of town on Sunday afternoon.[4]

Chapter Five:
The National Championship Years

The period of 1951 to 1955 represents another pivotal step in the further growth and expansion of the rally. In 1951, representatives of the Motor Maids organization, a national association of women riders, visited Sturgis to check out the site for future meetings. Most significant, however, was Sturgis' selection as site of the AMA Five-Mile National Championship Race in 1952, 1953, and 1954, and the six-mile national championship in 1995.

National press began taking note of the rally, and pictures of the Gypsy Tour were used on the cover of two national motorcycle magazines between 1951 and 1955. Seven of the 15 professional racers who participated in 1954 were ultimately recognized and inducted into the AMA Hall of Fame, and Harley Davidson Motorcycles began to make a dramatic impact on the racing scene at Sturgis. Capitalizing on the evolution of foot shifting in newer models, a young rider from Texas, Everett Brashear, made racing history with his win in 1952.

Community support continued to grow considerably during this period as well. By 1955, local organizations, service clubs and churches began establishing sites along Main Street as vendors of food, souvenirs and raffles, and local people began contributing prizes for the Friday night awards program. They also contributed awards and trophies and performed by singing and acting in humorous skits. Also in 1955, the "Friday Night Feed", established earlier for rally visitors and riders, had become so popular that the number of locals crashing the party began making a serious impact upon the amount of food prepared for the visitors.

August 10-12, 1951

The 1951 Classic, now officially a three-day event as advertised by race posters and fliers, was scheduled and held on August 10-12. Excitement was high by the first week in August. According to the *Sturgis Tribune*, Ed Kretz, the "Ironman" of Indian motorcycle fame, had mailed his application to participate in the 1951 Black Hills Classic race program.[1] Kretz, a native of San Diego, California, had won every major motorcycle race in America with the exception of the "Springfield Mile." (Rally planners later realized that it was Ed Kretz, Jr. who had registered to race.) A field of other expert riders was slated to join the 1951 events, including Chet Dykgraff, Bill Tuman, Dick O'Leary, Warren Meyer and Dick Klamfoth. It was becoming clear to all involved that Sturgis was a recognized event in the national motorcycle racing community.

Recognition, however, was not limited to the just the racing. A 1951 visitor noted that a picture of the annual Black Hills Gypsy Tour had been used, for the past three years, as a cover for the American Motorcyclist magazine published by the AMA.[3] This publicity, along with the resounding endorsement of rally visitors, was seminal in promoting the non-racing riding experience of the rally. The 1951 Tour took the established route south through the Hills and back, enjoyed a lunch provided by Pearl Hoel and the Jackpine Gypsy women, and featured the evening "feed" and entertainment program. One notable addition in 1951 was a tour of the Black Hills Passion Play Amphitheater site.

The Passion Play, imported to the Black Hills from Germany, was becoming a regional tourist attraction in the upper Midwest. Joseph Meier from Lunen, Germany, transplanted the Passion Play, an Easter Celebration initiated in 1242, to the Black Hills. Leaving Germany in 1932, Meier and the total cast of players emigrated to America and initiated the production in Spearfish, South Dakota in 1939. The Gypsy Tour members were able to visit the outdoor amphitheater and have tours conducted by Meier, who always played the part of Christ in the pageant.[5]

The Friday night program was held in the city park. Events included a welcome by Mayor Katherine Soldat, who presented the visitors with the "Key to the City". The Meade County Sheriff, Carl Aga, sang several songs and led the group in singing. The best dressed Male and Female Riders were Mr. and Mrs. Charles Sweeney from Jackson, Michigan. Since they were married, they also won the Best Dressed Couple award. The Best Dressed Club award went to a club with the unique name of "Gravel Gremlins" from Denver.[6] Jean Jensen, Pine Bluffs, Wyoming was selected from a group of 16 lady riders as the "Queen of the Classic."

A particular funny experience occurred during the presentation of the longest distance prize, which was awarded to brothers W.L. and J.B. Simpsons, who had trav-

Bill Tuman, #51, and other racers compete in the 1951 races. (Neil Hultman Collection)

eled to the rally from Long Island, New York — over 1800 miles. The judges were stumped when it came down to deciding which brother had actually come the farthest. According to the brothers, they both lived in the same house and slept in the same bed. Pappy Hoel solved the problem by giving them duplicate prizes. In the end, over 260 riders participated in the 1951 Gypsy Tour.[7]

Races

Interestingly, the 1951 AMA races at Sturgis were changed to three mile heat races and a five mile final. The switch from five and eight mile races held in previous years is noteworthy. Because Sturgis could only hold one race in the AMA National Championship category, the request for the five mile distance had been granted to the 1951 Classic.[8] Bill Tuman, the 1947 winner, won the "Expert" final in 1951, edging out Dick O'Leary, his traveling partner who took second. And despite winning his preliminary heat, Dick Klamfoth, the 1949 winner, did not place in the final.[9]

Ed "Eddite" Kretz, Jr. did participate in the 1951 races. According to Eddie, he had initiated a Midwest tour with another racer and Sturgis was their first event. Unfortunately Kretz broke his collarbone in one of the Saturday heat races. Unable to complete the planned tour, he returned to his home in California.[10]

The year 1951 was significant in establishing a deeper sense of respectability for the Sturgis experience, thanks due in large part to the increasing attendance of many nationally recognized racers and coverage of the Gypsy Tour on the cover of the *American Motorcyclist* magazine. A visit by members of the Motor Maids Organization, the national organization of women riders was also very important. Two representatives,

Mrs. Coleen Blackman of Sidney, Nebraska, and Mrs. John Melches of Salt Lake City, Utah, competed for the title of queen and were joined by four other Motor Maid riders.[11]

The combination of forces was helping the American public realize that motorcyclists were nice people who were able to tour and enjoy the natural beauty of the Black Hills. The welcome by the Mayor and the songfest led by the County Sheriff also demonstrated increasing local acceptance by local Black Hills residents. Pappy Hoel happily reported to the *Sturgis Tribune* that, in the three day event, only three riders had been reprimanded for speeding and an additional three for "too much noise."[12]

The nature of the rally was quietly shifting in 1951. Without realizing it, residents, riders and everyone involved were beginning to see that the rally was a fun, wholesome, generally entertaining event that was actually emerging as a unique recreational experience much larger than a series of weekend races. The idea of visiting Sturgis for simply having a good time was beginning to gel.

1951 Expert Champion: Bill Tuman

After his first win at Sturgis in 1947, Tuman went on to a brilliant career as a motorcycle racer. In 1951, he brought his son to Sturgis and had a great time hanging out with Dick O'Leary. They rode mules to the top of Bear Butte and had a lot of fun in Sturgis and at Wall Drug on the way home. At one point during the Bear Butte excursion, Tuman got off his mule for no apparent reason, placed the mule's ears in a vee and started peering at Harney Peak to the southwest of Sturgis. Allen Davis, another racer in the mule troop, asked him what he was doing. Tuman replied that he was using the "old mountain man telescope" and that the vee made by the mule's ears magnified everything in sight! Davis just laughed, but Tuman later noticed him trying the "mule scope" out for himself![1]

Although "sponsored" by Tri-City Indian Sales with the assistance of Indian Factory Representatives, Tuman had to work other jobs to support his family of five children. As a result, he became famous in racing circles as an outstanding tuner and engine builder.[2] He always made his own racing shoes, preferring to use the rear bumper from 1946 Ford automobiles which "just fit his boot."[3]

Tuman's first major win at the National level was the AMA Five-Mile National at Des Moines, Iowa in 1950 — a great day for Tuman and Indian motorcycles. He won his heat, the semi-final, and the final with the only Indian in the main event. Tuman had to compete with nine Harley Davidson riders to maintain the slogan "Indian Wins Again". Tuman's next major victory was a win at the AMA Grand National at San Mateos, California in 1952. In 1953 Tuman won the famous 200-mile National at Dodge City Kansas riding a Manx Norton. According to Tuman, he knew that his Indians were running pretty thin when it came to replacement parts and engine blocks. Since the Indian Company was importing Nortons, BSAs and Ariels, Tuman tried all three makes in racing. Later he became concerned about the long wait for parts

Bill Tuman on a Norton Manx at the Dodge City, Kansas 200, 1951. (Bill Tuman Collection)

(which had to be shipped from England) and because race officials had to "measure" his bikes' every time he went to a different race. He finally gave up on the British machines and finished out his racing career on his beloved Indian Scouts. He retired in 1955 when he could no longer maintain the vintage engines.[4]

In all Bill Tuman won five Grand National Championships, including his ultimate goal, the Springfield Mile in 1953, using a borrowed Scout engine. He had worn out all of his own engines out in the County Fair Circuit. For this win, he was awarded the coveted number one white plate — the last number one plate winner for Indian.[5]

After he retired, Bill Tuman continued with his engine building and tuning for other racers. In 10 years of professional racing, he suffered only one injury – a sprained ankle.[6] For a time he traveled the circuit for BSA and later started a Honda motorcycle dealership. At 81 years of age, Bill Tuman is vital, knowledgeable and interesting. Both his vigor and keen memory are impressive. He and his wife, Betty, still perform their responsibilities as AMA representatives for District 17. Bill Tuman was inducted into the AMA Hall of Fame as a Charter Member in 1998. He is also a Charter Member of the White Plate Flat Trackers organization[7]

August 8-10, 1952

1952 was a year of big news for the Black Hills Motor Classic. The most significant dimension was the hosting of the AMA Five Mile National Championship Race and was touted by the *Sturgis Tribune* as the first "national event in the northwest since the Dempsey Gibbons 1923 boxing match in Shelby, Montana".[1] The 1951 National Five Mile Champion, Lowell Retinger of Indianapolis, was expected along with Bill Tuman, the winner at Sturgis in 1947 and 1951.

Second, rally planners were expecting a large number of reporters and photographers from national motorcycle trade publications and the national press. The third exciting news was that the Motor Maids of America organization was planning to hold their Five State Convention during the Classic.[2] Apparently, the six Motor Maids who attended the 1951 rally were impressed with the good time, the Black Hills scenery and Sturgis hospitality. The regional president, Mrs. John Melches of Salt Lake City, was to preside, and the "maids were to be guests of the Chamber of Commerce for a welcoming breakfast at the Cozy Corner Cafe on the morning of August 7." In her letter to the Jackpine Gypsies, Dot Robinson, Founder and President of the Motor Maids indicated that she was "looking forward to the Sturgis meeting and would do "anything possible to make it a success."[3] Ms. Robinson, who lived in Detroit, Michigan, was voted the Most Popular Girl Rider in the United States in 1950.*

Full Week

1952 also saw the first steps in expanding the rally beyond three days. Bruce Barnes, now the Mayor of Sturgis as well as the "Manager of the Motor Cycle Classic" announced that the carnival had been engaged for the full week.[5]

The Gypsy Tour, generally limited to Friday, was also expanded. An initial tour to Hot Springs left Sturgis on Thursday, August 7 and was joined by a second group on Friday. Both groups met in Custer State Park at the Coolidge Inn for lunch on Friday. A buffalo feed and program of entertainment was held on Friday evening at the Bear Butte Park picnic grounds. The Main Street venue, first tried in 1949, was once again

The Gypsy Tour, 1951. (Pearl Hoel Collection)

---

* Robinson was inducted into the AMA Motorcycle Hall of Fame in 1998 for founding the Motor Maids.[4]

Souvenir Program

NOT FOR SALE

American Motorcycle Association

5 Mile National Championship
RACE

For the Year 1952

Sturgis, South Dakota

In the Black Hills

August 10th, 1952

Manufacturers of the World's Finest Motorcycles

This Program is given to you with the compliments of the INDIAN SALES CORP., of Springfield, Mass., and your local INDIAN MOTORCYCLE DEALER. J. C. HOEL, STURGIS, S. DAK.

Souvenir Program, First Sturgis National. (Gary Landeen Collection) omitted. The program of entertainment, similar to the previous years, included a new element – the Motor Maid Awards.[6]

Charley Clark of Long Island, New York took the award for longest distance rider. Apparently, the Simpsons brothers, who had won the award in 1951 also from Long Island, were unable to complete two 3,600-mile trips in consecutive years. The longest distance female rider (non-Motor Maid) was Nita Metz from Springfield, Ohio. Best-dressed male and female riders were Vern Couch of Sidney, Nebraska, and Evelyn Jasper from Centralia, Illinois. The oldest rider was Ellery Tremaine of Ogden, Utah. According to the *Sturgis Tribune*, "Almost every state in the nation" was represented in the 1951 tour.[7] The Motor Maid award for longest distance was presented to Nicki Hero, who rode her own motorcycle to Sturgis from Pensacola, Florida. And of course, the Motor Maids won the Best Dressed Club Award.

In a comedy routine enjoyed by all, Dick O'Leary, one of the Expert racers, was placed on a table on stage while a doctor and a nurse removed screw drivers, gears and balloons from his stomach so he would be able to ride in the Saturday races. And in a hotly contested contest, Betty Dimmit from Bell Garden, California, was selected "Queen of the 1952 Motor Classic."

Races

A crowd of 7,500 was present at Sunday's Five Mile National AMA Championship Race, which was won by Everett Brashear from Louisiana. Brashear completed the 10 laps in 4 minutes, 39 seconds. Second place went to Albrecht, and third to Byars. Although he did not place in the championship race, Dick O'Leary placed second in the championship consolation race.[8] Brashear was inducted into the Charity Newsies Motorcycle Hall of Fame in 1978 and the AMA Hall of Fame in 1998 as a "1950s AMA Dirt Track Racing Champion". Both he and O'Leary are charter members of the White Plate Flat-Trackers Association.[9]

Rally officials were to later learn that Brashear's win created a good deal of national publicity for the Black Hills Motor Classic. Brashear had used a new model Harley Davidson racing bike to win. Since it was the first major victory for this motorcycle, the Harley Davidson publicity staff spotlighted the win, and incidentally Sturgis, in their major advertising efforts over the winter of 1952-53. The Classic gained a good deal of indirect exposure as a result.

It is interesting to note the gradual expansion of the rally towards its present full week program. Little by little, the positive elements of the Sturgis experience were becoming rooted in people's attitudes. For non-racing participants, the rally in 1952 had grown to four days, and the weeklong carnival may have been a harbinger of future Classics. It is also interesting to point out that this expansion was related to participants rather than racers. While touring had always been secondary like the dressing on a "Sturgis Salad", it was fast becoming a good portion of the lettuce itself.

1952 Expert Champion: Everett Brashear

Everett Brashear was born in Beaumont, Texas, in 1927, and his interest in motorcycles began in 1946 after his discharge from the Armed Services. Brashear's first dirt-track bike was an Indian Scout. In 1948, he entered the professional ranks as a Novice. After banging around the Texas and Louisiana dirt-track circuit, Brashear started racing on a WR Harley Davidson in 1949. He earned his Expert license in 1951. His professional career really took off when he won the National Five Mile Championship at the very first AMA National held in Sturgis in August 1952.[1]

In the early 1950's, the Harley Davidson Company, concerned about the outstanding success of the Indian racers, developed the KR750, a new 45 cubic inch racing bike that featured a hand clutch, a foot shifter and hydraulic forks. Prior to this model, Harley Davidson racers had been dependent on a highly tuned version of the WR model. This older design had been consistently out-running the KR750s in the early going.

Brashear established a milestone for Harley Davidson, and a lot of publicity for the Black Hills Motor Classic, when he defeated the five-time National Champion, Paul Albrecht, who was riding the older WR model in the 1952 three mile AMA National Championship race at Sturgis[2] Some of the spectators at Sturgis attributed Brashear's win to strategy. According to Neil Hultman, Brashear went wide in the fourth turn to improve his traction in the softer, moister dirt, thus increasing acceleration into the final straight.[3]

He was to repeat this strategy on other occasions, especially in his win of the 25-Mile AMA National at Springfield, Illinois, in 1955. In this race he edged out Bobby Hill, who had drafted Brashear for the entire race, and then passed him in the third turn. Everett went wide—the Sturgis move—and beat Hill by a bike-length. The Springfield Mile was

Brashear's best race. He repeated his Springfield victory again in 1956, edging out Charlie West (1956 Sturgis Champion) by about four inches, the length of his front tire. Brashear took second place behind Joe Leonard at Springfield in 1957, and in 1958 he took the mile National at San Jose riding a BSA. In total, he won 15 National Championship Races (eight at the mile and seven at the half-mile venues) between his initial win at Sturgis and his retirement. He was able to accumulate enough points to finish in second place in the National Series rankings for 1955. His other top-ten total point positions included fourth place in 1956, fifth in 1957, third in 1958 and sixth in 1960.[4]

In 1957, he was "canned" (his own words) by Harley Davidson after riding a BSA Goldstar as a favor to a dealer friend.[5] As a result, he entered and won the Grand National Mile Championship at San Jose, California, on a British bike. Using his tried and true "mile turn talent—get-

Everett Brashear, 1952 Expert Champion at Sturgis with new White Plate number 25, 1952. (Everett Brashear Collection)

ting traction on the final turn groove, for a drive to the checkered flag," Brashear was able to pass both Sammy Tanner and Caroll Resweber in the final stretch and win the race by two lengths.[6]

Brashear returned to Harley Davidson in 1959 but experienced a marginal season. For a short time he took a job working for a Triumph distributor in California in 1960, but returned to racing, winning his final AMA national in Sacramento on July 17. His final race, however, was in 1964. Performing his best and placing sixth at the Daytona 200 on a Matchless motorcycle, Brashear realized that, at the age of 37, it was finally time to quit.[7]

In his retirement from racing, Brashear managed a Harley Davidson dealership, served as a district manager for Triumph, sold insurance, and worked as a sales manager for Yamaha, Kawasaki, Husquavarna and various after-market manufacturers. He also served on the Board of Directors of the Motorcycle Industry Council for the 1973-74 sessions. He is retired and lives in San Diego, California.[8]

Harley Davidson promotional materials highlighting the victorious "K" motorcyles. (Everett Brashear Collection)

Harley Davidson History

The first Harley Davidson Motorcycle was assembled in 1903. Using an engine designed in 1901 and 1902, William S. Harley and Arthur Davidson attached this engine to a bicycle chassis and a legend was born. The engine had a bore and stroke of 3.0 x 3.5 inches and functioned with a carburetor designed by Ole Evinrude of outboard motor fame.[1]

In 1906, the two proprietors, with the assistance of one employee, produced 50 motorcycles and characterized them as "Silent Gray Fellows." In 1907, the long standing rivalry with Indian motorcycles, or "Indian Wars," began. Harley Davidson was incorporated and established a factory racing team in 1908. These early competitions consisted of Endurance Runs and board track races. The team won their first Endurance Run in 1911, after Harley Davidson had developed its first twin. This machine had a displacement of 61 cubic inches, or 1000 cc, and was used in board track competitions.[2]

In 1916, Harley Davidson motorcycles saw service against Pancho Villa, and 20,000 units were used during World War I (1917-1918). In fact, the first person to enter occupied Germany at the end of the war was Corporal Roy Holtz on a Harley Davidson dispatch bike.[3]

By 1920 the company boasted dealers in 67 countries, and the name HOG was introduced to the motorcycle riding community. The name supposedly evolved from the practice of a Midwest pig farmer who developed into a skillful and successful amateur racer. This gentleman would bring his pet pig to each race as a mascot, and upon winning a race, he would take his victory lap with the pig riding on the gas tank. The fad caught on all over the Midwest, and Harley Davidson riders became known as "Hog Boys" and their bikes characterized as "Hogs."[4]

The Great Depression seriously affected the production of motorcycles. By 1933 production had decreased to 3,700 units. In 1935, the factory licensed the Sankyo Company to build motorcycles in Japan. In 1936, the firm introduced the EL model, a 61 cubic inch "Knucklehead" engine motorcycle. This machine was such a success that many cycle historians credit this model with saving the company from its depression-related financial problems. The famous 74 inch (1,200 cc) Knucklehead was introduced in 1941, and this motorcycle, along with the shaft driven model XA BMW clone, accounted for the over 90,000 cycles Harley Davidson manufactured for the Allied Forces during WWII.[5]

After the war, hundreds of returning GIs bought war surplus motorcycles and started chopping parts off of them to make them lighter for racing. The word "Chopper" was quickly coined, and essentially refers to a modified wartime 74 cubic inch Panhead.[6]

In the early days of dirt track racing, the Harley Davidson cycles generally had a tough time competing against the racing Indians. Whether this was due to the function of speed or durability of the engine and frame configuration has never been determined. Everything changed, however, in 1953 when the newly developed KR750 racing model began winning. Skeptics suggest that the early success of this motorcycle was due in large part to the AMA ban on overhead camshaft racers (which limited the Norton Manx and other British machines to 500cc's) and the demise of the American-made Indian "Scout" racer. Whatever the cause, Paul Goldsmith won the Daytona 200 on one of the new KR750s, and Harley Davidson was back on the racing scene.[7] The AMA National Championship titles of Brad Andres (1955), Joe Leonard (1956-1957), and Carol Resweber in 1958 are all evidence of the viability of the KR750 as a racer.

By late 1960s, the Harley Davidson company, again feeling threatened in the racing world by improved British iron, began scrambling to develop a viable racing bike. As a stop-gap measure, an initial model — dubbed the XR750 — was released to the public. Based on the Harley Davidson Sportster production bike's 45 cubic inch engine with cast iron sleeves, the racer was moderately successful in the racing world.

In 1972, a replacement bike, also dubbed the XR750, became available. This racer, an instant success, featured an alloy engine and went on to win 20 of the next 27 racing seasons. These "Alloy XRs" can still be seen roaring around American dirt tracks and winning races.[8]

The Alloy XRs began dominating at Sturgis in 1974 when Steve Droste of Waterloo, Iowa unexpectedly outran the touted Triumph riders of the Pacific Coast Regional Half-Mile Championship. This was to continue in 1975, when all three places (Mike Kidd, Mike Collins, and Paul Pressgrove), were taken by XR750 racers.

August 6-9, 1953

In early 1953, Pappy Hoel, his son Jack, Neil Hultmann and Frank Miller – all from the Sturgis area – attended the AMA 200 Mile National at Dodge City, Kansas, to see Bill Tuman and Chet Dykgraaf compete. Jack Hoel, Neil Hultmann and Frank Miller all served as corner flagmen on the two-mile dirt track According to Hultmann it was 110 degrees and windy![1] Tuman won the 200 Mile National and Dykgraaf, who had participated in previous "Classic" races, winning in 1950, unfortunately suffered a broken leg when his cycle crashed and burned. Dick Klamfoth. one of the leaders, had to drop out when his oil line ruptured. Tuman and Klamfoth both signed the entry blanks supplied by Hoel and Hultmann, indicating that they intended to race at Sturgis. The 1953 Classic promised to be an exciting event according to Hoel, due to

The Gypsy Camp in Hoel's backyard, early 1950s. (Sturgis Museum Archives)

Riders Entered for Sunday's Races

(Courtesy of J. C. HOEL, Local INDIAN DEALER, Sturgis, S. D.)

	EXPERTS		Machine	Time
1	BOBBY HILL	Ohio	Indian	29.67/12
2	DICK KLAMFORTH	Ohio	Norton	30.29/9
7Y	GEORGE COOPER	Calif.	Triumph	30.80/17
15N	BILL McCONNELL	Colo.	H. D.	30.30/8
13	JOHNNY KNAPP ✕	Mich.	H. D.	
4M	JAMES SPIRK	Colo.	H. D.	30.89/4
25	EVERETT BRASHEAR	La.	H. D.	30.71/19
26E	AL KNAPP	Mich.	H. D.	30.47/1
37X	CHUCK BASNEY	Calif.	H. D.	29.60/15
51	BILL TUMAN	Ill.	Indian	29.78/13
54	ALBERT GUNTER	Calif.	B. S. A.	30.24/5
56V	FRANK WEIMER ✕	Mich.	Norton	
63	TOMMY BYARS	Texas	H. D.	30.59/3
66	RICHARD McDOUGALL	N. Mex.	H. D.	30.48/6
70	LLOYD ENSMINGER	Colo.	H. D.	30.64/2
81	BOB SLACK	Mont.	Triumph	31.03/19
82	WILLIAM PETRI	Wis.	H. D.	30.40/11
84Q	TROY GEORGESON	Mont.	H. D.	31.17/14
88K	DON HUTCHINSON	Mo.	Triumph	31.03/10
89Y	HUGH McAFEE	Calif.	Triumph	30.26/18
90	RAY KUBAL	Colo.	H. D.	31.27/7
97	CHARLES CAREY ✕	Ill.	Indian	
97G	MILTON LASSITER ✕	Wis.	Indian	
98	JOE LEONARD	Calif.	H. D.	30.18/16

	AMATEUR		Machine	Time
11L	ROBERT JOHNSON	Ala.	H. D.	30.19/14
13K	NORMAN McCLURE	Mo.	Triumph	31.93/2
14Y	NORMAN SMITH	Calif.	B. S. A.	29.69/13
25S	ARNOLD BANDY	Ill.	Indian	31.15/5
25N	ROBERT WEBSTER	Colo.	Triumph	31.70/3
44N	LEO WALTER	Kans.	H. D.	31.11/11
54K	RAY HENDERSHOT	Mo.	Triumph	32.40/9
47C	DON SMITH	Fla.	Triumph	30.90/8
64K	AL BURKE	Minn.	B. S. A.	32.67/4
75W	JAMES HAYES	Utah	H. D.	31.28/12
77Q	BILLY HUDSON	Colo.	Triumph	31.37/7
81N	LOUIS STADLER	Colo.	Indian	32.37/6
98N	MELVIN FLINT	Colo.	Triumph	30.65/1
84J	HAL SPRICK	S. Dak.	H. D.	30.73/10

1953 Race Program score sheet. Note the time trial times and scratched (X) riders. (Pearl Hoel Collection) national publicity and word of mouth as indicated by the "high praise from cyclists and spectators" at Dodge City.[2]

Officially established as a four-day rally in 1953 (August 6-9) with two days of Gypsy Touring and two days of racing, the Sunday racing calendar again included the Five Mile National Championship. The Gypsy Tour repeated the 1952 route with Thursday riders touring the southern hills, spending the night at Hot Springs and then linking up with the Friday Tour at the State Game Lodge in Custer State Park for a noon lunch. A Gypsy Tent was set up as tour headquarters behind Hoel's Indian Motorcycle Dealership. The Friday night program included a special guest: nationally famous Johnny, the singing bellhop from Phillip Morris Cigarettes, made an appearance.[3]

On Sunday, Johnny presented a corsage to Shirley Couch of Sidney, Nebraska, the 1953 "Gypsy Tour and Race Queen." It was Shirley's third trip to Sturgis riding on her own motorcycle. Over 250 riders participated in the two days of touring.[4] Joe Leonard of San Jose, California, was crowned the National Five Mile Champion after winning the Sunday feature race. Bill Tuman (1947,1951 winner) came in fourth.[5]

Johnny, the Philip Morris Cigarettes mascot, at the start of the 1953 Gypsy Tour. Clarence Hoel, facing the assembled riders, gives last minute instructions to the group. Neil Hultman, at front left, takes the road captain position. (Pearl Hoel Collection)

1953 Expert Champion: Joe Leonard

A native of San Diego, California, Joe Leonard spent his childhood near an open area where the local motorcycle club held field events, which allowed him to observe and later participate. As a youth too young to be licensed to ride, Leonard began teaching sailors form the San Diego Naval Station by riding as a passenger.[1]

Joe Leonard was born on August 4, 1932 in San Diego, and in 1951, at the age of 19, he moved to San Francisco and got started in racing. At first he raced Triumphs at the local tracks and developed a reputation of being an aggressive racer with a lot of promise. Tom Sifton, a well-known engine builder who owned a Harley Davidson dealership in San Jose, spotted Leonard. Leonard soon moved to San Jose and began to race for Sifton.

By 1953, as a Rookie Expert, Leonard was involved in a serious street accident, which resulted in a month-long hospitalization.[2] After recuperating, Leonard was still able to win four AMA Nationals in 1953, one of which was the second five-mile national held in Sturgis in August. He was to return to Sturgis several times, winning the "Classic" Championship again in 1957.

Leonard's memories of his times in Sturgis are quite interesting, including a particular experience arriving in Sturgis in 1954 with traveling partner Charlie West (Sturgis Champion, 1956). According to Leonard, the last few miles of highway coming into Sturgis were graveled. The gravel was really loose under the railroad underpass at the edge of town, and their old Nash tow car met a vehicle at the underpass. West hit the brakes, the Nash went into a slide, the trailer carrying the two racing bikes jack-knifed and they hit the other car. The woman who was driving got out and said that they would have to call the police. Leonard talked her out of doing so by giving her a hundred-dollar bill and the two racers pushed the car into town.[3]

In the meantime, Dick Mann, teaming with Al Gunter, was making his first trip to Sturgis as an Amateur. The two BSA riders met up with Leonard on Main Street, a few doors West of Gunner's Lounge. According to Mann, Leonard was standing beside the old Nash, and he could see Charlie West's two feet sticking out from underneath the car. West was under the car attempting to repair the drive shaft, which had been damaged in the accident. Apparently the Nash was repaired, and the four racers went into Gunner's for a beer. Later another racer, Don Hawley, attempted to start a fight and so everyone jumped into the Nash and drove to Deadwood. About a mile out of Deadwood, the Nash had a flat tire and West drove it into Deadwood on the rim. Al Gunter, Dick Mann and Leonard continued to party while West went looking for a new tire. After partying late into the morning, the riders returned to Sturgis and went to sleep. From Dick Mann's perspective, his first experience in Sturgis was quite exciting.[4] Albert Gunter went on to win the National Championship race on Sunday, and Leonard finished third in 1954.

In 1956, Charlie West came to Sturgis alone and won the Sunday feature. Leonard was racing somewhere else that year but returned in 1957, winning Sunday's feature race and beating out Dick Klamfoth and Dick Mann, who by then was riding as an Expert.

Joe Leonard, the 1953 Expert Champion at Sturgis, pictured here at the 1969 Indianapolis 500. (John Tibben Collection)

When he finished his motorcycle-racing career, Leonard began racing automobiles. He was leading the pack at the 1968 Indianapolis 500, but with only nine laps to go, his turbine engine racecar suffered a fuel injection failure.

Joe Leonard lives with his wife and granddaughter in San Jose and travels to motorcycle races whenever he can, especially enjoying the Daytona Beach Racers Reunion in 2002 at Daytona. At this party, he asked Jack Hoel if the backstretch at Sturgis was still a downhill. Jack, who has lived in Sturgis all his life, was astounded. When he returned home to Sturgis from Daytona, Jack drove out to the half-mile track and, sure enough, Joe Leonard was right.[5] For the past 65 years, the track has had an additional feature unrecognized by anyone in Sturgis. Championship racers like Joe Leonard had to be able to spot any advantage they could in winning races.

Joe Leonard was inducted into the AMA Hall of Fame in 1998 as a Charter Member and is also an inductee of the National Motorcycle Hall of Fame. In 1991 he was inducted into the prestigious automobile-racing dominated Motor Sport of America Hall of Fame, selected for one of the few slots allocated to motorcycle racers. He is also a Charter member of the White Plate Flat Tracker's Association.

The Rigors of Racing

Today, the average visitor to the Black Hills Motor Classic probably spends more money in one day than the average winning racer of the 1940s, 50s and 60s earned in two days of racing. In the early days when a rider was broke or injured, the other riders generally got together to help the fellow out in some way. These gentlemen, in the early years of racing, lived by a code that included the elements of sharing and mutual support.

According to Dick Mann, no one made any money at dirt track racing. Even as late as the 1960's when he was Number 1 and the AMA National Championship Racer, he had to have a winter job. During the short summer racing season, Mann made about as much as a plumber and felt that this made it a high- paying job. In most cases – a general average according to Mann – if you were able to win both your heat and the final race, there was about $125 for the weekend. In those days, however, a racer could buy a pretty good racing bike for about $700, and one of the ways Mann earned money to survive between races was changing tires on the racer's machines. At times he would take a chance. Instead of charging his regular $5.00 fee per tire, he would gamble with the other racer for half of the purse. Sometimes he won as much as $25 for a tire change.[1]

Mann also reflected on the problem of modifying motorcycles to work properly in a racing mode. Early racers always worked on their own bikes. Even when he was National Champion, Mann designed and built his bike's frame, hopped up and tuned the engine, painted the bike and the trailer, drove from race to race, loaded and unloaded his own bike, and rode it in the races. Much of this independence ended in the early 1970's when manufacturers began to provide motorcycles especially designed for racing.[2]

Broken bones were also a common theme in racing. Mann described the "racing cast," which was constructed by a rider to qualify for racing after carefully removing the full-sized "doctors cast". Using a woolen stocking from JCPenny, and plaster of Paris from the local drug store, Mann and his fellow racers got to be pretty good at hiding their injuries.[3] Neil Keen whose early nickname was "Peaches" and later "Peachy Keen" read everything he could on injuries, fractures and broken bones. Keen became very good at constructing temporary casts using duct tape. As his reputation spread, Keen's nickname evolved into "Dr. Peach."[4]

Life on the road was no picnic. Ed Youngblood, in his recently published biography of Dick Mann, *Mann of His Time,* described some of the rigors early racers experienced driving from race to race. Mann, living in California and competing on the national circuit, was required to make four cross-country trips per year on two-lane highways in those pre-Interstate days. The first trip was to Daytona in March, and the second trip in the Spring included Lacomia, New Hampshire; Heidelberg, Pennsylvania; and Columbus, Ohio. The third trip started with Sturgis and the "Kansas Circuit", followed by Peoria and Springfield, Illinois. Finally, a return to Pennsylvania for the Langhorne race closed the season. The time record from Oakland to Daytona was 58 hours on two lane roads. After the Interstate highways were opened, this record was reduced to 52 hours according to Dick Mann. Riders relied on a wide range of vehicles, including worn out automobiles or panel trucks, home-made trailers, and an occasional pickup. Joe Leonard liked to use Nash automobiles because the seats could be converted into a bed for sleeping. In the early years of his career, Gary Nixon, who was always broke, often mooched rides or was towed behind someone's pickup. On one occasion, Nixon was able to get Dick Mann to tow both his broken-down Lincoln and the trailer behind Mann's vehicle.[5]

Lodging was yet another problem. Some of the racers tried sleeping in their cars while others would park near a motel early in the morning

One example of what a racer might do to transport his or her machine —
Pappy Hoel and his side-car mounted racer rig. (Pearl Hoel Collection)

and catch an open door when someone checked out of their room. They would then hurry into the abandoned motel room, take a shower and then catch some sleep until the maid showed up to clean the room. When anyone could afford a motel, four or five riders would join him, take the beds apart, and then sleep on the mattresses and the box springs. Joe Leonord would often hit camping trailer dealerships at night and after finding an open door, set his alarm clock, sleep-in and then take off. Once his alarm did not go off, and Leonard was discovered by a customer who was doing a walk-through with the camping trailer salesman.

When racing in the Midwest, "The BSA Midwestern Racing Headquarters" became John Lund's dealership in Decatur, Illinois, where racers met to work on their bikes, sleeping on the front and back porches, in the yard or in the shop itself. Food was also a problem. In August, most of the riders would raid Midwestern cornfields and boil the stolen ears in a hubcap.[6]

Clothes were often washed in a creek or pond and draped over the handlebars. In the early days at Sturgis most of the racers would head for Bear Butte Lake, after the races to wash their clothes and skinny dip.[7]

These early riders would often caravan from race to race. This was probably because of the marginal vehicles they used in transporting their motorcycles. If one of the rigs broke down, the others would help by either fixing the vehicle or shifting around to haul each other's racing bikes. Sometimes to overcome the boredom of driving four wheeled vehicles, they would form up into a bumper-to-bumper configuration called a "train", douse all of the headlights (except for the leader's) and then race down the two-lane roads at 80 miles per hour.[8]

Today's riders travel in elaborate motor coaches, often sleeping in first class hotels and dining in the best restaurants. They are assisted by support teams, which include mechanics, factory reps, and even publicists. In contrast, the racers of the 1940s, '50s and '60s were not necessarily members of the Jackpine Gypsies but they actually were the real Gypsies of their day!

August 12-15, 1954

Although 1954 proved to be an exciting year for the Classic, it began on a sour note for two local riders. Bill Hunn, a linotype operator at the *Sturgis Tribune* and supporter of rally events, was injured prior to the rally when his motorcycle was rear-ended as he attempted to make a left turn. Hunn, a member of the Jackpine Gypsies Motorcycle Club, was on his way to help lay out the hill climb course at the 1954 rally.[1] In those days prior to electric turn signals, the driver of the car maintained that he did not see or understand what Hunn was doing extending his arm as a turn signal. He later stated that he thought he was just waving his arm.[2]

Another injury was reported on August 5th when the youngest son (no name given) of Mr. and Mrs. Harold Huntley was reported to be recovering in the Deadwood Hospital from injuries when his motorcycle crashed, catching his ankle in the chain.

As for excitement, the AMA Competition Committee again selected the Sturgis venue for the National Five Mile Championship. Officials of the Black Hills Classic were exceptionally pleased and Bruce Barnes, the all-time pragmatic race manager and promoter, guaranteed that the track would again be dust proof on race day![3] According to Jack Hoel, track preparation required initial blade work by a grader, then water had to be worked into the sub-surface prior to a final treatment of calcium chloride which would act as a chemical agent to draw moisture from the subsoil and from the air, providing a dust free racing surface.[4]

Clarence "Pappy" Hoel, who was chairing the publicity effort for 1954, indicated that rally information was going far beyond the Black Hills area to include coverage in national magazines. Two days of touring were scheduled (August 12-13), starting on Thursday and again on Friday, maintaining the four-day rally format of previous years. The Friday night feed would include barbecued venison and would again be held, with an accompanying program of entertainment, in the City Park.[5]

Of the 15 "Expert" riders entered, six were future AMA Hall of Fame inductees. They included Paul Goldsmith, the 1953 Daytona 200 winner; Albert Gunter, Dirt Track Racing Champ 1950s and 1960s; Bobby Hill, 1951-52 AMA Grand National Champion; Joe Leonard 1954, '56, '57 AMA Grand National Champion and two time winner of the Daytona 200; and Bill Tuman, 1953 AMA National Champion.[6] Another rider, registered as an amateur in 1954, was Richard (Dick) Mann, who was to become the 1963 and 1971 AMA Grand National Champion as well as winner of the 1971 Daytona 200.[7]

By 1953-54, many of the lighter, more maneuverable English motorcycles were becoming a part of the riding scene in the Black Hills Area. Cycles from BSA (Bir-

Peggy Burke, Black Hills Motor Classic Queen 1954. (Al Burke Collection)

mingham Small Arms Ltd.), Triumph, Norton, AJS, Matchless and the new light-weight Indian Arrow and Warrior were replacing the older, heavier Indian and Harley Davidson machines.[8] Because of these new motorcycles, two additional events were added to the 1954 rally: a polo match and trail ride.

The polo match was scheduled for Saturday night after the races and featured the Jackpine Gypsies of Sturgis and the Rapid City Pioneers Motorcycle Club. It was essentially a good-natured contest between local riders. The trail ride was scheduled as an option in place of the Friday tour and would feature back roads, logging roads and deer trails. It was touted as being designed "for those who feel that road riding is too tame."[9]

Riders began streaming into Sturgis on Tuesday, August 10, two days before the official opening of the Classic. Pappy Hoel estimated that there were over 1,000 visitors and that 560 AMA members had registered in the Tour Book. On Friday evening, the visitors consumed 30 gallons of potato salad and over 400 pounds of venison. At the program, Peggy Burke of Bloomington, Minnesota was selected from a field of over 20 entries as the "Queen of the Classic". Best dressed male and female rider awards went to Ken Trapp of Hastings, Minnesota, and Cathy Anderson also from Bloomington. The distance award was presented to Harold Rebaclow, who rode in from Miami, Florida. The oldest rider was Bill Wheeldon from Mitchell, South Dakota. The Dusty Riders from Des Moines, Iowa were the best-dressed club, and Mr. and Mrs. Howard Knapp, also from Des Moines won the newlywed prize. Sturgis Chief of Police, Fred Ritchel reported that no arrests were made during the four-day event and that this was the best behaved group ever to visit Sturgis.[10]

In Saturday's races, the Expert final was won by Charlie West, followed by his traveling partner Joe Leonard in second and Billie McConnel in third. On Sunday, the National Five Mile Championship saw AMA Hall of Fame riders in the first 4 positions.

The feature race winner was Albert Gunter with a time of 4:46:02. Riding a BSA motorcycle, Gunter from Los Angeles, California and nick-named the "Stockton Comet", found enough power in the final lap to beat out Klamfoth, Goldsmith, and Leonard, all nationally-ranked racers. According to Pappy Hoel, these four riders were closely packed the entire race, especially in the corners. Placing only third in his qualifying heat race and sixth in his time trial, Gunter used determination and skill to win this National Championship. Dick Mann of Richmond, California (and Gunter's traveling partner at this time) began his first tour away from California as an Amateur, taking second in the Junior race behind Al Lauer, who won the National Amateur title riding a new K model Harley Davidson. Mann went on to become one of the most outstanding dirt-track racers in history of the sport. Both he and Gunter were touring the country riding "Beesers" for a California BSA dealership.[11] Both Gunter and Mann were eventually inducted into the AMA Hall of Fame and were also elected to membership in the White Plate Flat Trackers Association.

Bill Tuman, the fifth Hall of Fame rider at Sturgis in 1954, did not do as well, placing fourth in one of the heat races on Saturday and third in the Five Mile Consolation Race on Sunday. Apparently Tuman's Indian racers, last produced in 1950, were beginning to give him trouble. According to Jack Hoel, after Indian quit producing 500cc vertical twins, they began importing Norton and Matchless machines from England. The Indian factory, in turn, encouraged their racers to use these British bikes in competition. This worked well, especially in regard to the 498 CC Norton Manx, until the AMA began limiting the DOHC engines. Both Tuman and Klamfoth raced successfully on Nortons for a few seasons.[12]

NO.		NAME	MACHINE	TIME
5 MILE AMATEUR HEAT—WINNERS TO AMATEUR FINAL				
71N	1st	G. Lake	HD	5:01:81
83Y	2nd	R. Mann	BSA	
71H	3rd	D. Major	HD	
5 MILE EXPERT HEAT—WINNERS TO CHAMPIONSHIP RACE				
98	1st	J. Leonard	HD	4:49:12
58	2nd	H. McAfee	Triumph	
3	3rd	P. Goldsmith	HD	
5 MILE AMATEUR HEAT—WINNERS TO AMATEUR FINAL				
2Y	1st	A. Lauer	HD	4:57:63
96P	2nd	A. Bergquist	Indian	
27Y	3rd	C. Eastman	HD	
5 MILE EXPERT HEAT—WINNERS TO CHAMPIONSHIP RACE				
21Y	1st	C. West	HD	4:46:00
54	2nd	A. Gunter	BSA	
2	3rd	D. Klamfoth	BSA	
5 MILE AMATEUR CONSOLATION.				
66K	1st	J. Marcell	BSA	5:06:67
68M	2nd	R. Nelson	HD	
81N	3rd	L. Stadler	Indian	
5 MILE EXPERT CONSOLATION				
52	1st	C. Mook	HD	5:09:35
84Q	2nd	T. Georgeson	HD	
1	3rd	B. Tuman	Indian (Didn't run)	
5 MILE EXPERT CONSOLATION				
71	1st	B. Hill	Indian	4:52:37
30	2nd	B. McConell	HD	
70	3rd	L. Ensminger	HD	
5 MILE AMATEUR FINAL—WINNERS IN HEATS				
2Y	1st	A. Lauer	HD	4:58:52
83Y	2nd	R. Mann	BSA	
96P	3rd	L. Bergquist	Indian	
THE 5 MILE AMA NATIONAL CHAMPIONSHIP FOR 1954				
54	1st	Albert Gunter	Calif	BSA	4:48:02
5	2nd	Paul Goldsmith	Mich	HD	(98-31-58-
2	3rd	Dick Klamfoth	Ohio	BSA	54-3-2)

1954 Score Sheet with winning times. (Pearl Hoel Collection)

1954 Expert Champion: Albert Gunter

Albert Gunter was an excellent racer and competitor who placed in the top 10 of the Grand National Series every year beginning in 1954 through 1962 with the exception of 1958. Although he was never awarded the National Number One honor, he did place second in 1957, and third in 1956. In 1954, the year Gunter took the five-mile National crown at Sturgis, his overall season point record placed him at number five behind Joe Leonard, Paul Goldsmith, Charlie West, Dick Klamfoth and Bobby Hill, who were tied at fourth place. All of these racers, with the exception of Goldsmith, were champions of Sturgis in the 1950s.

Albert, a somewhat controversial figure in the racing community, was born in Houston, Texas in 1933. He became interested in motorcycles, hanging around one of the local motorcycle shops. His initial experience in racing began in Texas and Louisiana, where he attracted the attention of Vern Gardner, a Triumph dealer from Oakland, California. Gunter soon moved to California and began working in Gardner's dealership and racing Triumphs. According to Neil Keen, he later "skipped" to BSA and moved to Los Angeles.[1]

Dick Mann describes Gunter as an individualist, a free thinker, a great mechanic and one of the smartest and shrewdest riders he ever knew. Mann indicated that Gunter's mechanical ability and insights about engines were always ahead of his time. As a racer, he was secretive, a loner, and always played mind games with the competition, which led to his dislike among many of the other racers. Like the baseball player who fiddles with the pitcher, stepping in and out of the batter's box, Albert would delay the start of a race by adjusting his gloves, jockeying his bike and adjusting his goggles in the hope of psyching out and irritating the other riders at the starting line. He was quite good looking, was fastidious about his appearance, wore tailored leathers and affected a Marlon Brando pose.[2]

Mann met Gunter when he was asked to team up with him in the summer of 1954, by Louis Thomas, a Los Angeles BSA tuner. Consequently, Mann's first experience at a National was at Sturgis, racing as an Amateur. The trip to Sturgis with Gunter was quite an adventure for

the young racer. Gunter went on to win the 5 Mile National Championship race on Sunday while Mann took second place in the Amateur
final. Both riders were lifelong BSA afficianadoes.[3]

According to Neil Keen, Gunter was "handsome to a fault, as charm-
ing as a bird, and as eccentric as the March Hare." He was so set in his
ways that, "despite his brilliance as a rider, most of his great ideas were
for naught." Albert's major contributions, according to Keen, included

*Al Gunter (at right),
with fellow BSA racer
Neil Keen in the early
1960s. Gunter won
the 1954 National at
Sturgis. (Courtesy of
Ken James)*

representing the riders at the AMA Rules Committee meeting regarding rider insurance, prize money, and motorcycle modification rules. Later in his career, Gunter became a vegetarian and associated it with clean living. In the interest of becoming a better racer, Gunter neither drank nor smoked.

There are several stories regarding Albert's behavior in restaurants. Since most of the other racers patronized beer and hamburger dives, Gunter always had difficulty ordering vegetarian meals in these biker hangouts. One waitress was exceptionally frustrated by Albert's request for "dry poached eggs." After being sent back to the kitchen twice, she returned a third time with the eggs on a separate plate and then promptly turned them upside down on top of his toast and walked away in disgust.[4]

One of the problems with the vegetarian diet, according to Dick Mann, was that Albert lost a lot of weight and strength, and in a 50 mile National at Springfield, Illinois, after taking the lead early in the race, Gunter's legs gave out in lap 26. After this race, Gunter gave up on being a vegetarian and went back to eating in hamburger shacks with the rest of the racers.[5]

In his biography of Dick Mann, *Mann of His Time,* Ed Youngblood describes Gunter as "getting away with abrasive behavior through the sheer heat of his genius." Although Gunter never graduated from high school, Youngblood describes him as being very bright, and an accomplished engine builder who could always make his bikes run faster and better than anyone else's machines. Gunter was also the designer of the first full coverage helmet "having designed the 'Bell Star' while working for the Bell Corporation."[6]

Everyone in the 1950's racing community has a different version of one of Gunter's most infamous escapades at the 1957 Daytona. It seems that he and Mann were testing their BSA Goldstars on a backwoods dirt road near their motel. They had stopped and Mann had pulled his spark plug to check his mixture when the local Sheriff drove up and attempted to arrest both of them for speeding, excessive noise, and riding their bikes without lights or license plates. Gunter, whose bike was not disabled, took off in a flash leaving Mann with his crippled racer. The Sheriff threw Mann into his cruiser, and took off after Gunter. He called in Gunter's number 54 plate which he had noted on Albert's bike and put out an APB. Interestingly, another policeman arrested an Amateur with the same number who was lining up at the Daytona track for a heat race. After a good number of law enforcement people were deployed, Gunter was finally located and arrested in his motel room, where he was calmly watching television. Since the back road and the motel were in different counties, the BSA boss, Ted Hogdon had to post bond and bail them out of two different county jails in time to compete in the Daytona 200. Gunter took second in the race and won $1500, but ended up using most of it to pay his fines.[6]

One of the typical problems that faced injured riders in those early days was a concern about ambulance and hospital bills. A common practice was to have another rider sneak the rider out of the hospital as soon as it was at all feasible to do so. When Dick Mann wrecked his knee in a race at Stockton, Kansas, he ended up in the Ft Hayes, Kansas hospital while all of his pals and his partner Gunter left for the Minnesota State Fair to compete in the seven mile National race. Albert, who won this race, and loyal to his racing partner, returned to Kansas and smuggled Mann out of the hospital in a wheelchair by telling the nurses that he was taking him out for a haircut. In about 10 minutes they were in Gunter's pick-up on their way to California.[8]

Gunter was a perennial champion at Ascot Park racetrack in Los Angeles for nearly 10 years. When his racing career began to wind down in the late 1960s, he suffered a head injury at Dodge City, Kansas and never really recovered. His eccentric temperament and negative behavior became more and more pronounced. At a race at Ascot Park he ran into a fence at the end of the front straightaway on a borrowed motorcycle and was paralyzed from the chest down. About a year later, despondent because he could no longer race motorcycles, he took his own life.[9]

Birmingham Small Arms Company

Birmingham Small Arms (BSA) motorcycles didn't arrive on the American motorcycling scene until after World War II. In an effort to protect American manufacturers and the domestic economy during the Great Depression, Congress passed the Smoot-Hawley Tariff act, which established high tariffs on imported goods. And while Great Britain probably produced a wider variety of motorcycles than any other nation, the price of these machines, including the high tariff, discouraged importation to the U.S. Consequently, by 1940, the only two marquees available to American motorcyclists were Harley Davidson and Indian.[1] Later, the Economic Cooperation Act of 1948 empowered the Marshall Plan to encourage the economic reconstruction in Europe. This action assisted rehabilitation efforts in Great Britain and Western Europe's industrial infrastructure and also encouraged international trade, thus eliminating the Smoot-Hawley Act. A variety of British and European motorcycles were soon imported by far-sighted dealers, and American riders were exposed to a variety of small, medium, and large English bikes. This variety in machines actually expanded the sport of motorcycling because new riders who could not or did not want to deal with the larger Harleys and Indians were able to purchase these smaller and less expensive machines.[3]

Dick Klamfoth's 1949 ride, the Beart-prepared Norton Marx used in winning the Daytona 200, was kind of an interim example of this Marshall Plan development. By 1950, the Indian Motorcycle Company was thoroughly involved importing Nortons, and as a result, Klamfoth's 1950 Marx was sponsored in part by an Indian dealer in Ohio and the Indian factory.[4]

The Birmingham Small Arms Company began in 1865 when a group of craftsman joined together and began producing small caliber firearms. They began producing bicycles in the 1880s, and like Harley Davidson and Indian, BSA began building motorcycles around the turn of the century. Starting in 1906, BSA went on to become Britain's largest manufacturer of motorcycles, producing in excess of 75,000 motorcyles annually in some of the years following World War II. The focus of the firm from 1906 to 1945 was the production of reliable motorcycles, suitable for general recreation and transportation. These early motorcycles were simple in design and construction, and BSA was rarely involved in racing.[5]

In early years, BSA developed a cheap, reliable and popular 750cc motorcycle with a Harley Davidson/Indian V-twin configured engine. This bike was both successful and popular, and because of its large engine was used by a great number of English riders as a sidecar rig. In 1930, BSA developed the "Sloper," named for its large single cylinder 493cc engine sloped to the front of the bike. The British public loved this machine, and it was used widely in the 1930s for transportation and the occasional sporting event. The Sloper was improved and adapted in the late 1930s, and the revised model, the M20, saw wide usage by the military during World War II. Over 125,000 of these 500cc motorcycles were supplied to the Allied Forces.

In 1946, BSA launched their 500cc Star Twin. This motorcycle was expanded to 650cc by 1950, and reconfigured to a unit construction drive train by 1952. At the same time, work began on improving the 500 cc single cylinder design, which became a favorite of competition riders during the 1950s. This motorcycle, the BSA Gold Star or "Goldie," is still regarded as the ultimate British single.[6]

In 1962, BSA introduced the Fighting Clubman, a 650cc vertical twin that cranked out 53-horse power. Although a fine machine, the Clubman never achieved the equivalent success of similarly sized Triumphs and Nortons. It was also threatened in the American market by the flood of Japanese motorcycles. By 1970, BSA began to experience financial difficulty and was absorbed by Norton-Villiers-Triumph in 1971. Development of the three-cylinder BSA Rocket soon concluded, and the BSA marquee was abandoned by Norton-Villiers-Triumph in 1973.[7]

Many of the racers at Sturgis during the 1950s and 1960s rode BSA motorcycles, including Albert Gunter, Dick Mann, Neil Keen, Sammy Tanner, Bill Tuman and Dick Klamfoth. Although some of them used the Star Twin model, the vast majority of them rode the Gold Star singles.

August 11-14, 1955

In 1955, the street carnival included booths run by 4-H Clubs, the Business and Professional Women's Club, Girl Scouts, Explorer Scouts, the Women's Literary Club, both Veteran's Organizations and, of course, the Jackpine Gypsies. Apparently, respectability and the good, old American concept of making a buck for charity had evolved in the Sturgis experience. The dance had also been converted to a free street dance with a format focused on square dancing. Pappy Hoel, manager of the Black Hills Classic, reported that invitations had been extended to square dance clubs from all over the Black Hills.[1]

Several nationally-recognized racers were registered by August 11 for the big weekend of racing. Albert Gunter, the 1954 winner at Sturgis, and Dick Klamfoth (Sturgis 1949), the National Six Mile Champion, were signed up. Also registered was Brad Andres, a new rider to Sturgis, who, by mid-summer 1955, had accumulated the most points and was leading everyone else for AMA top racer of the year. He went on to become the 1955 AMA Grand National Champion and winner of the Daytona 200 in 1955, 1959 and 1960. Andres became a Hall of Fame Inductee in 1998.[2]

Hoel reported that hotels and motels in the area were nearly filled and that mail-in reservations were coming in daily. He also indicated that excitement was high about the amount of local interest and participation in the street carnival.[3]

On Sunday, August 7, 1955 the *Rapid City Journal* carried a feature article, educating the local Black Hills population about the sport of motorcycling. This piece was

Members of the Jackpine Gypsies and the newly-arrived Royal Enfield Indians. (Pearl Hoel Collection)

directed towards the generally negative public attitude towards motorcyclists and attempted to explain that the majority of the riders visiting during rally week were really good, self disciplined, conscientious, law-abiding people. Apparently the impact of the Sturgis rally, already well accepted in Sturgis, was beginning to bother folks in Rapid City.

The author of the piece, Jack Cannon, Sunday Editor at the *Journal*, informed his readers that these riders were not "scatter-brained speed-crazed individuals" but rather members of AMA regulated motorcycle clubs who, as part of their own efforts, were fighting an up-hill battle against misunderstanding and false attitudes on the part of the general public.[4] Cannon went on to explain that the AMA and its member clubs, like the Gypsies and the Rapid City Pioneers Motorcycle Club (RPMs), were working hard to eliminate "outlaws" or those who defied the rules for safety and noise. He then cautioned motorists to be aware of the common courtesies that drivers should extend to rally visitors.[5]

The remainder of the article explained some of the year-round activities of the local clubs, including scrambles, the slow-race, broad jumping and fun-filled events like the egg races and the suitcase drills where the rider has to ride to a point, change clothes, and return to the starting line in the least time.[6] It is interesting to note that the community support recognized in Sturgis was expanding to the Rapid City area by 1955.

Gypsy Tour

Over 400 riders registered for the two days touring and about 800 riders returned to the Sturgis Park for the Friday night Barbecue. Darlene "Bunny" Wellner of Richfield, Minnesota was chosen as Queen. Best dressed riders were Don Davis from Mitchell, South Dakota, and Delores Beise from Hastings, Minnesota. Distance trophies were won by Jerry Green of Zanesville, Ohio (a female rider) and Jim Baker of Bangor, Maine. The couple riding double the longest distance was Mr. and Mrs. Earl Moore of Washington, DC, and the oldest rider, Jay Dahl, age 66, rode in from Spirit Lake, Iowa. The Best Dressed Club came from South St. Paul, Minnesota.[7]

After the trophies were awarded, a visiting pastor, Reverend Webster gave a talk about the quality of management and organization of the Gypsy Tour. Reverend Webster, having ridden on several motorcycle tours around the United States, stated that this tour was the best of them all.[8]

Races

The distance prescribed for the 1955 National Championship was six miles. After a dry dusty series of races on Saturday, a drizzle developed on Sunday morning and by race

Darlene "Bunny" Wellner of Richfield, Minnesota sits on her throne as Queen of the 1954 Black Hills Motor Classic. (Sturgis Museum Collection)

time, the track was quite damp and slippery. The race announcer commended the grandstand crowd for their patience as they sat for several hours while 50 cars and a roller truck dried and packed the track. When the races were finished, a new Champion, Don Tindall from Portland, Oregon was the new AMA National Six Mile Champion. His brother Ron won the Amateur final, making the day complete for the two Tindalls. Second and third place money was taken by Joe Leonard and the currently famous Brad Andres. Both of the Tindalls and Leonard rode Harley Davidsons. Dick Klamfoth placed third in the Expert Consolation Race. Only two injuries were reported during the Saturday races. Al Burke injured his foot in one of the Expert heat races and Don Mulowney fractured two vertebrae in one of the Saturday novice finals.[9]

1955 Expert Champion: Don Tindall

Don Tindall was born in Salem, Oregon on April 22, 1931. When he was a child, the family moved to Portland, where his father worked for the Greyhound Bus Company. Tindall's Dad was an accomplished motorcycle racer, recognized in the Portland area for his expertise in hill climbing and enduro racing. When Don was 15, his dad bought him a 1941 61 cubic inch Harley Davidson that had been stroked to 68 cubic inches. Don and his brother Ron rode their bikes frequently, using the local gravel roads to evade the police. Don was eventually caught with just a learner's permit and had to quit riding the Harley because the police were watching for it. He then got a 1947 21 cubic inch Velocette. A dealer was in the process of converting it to a 30.5 cubic inch racer when he decided to buy another bike — a 1948 BSA 500cc single.

Tindall lied about his age and applied for his AMA novice license in 1948 at age 17. He raced in the Portland area, moving to Amateur in 1949 and to Expert by 1950. After winning several races in 1950 and 51, Tindall enlisted in the US Navy and was stationed in the Japan/Korea area aboard the aircraft carrier USS Bataan.

Early in 1955, his ship docked in San Francisco. Don had not been on a bike for two years, but on shore leave he visited some motorcycle shops and noticed a poster in a Triumph shop advertising a road race at Willow Springs, California. He told the Triumph dealer that he had an Expert license and really wanted to race. He then called his dad in Portland and told him about the race. His dad called him back and told him that George Shanton, a Harley Davidson dealer in Portland, would bring a new KR 750 Harley Davidson to race at Willow Springs. Tindall went to the race, and after a disagreement with the officials about his choice of "Grasshopper" tires, was allowed to enter the race. He took second in his time trial (behind Ed Kretz, Jr.), and got a good start in the feature race. He had lapped the second place rider and was between the 75th and 76th mile lap when the KR's lower end failed. As he was pushing the bike back into the pits, two gentlemen in suits approached him and one of them asked, "Those Harleys are just no good, right?"

Tindall's response was, "Best ride I ever had." He later found out that it was the correct response. The two "suits" were Bill Harley and Walter Davidson. He was later contacted by John Gayle, a dealer in Montavo, California and was asked if he would race for him. Tindall's ship was being decommissioned and he had been assigned to a different ship tied up at Ventura, California. Since he was still in the Navy, he couldn't commit to Gayle, but soon discovered that the Harley Davidson folks had sped up his discharge papers, and he was to race in the road race at Laconia, New Hampshire. Gayle gave him an airplane ticket; he flew to Milwaukee and then on to Laconia and was in second place behind Joe Leonard when he crashed at the 75-mile lap.

By August of 1955, he and his brother Ron, working their way back to Portland, decided to take in the Kansas Circuit, "cherry-picking" the easy races. According to Don, his brother Ron was a master mechanic and they would always overhaul the lower end of the engine after every third race program. At this point in the year, the two riders had no intention of competing at Sturgis.

One the way home to Portland, the Tindall brothers pulled into a gas station in Nebraska with their trailer rig. The attendant asked if they were going to the races in Trenton, Nebraska. They were not, but assured the attendant that they were, and then proceeded to Trenton. When they got there, they drove their car around the track to check the actual distance and decide on gear ratios. They then noticed some riders in a group by the grandstand. They went over and were asked, "What were riders from as far away from Oregon doing here at Trenton?" Ron mistakenly blurted out, "Cherry-picking!" — the worst possible reply. The next day they placed first and second in Trenton's feature race, and after the race one of the other racers asked if they were going to Holyoke Kansas. The other racers told this guy to shut-up, and the two brothers went to the car, got out their map and located Holyoke. They made the quick trip and repeated their first and second place victories.

Don had pulled the ligaments in his left knee at Holyoke and was in the pits wrapping it with Ace bandages when Ray Cook, a Harley

Davidson dealer from Denver, approached and asked if they were going to Sturgis the next week. Don's knee was really bad, and they said that they were not going. Cook insisted that they go and promised that a new KR 750 racer would be waiting there for Don to ride. The brothers went on to Sturgis and after seeing the new racer, Don insisted that Cook's mechanic change the handlebars and use the rear suspension from Tindall's bike. After a long argument with Cook's mechanic, they finally got the bike rigged out.

During the time trials, Tindall who was using the regular four inch Harley Davidson tires that came on the bike, realized that Sturgis, like the tracks in Oregon, was a "sticky" track and the KR would be faster if he changed his wheel configuration. He switched to a 21-inch front

Don Tindall, 1955 National Champion at Sturgis. (Courtesy of Ellie Tindall)

wheel with a 3.00 tire, and mounted a 3.50 x 18 tire in the rear. In the first turn, Tindall was on the inside of Joe Leonard, who was riding a Sifton-tuned KR750. Coming out of the turn, Tindall went through the motion of shifting out of third gear. Leonard immediately followed his lead, shifting into fourth gear, but Tindall had really left his bike in third gear. He was able to accelerate out of the turn, get ahead of Leonard, and lead to the finish line. "I was lucky to have the lead," he said. "Because with my left knee in such bad shape I couldn't use my iron shoe in broad sliding the corners." Don's Brother Ron won the Amateur final, making the 1955 Classic a Tindall sweep.

After winning the National at Sturgis, Cook asked the Tindall brothers to come to Pike's Peak for the National Championship race up the mountain. Since Cook had already signed a Denver rider, Billy Myers, to ride the bike, Don would be held in reserve to ride Cook's motorcycle in the event that Myers was incapacitated. The Tindall brothers came

Don Tindall with a Trophy Girl, somewhere in Oregon. (Courtesy of Ellie Tindall)

anyway, opting to ride their own bikes in the competition. Cook also had two "Indy" cars entered in the Pike's Peak race. "I was sitting in one of the cars, and after awhile, everyone assumed I knew how to drive it," said Tindall. "I didn't even know how to start it." He asked someone, watched the others, got the car started, and ended up in a practice run. Cook's contracted driver placed 13th in the time trial and Tindall placed fourth. He was about to be entered in the auto race when internal politics in Cook's crew eased him out of the ride. "I really had fun listening to that Offenhauser engine on my time trial," recalled Tindall.

Don's brother Ron was seriously injured in practice on his motorcycle, and Tindall spent the night with him in the Colorado Springs hospital. The next day, he came to race and passed Bill Myers, Cook's contract racer, on the way up. He went on to win the Pike's Peak motorcycle race in 1955.

After the Pike's Peak win, Don waited until his brother Ron recovered, and the two brothers returned to Oregon. He retired from professional racing shortly thereafter in 1956 at age 25.

After racing Don Tindall worked in the car business until the early 1970 and then became a General Contractor in Oregon and California. He was a builder and property developer until his retirement in 1994. He presently lives with his wife, Ellie, in Portland, where his hobbies include "traveling and staying out of trouble!"

Bobby Hill: A Classic Favorite

Although he never won the feature race at Sturgis, Bobby Hill was a favorite of Black Hills Classic fans and a true gentleman in the racing circuit, traveling to Sturgis in the early 1950s with life long friend, Bill Tuman. Hill often placed in most of the races and won the Consolation final in 1953. He had a spectacular career at the national level, and was AMA National Champion in 1951 and 1952 by winning back to back championships at the Springfield Mile.* He was also elected the AMA's Most Popular Rider in 1951.[1]

Allen Robert Hill was born in Triadelphia, West Virginia on July 22, 1922.When he was a teenager in West Virginia, his older brother worked in the local Harley Davidson dealership. By the time he was 14, he began fooling around with motorcycles. His mom cashed in on a life insurance policy to help out, and Bobby purchased his first motorcycle, a WLD 45 cubic inch Harley Davidson for $327. He was 16 at the time and joined the Wheeling, West Virginia "Roamers". Hill soon became involved in "Closed Club Event" dirt track racing on his older brother's WLDR Harley Davidson, a racing conversion motorcycle. According to Hill, he and his brother would ride to the race, remove the lights and the front fender and compete. After racing, they would replace the lights and fender and ride home. Using this bike, Hill started competing in these local club events in 1938. He continued to compete in this manner during 1939, '40 and '41.

In 1940, he was 18 and secured his Novice license from the AMA. In 1942 he won seven out of the seven races he entered in Ohio and was noticed by Ralph Shops, the owner of "Shoppes Indian Sales" in Columbus, Ohio. "I didn't even know that they made Indian Motorcycles before the war," Hill said. After serving in the Marine Corps in the South Pacific and China during World War II, Hill came home and "found my self sitting on a brand new Shoppes Indian."[2]

---

* Prior to 1954, the AMA Championship and the coveted Number One Plate was awarded to the rider who won the National Championship Race. Before World War II, this race was generally held at Daytona Beach; Langhorne, Pennsylvania or Atlanta, Georgia. In 1946, however, the Springfield Mile was selected for the National Championship. Beginning in 1954, the AMA established a point system to determine the number one rider in the nation. A series of races, known as the Grand National Series (GNS), were held at various locations around the country and the rider with the most points at the end of the season received the Number One Plate. To test this idea, the AMA kept records of points earned by each rider in 1953 to determine the feasibility of the proposed system. It is interesting to note that Bobby Hill was the points leader for 1953, but since he did not win the Springfield Mile, he was not champion that year. Had the GNS point system been in place a year earlier, Hill would have been Number One for three consecutive years.

Bobby Hill, a favorite of Black Hills Motor Classic fans. (Bobby Hill Collection)

Hill raced this Indian in 1946, and by 1947 he had earned his Expert license and competed in the Daytona 200. He was leading the race winner, Johnny Spiegelhoff (Sturgis champion in 1938, '39, '41, and '46) by 15 seconds when at the 180 mile lap, he bumped or was bumped by another rider and crashed out.[3] In 1948 Hill and Billy Huber both won the National at Atlanta, Georgia finishing in a dead heat. It remains the only "tied championship" in AMA history.

While riding for Ralph Shops, Hill learned to work on his own engines. He became quite skilled at mechanic work and tuning. He also worked to improve his riding skills, always picking up the finer points of racing from veteran riders. When he started racing in earnest, Hill stopped riding on the street. According to Hill, "Good racers are sensible. They may look wild, but once you get the art of racing down it is safer than the streets."[4]

With regard to Sturgis, Hill indicated that he liked the adventure of seeing the "Real West" and especially the Black Hills. He loved the Friday night buffalo feed and seeing real American Indians. He still treasures the welcome he always received from the Jackpine Gypsies, the fans and, especially from Pearl and Clarence Hoel. He did not, however, enjoy the wide-open spaces he had to cross in riding to Sturgis from Western Iowa. "It was a real challenge. The two lane highways, the zigzagging route changes and nothing to see! Wall Drug was the first water stop and the first place where you could even get a sandwich!"[5]

Hill traveled alone to Sturgis in 1950. During the off-season that year, he and Bill Tuman began a six-week tour of Indian dealerships in Texas and the Southwest, promoting for the Indian factory. They became lifelong friends on that trip and still spend a good deal of time together.

In 1954, Hill won at Daytona on a BSA. He also rode Manx Nortons at times but always loved his Indians best! During his racing career, Hill

Bobby Hill at work. (Bobby Hill Collection)

*Bill Tuman, at left, and
Bobby Hill in 1989.
(Bobby Hill Collection)*

competed in 50 to 60 races each year. These races included short-track half-miles, miles and special races like Daytona. In a good year Hill won $7,000 to $10,000. The biggest purse in those days was the Daytona 200 which paid the winner $2,500. First place at the Springfield Mile was $1,175.

Bobby Hill retired from racing in 1959 and went to work for The Standard Oil Company. In 1977, he was inducted into the very first ever Racing Hall of Fame in America. This "Charities Newsies" Hall of Fame is located in Columbus, Ohio and Hill was the very first Inductee. He is also a charter member of the National Motorcycle Hall of Fame, the White Plate Flat Trackers Association and the new AMA Hall of Fame. Hill retired from Standard Oil in 1984 and now lives in Grove City, Ohio with his wife, Nancy. The couple has three grown children.[6]

Bobby Hill loves to travel to Vintage motorcycle events, especially when he can hang out with his old pal, Bill Tuman (Sturgis Champion 1947 and '51). He returns to Sturgis on a regular basis to visit Pearl Hoel and the other old friends in the Jackpine Gypsies. The major difference in Sturgis from his years of racing there, according to Hill, is that "in the 1950's, everyone who rode a motorcycle knew about the races and knew the names of the racers. It's not the same now!"[7]

Bobby Hill also attends the Sturgis Hall of Fame ceremonies and the White Plate Flat Trackers annual meeting at the Gypsies Clubhouse. "It's just like family," says Hill. "I wouldn't miss it!"[8] He did, however, miss the Classic in 2002 due to hip surgery in June, but plans to return in 2003.

Chapter Six:
Transition and Evolution

The years 1956 through 1960 are best viewed as an era of peaceful transition in the evolution of the Classic. Although continuing to grow annually in the number of visitors, the format of the four-day rally remained essentially the same during these five years. There was, of course, the continued participation of nationally recognized racers, enhancement of purse money, and a continuing problem in feeding the locals at the "Feed." Community support and participation continued to grow at a steady pace as evidenced in the Friday night program, which began to include public prayer and community songfests led by one of the local pastors. Locals were also informed that they were not eligible for prizes.

For a larger number of visiting riders, touring the Black Hills was beginning to become as important as racing, and two new events for local "sportsmen" were introduced: a moonlight trail ride and a scrambles race.

It is interesting to note that although the race headquarters had been moved to a downtown location by the Chamber of Commerce, the Hoels continued to serve coffee and doughnuts and provide an informal meeting place with sleeping space. Each year, the Hoels would lease a large circus tent from a firm in Rapid City and pitch it in the open area behind their motorcycle shop.

In 1958, a glitch in planning limited attendance at the half-mile races. The Chamber of Commerce/Black Hills Motor Classic Committee and the Meade County Fair Board scheduled both events for the same weekend. Although touted as a cooperative effort in the interest of promoting the community, this decision resulted in limited participation at both venues.

By 1959, both housing and camping space were becoming a problem due to the large numbers of visiting riders. In 1960, people began coming on Tuesday in anticipation of the Thursday opening and the campground was full by mid-day Wednesday. Classic organizers were begging local families to provide sleeping rooms in their homes.

August 9-12, 1956

A significant milestone in access to the Black Hills Motor Classic was made evident to the visiting rider in 1956. Survey crews and other basic elements of road building could be noted to the North and to the South by riders traveling to the Sturgis area via Rapid City. Interstate 90 through Meade Country had been approved, and the right-of-way was undergoing preliminary construction efforts.[1]

Although the public was invited to the traditional Friday night program following the second day of "Gypsy" touring, they were informed that the barbecue beginning at 6:30 was "free" for motorcyclists only! Apparently the event was becoming more and more impacted by the non-riding public.[2]

The traditional program itself began at 8:00 pm and provided a few innovations or additions. First it was opened with a prayer, and included group singing led by Revered Munck. Another innovation was a dance program provided by the Don Crosby School of Dance. A new category was also nested in the list of traditional riding awards: "Youngest Rider as a Passenger." With attention to earning and exploiting respectability (ever present in the planning efforts of the "Classic" staff), the 1956 program was capped with a presentation and recognition of the members of the Jackpine Gypsies "who made the rally happen."[3] It was probably true that everyone in town, as well as a good number of visitors, knew that credit was due, yet this was the first time such public recognition was noted.

Gypsy Tour riders enjoy one of Pearl Hoel's many mid-day lunches in the Black Hills. (Pearl Hoel Collection)

Charlie West of San Jose, California, riding a Harley Davidson, won every race he entered and capped his performance by winning the Five Mile Feature race on Sunday. Only nine Amateur/Expert riders were entered, too few for a field in each class, but there were 27 Novice riders.[4] The Six Mile National Championship Half-Mile had apparently been moved to a different venue in 1956. This limitation, although disappointing to persons in the inner-circle, was lost in regard to the spectators. A crowd of 4,500 spectators was treated to spills and thrills including that of a Huron, South Dakota Amateur, Robert Dempster, who "went down" in one of the Sunday heat races. His injury was limited to a twisted knee.

There was another exciting heat race on Sunday that ended up as a virtual photofinish between two Amateur racers: Joe Finley of Salem, Oregon, and Don Smith of Richmond, California. Since photofinish equipment was unavailable, the heat was awarded amid a series of boos and cheers, depending on the perceptions of each individual spectator.[5]

Although major national star racers were not entered in the 1956 races, Bill Tuman, Hall of Fame recipient and Sturgis Champion (1946, 1951) who had retired from racing, served as the official starter. Dick Mann of Richmond, California, who would become the 1971 AMA Grand National Champion and dual winner of the Daytona 200 (1970, 1971) was present, as was Al Burke, who became a co-founder of the White Plate Flat Trackers Association (WPFTA) with Clarence Hoel in 1980. Burke won his heat on Saturday and Mann placed in all of his races.[6]

There was no coverage of the Friday night program in the post-rally edition of the *Sturgis Tribune*. The editor, although seemingly limited in the 1956 coverage, did compose a highly supportive editorial stating, "The Black Hills Motor Classic is probably one of the best attractions in the Black Hills and it will continue to draw crowds, who thrill to the roar of the motors and daring of the riders for many years to come."

1956 Expert Champion: Charlie West

Charlie West first came to Sturgis in 1951. In 1953, '54, and '55, he traveled with Joe Leonard (Sturgis Champion 1953 and 1957), serving as his mechanic and also competing in racing. In 1956, Leonard was racing elsewhere and West came to Sturgis alone and won the half-mile championship.

Charlie West was born in San Jose, California on November 30, 1925. His affair with motorcycles began after his discharge from U.S. Navy in 1946. His first cycle was a 1940 61-cubic inch Harley Davidson knucklehead, which he rode to a couple of races and decided to try racing. He then purchased an Army surplus 45-cubic inch Harley Davidson and began converting it into a dirt track racer, lightening the engine to get it to turn faster. After two years he decided to replace the original engine and purchased a brand new WR engine and installed it into the Army frame. West continued to upgrade this machine for a time and then purchased a whole new WR model. By the time he began racing in Sturgis he was using a KR750 Harley.

According to West, he always enjoyed the mechanical work more than the actual racing. When he was going through the process of upgrading his motorcycle, he was guided by Tom Sifton, a nationally fa-

Charlie West, 1956 Expert Champion at Sturgis, waiting for his heat race. (Dick O'Leary Collection)

mous tuner from the San Jose area. "I really learned a lot from Sifton," said West.

Not surprisingly, Charlie's mechanical ability was well recognized by the racing community of his generation. He was a master mechanic and motorcycle tuner. One story always attributed to West is the phrase, "Charlie's Harleys run the best." According to West, this is a mistake that started at a race at Columbus, Ohio where a local Harley Davidson dealer named Charlie Best was distributing tee shirts in the pits that stated "Charlies Harley's run the Best." One of the other racers picked up the idea that Charlie West had printed the T-shirts and spread the rumor! He has been teased about this ever since.

West says that he enjoyed being on the road while racing, especially when he could help the other riders with mechanical work. Several racers have testified to Charlie West's complete loyalty to Harley Davidson motorcycles. "They were the only bike around when I started," he said, but he admits to helping riders on other bikes, "I helped lots of people who had Triumphs and BSAs." One time in Sturgis, when Dick Mann spilled and his BSA Gold Star ingested a bunch of dirt, West traveled with Mann to Cheyenne, Wyoming — the closest available dealership with BSA parts — and helped him overhaul his engine.

West's first racing experiences were at Belmont Speedway, a quarter mile dirt track near his home. The track was also the first venue for Dick Mann (Sturgis Champion 1958 and 1966) who began racing there in the early 1950s.

In 1953, West traveled East with Joe Leonard, another racer from San Jose. To save money, Leonard generally purchased an old Nash beater to tow his bikes. The Nash cars were cheap, and after West and Leonard outfitted them with straight pipe exhausts (using ordinary water pipe says West), they generally had enough power to tow the bikes at a reasonably high speed. The big advantage in the old Nash cars were seats that converted into a bed for sleeping on the road. It was Charlie's job to keep these junkers running and tune the bikes for each race!

One time, coming into Sturgis, Leonard shifted into second gear to slow the Nash down on the hill into town. With no restraint on the engine because of the open pipe, the car was really bellowing by the time they hit the city limits. The city cop met them and "encouraged" them to leave town. Another time the two racers lost a universal joint on the driveshaft and West positioned the Nash to straddle the curb on Main Street so he could get under the car to make repairs. The policeman arrived again with a message that "they had a half hour to get out of town." All of the old timers at Sturgis still talk about Joe Leonard's Nash cars!

Charlie West's best year of racing was 1954. Although he did not take a Grand National race that year, he earned enough podium finishes and points to finish third in the Grand National Series standings behind Leonard and Paul Goldsmith. He repeated this in 1956, the year he won at Sturgis, by earning enough points to be ranked sixth in the nation. One of his biggest disappointments, though, was losing the Springfield mile to Everett Bashear in 1956. "I drafted him through the last lap, but I pulled out to pass him about a second too late," Charlie said. "He beat me by a tire length...not a wheel length, a tire length...about four inches of black rubber!"

All during the years following World War II, West was also involved in car racing. He raced midgets, stock cars ("hardtops and roadsters") in the off-season. At the end of the 1956 season, West returned to his job at an electronics firm in San Jose and was informed by the boss that he had to quit racing motorcycles if he wanted to keep his job.

With a wife and four children to support, Charlie decided to hang it up, officially retiring from motorcycle racing in 1956. He did, however, remain actively involved in stock car racing at local tracks while working at the electronics firm.

In 1970, he left San Jose and moved to Cascadia, Oregon where he worked for about a year as a mechanic in a small sawmill operation. After that he worked in the area as a mechanic and machinist until 1984 when he moved to Tacoma, Washington. At Tacoma he worked for a large mechanical contractor, welding and repairing steel building rigs, cranes and other heavy equipment. He later injured his knees in a fall and retired.

Charlie West (#54) edged out by Everett Brashear (#25) at the Springfield Mile, 1956. (Everett Brashear Collection).

Although retired, West kept involved in stock car racing, tuning his own racer and doing custom work for others. He continued to compete until age 73 when his arthritis started giving him trouble climbing in and out of the window of his Chevy-powered Pontiac Firebird racing car. His son, Charlie Jr. is still actively racing this car in the Seattle area, and Charlie Sr. is still doing the mechanic work.

Charlie West and Lorraine, his wife of 54 years, live in Tacoma, Washington.

August 8-11, 1957

Subtle modifications to the Gypsy Tour in the Thursday/Friday format were realized in rally plans for the 1957 Classic. Hesitant in moving to a five-day format, the Black Hills tour was scheduled for Thursday, August 8, rather than Friday because Friday afternoon's schedule would include a new event: the Sportsman's Hill Climb — a participatory competition for amateur riders. As a result, the Friday Gypsy Tour was relegated to a short, local-area morning ride in hopes of insuring spectator and contestant involvement in the hill climb.[1]

A Thursday evening program, which followed the big southern hills Gypsy Tour, was planned for the Gypsy Camp located behind Hoel's Motorcycle Shop. Pearl Hoel would provide coffee and doughnuts for the riders, and then Pappy would treat them to a two-hour outdoor movie about motorcycle racing in Europe.[2] It's important to note that, with the demise of American-manufactured Indians in 1953, Hoel had switched to selling Royal Enfield Indians, AJS, Matchless, and even Maico cycles.[3] The movie, provided by BSA, was probably an attempt by Hoel not only to entertain and inform but also to test the water about possibly taking on a BSA franchise.[*]

The hill climb, which matched a steep hill to "hill-climbers from all sections of the country," was to begin at 12:00 sharp. The meet was held at the junction of highways 14 and 24 (later State Highway 34)on the Hoel property East of Sturgis near Bear Butte.[4]

Awards Program

Priscilla Hammer of Omaha was crowned Queen of the Black Hills Motorcycle Classic at the Friday evening picnic and program. A Connecticut couple, Mr. and Mrs. Baird Robinson, won two trophies: the first for longest distance ridden to the rally and the second for being the longest distance, two-up riders. The longest distance female rider prize went to Shirley Allen of Champlain, Illinois and a motorcycle club from St. Paul, Minnesota took honors as the best dressed club. The best dressed male and female individual rider awards went to Benjamin Baines of Port Arthur, Texas and Mrs. Charles Snap of Kingsport, Tennessee. Oldest and youngest rider awards went to a "regular", Mr. John Dahl of Spirit Lake, Iowa, and Jerry Hinz of Tracy, Minnesota. A new award introduced in 1957 was given for the longest distance as a passenger in a sidecar. This honor went to Vera Anderson of Minneapolis.[5] The winners of the Friday afternoon hill climb were not reported.

Races

In the Saturday Amateur races, Sammy Tanner took first in his heat race and third in the final. Joe Leonard, from San Jose, California, Dick Klamfoth, and Albert Gunter all won their heat races, with Dick Mann, Al Burke and Bobbie Hill taking seconds. In the Saturday Expert final, Leonard was first, followed by Gunter, Klamfoth and Dick Mann. Leonard won again on Sunday, August 11. Al Gunter, Tom Cates, and

---

[*] Hoel selected a Yamaha dealership in 1960.

The Hill Climb at Sturgis. (Courtesy of Eva Satterlee)

Dick Klamfoth placed second, third, and fourth respectively in Sunday's feature race. Sammy Tanner won his preliminary heat and went on to win the Amateur final.[6] This was Leonard's second feature race win, having taken a first at Sturgis in 1953, winning the AMA National Championship for the five mile circuit. Leonard was inducted into the AMA Hall of Fame in 1998. He was selected as a Charter Member of the White Plate Flat Tracker's Association and inducted at the opening ceremonies. Sturgis was continuing to emerge as an outstanding touring and recreational destination for the American motorcycling public, and the fast Sturgis half-mile track continued to attract the nation's best racers.

1957 Expert Champion: Joe Leonard

Joe Leonard had a spectacular career at the national level. His overall win total of 27 checkered flags included 23 Grand National Series (GNS) wins, including two half-miles, eight miles, six TTs and seven road races. Short track was the only race in which he failed to have a national win, and the versatility he displayed in the professional motorcycle-racing world is still a subject of conversation among fans. His record in the Grand National Series puts him in 10th place overall. He won a total of three Grand National Championships in a career spanning nine years (1954-1961). He won the Daytona 200 twice, the Laconia Classic three times and was a seven-time winner of the Peoria TT. His first national victory at Sturgis came in 1953, just prior to the establishment of the GNS in 1954.[1]

Leonard's first national title year was 1954 when he won no less than eight GNS races. They included road races at Laconia, New Hampshire and Wilmot, Wisconsin; and three mile races in San Mateo, California; Springfield, Illinois; and Indianapolis. He won both of the TT races at Peoria and also a half-mile at Hammond, Indiana.[2]

In 1955 Leonard finished third in the Grand National Standings, winning the road race at Windber, Pennsylvania, one TT at Peoria and the half-mile at Milwaukee. In 1956 he was back as Number One, having amassed enough points. His two victories that year were the mile at San Mateo, California and the TT at Peoria. His GNS point total for

Joe Leonard, 1957 Expert Champion at Sturgis. (Mahoney Photo)

1957 earned him the coveted Number One for the second consecutive year. Before coming to the Black Hills Motor Classic in 1957, Leonard won the Daytona 200 road race on March 3, the 100-mile road race at Laconia, New Hampshire on June 23, and the dirt track mile at San Jose, California. After winning the Championship race at Sturgis, Leonard went on to Springfield, Illinois to take the mile.[3]

In 1958, Joe Leonard repeated his 1957 wins at Daytona and Springfield, the two most prestigious races in America. He ended up in second place in the point standings in 1958, losing first place by one point to Carrol Resweber. In 1959 Leonard slipped to fifth place in the standings, but he was back to second place in 1960. Both of these placements were from points garnered by podium finishes because he failed win any Grand National races in either year. In 1961, Leonard's last year, he won two nationals, the 100-mile road race at Laconia, New Hampshire and the mile at Sacramento. He was ranked second in 1961.[4]

The following year, Leonard switched to automobile racing. Leonard said that "good motorcycle racers can always do well at car racing, but very few, if any, car racers could ever succeed in a motorcycle race."[5] He went on to win two United States Auto Club (USAC) Championships in the 1970s, making him the only American racer to win National Championships in both venues.[6]

August 7-10, 1958

Pappy Hoel, apparently fired up about his son Jack's grass track (Grassbahn) experiences and championship while serving in the U. S. Army in Germany, decided to experiment with this racing venue in 1958.[1] On July 19, the Gypsies sponsored a 1/6 mile grass track racing event at Sky Ranch in Butte County, about 40 miles north of Sturgis.[2] Founded by Father Don Murray, Sky Ranch was a home on the plains for homeless abandoned and needy boys. This Sunday event focused on having a good time and raising some money for a worthy cause. Hoel was always sensitive to the public's view of motorcycling, and coupled with the Gypsies' sense for charitable activities, this move probably provided a win-win situation for everyone involved.

The purse for the 1958 half-mile races had grown to $2,400, and excitement was high about the quality of touring, racing and just having a good time. The program format paralleled the 1957 Classic with tours scheduled for all day on Thursday and Friday morning with the hill climb at 2:30pm on Friday. On Thursday, August 7, the Hoel's were again planning to serve coffee and doughnuts west of the motorcycle shop. An evening trail ride for those interested was to leave at dusk. Friday's events, including the short tour and hill climb, were to culminate in a free supper for the riders and a program for all. An interesting element noted in the *Sturgis Tribune* was an admonition regarding eligibility for awards. To win any prize, an entrant must have come to Sturgis by motorcycle. Entertainment was to be provided by the Alkali Troopers 4-H Club as this year's rally was being held in conjunction with the Meade County Fair.[3]

Races

On Saturday Bart Markel of Flint, Michigan won the Amateur final and made a repeat win on Sunday. In the Expert class, Saturday's winner was Joe Leonard, followed by Sammy Tanner, Gary Emmick, Glen Jordan and George Roeder. Dick Mann from Sobrante, California, riding a BSA, was the winner of the Championship race on

On the way to the top of the Sturgis Hill Climb. (Courtesy of Eva Satterlee)

Sammy Tanner after placing third at Sturgis, 1958. (Sammy Tanner Collection)

Sunday. Second place went to George Roeder and third to Sammy Tanner. Joe Leonard, the 1957 champion, placed fourth on Sunday after winning the feature race on Saturday. The grandstand crowd was only average, due in large part to the concurrent county fair events.[4]

Dick Mann, who was 24 years of age when he won at Sturgis, became a two-time winner of AMA Grand National Champion Award. Mann had an outstanding racing career in all of the AMA Grand National Series categories, including the mile, half-mile, short-track, TT, and road racing.[5] George Roeder who took second place in the championship race on Sunday also went on to a noteworthy national racing career. He was inducted into the AMA Hall of Fame in 1999 for his record in the Grand National Series (GNS) during the 1960s. In 1965, Roeder piloted a streamlined motorcycle with a 250cc Harley Davidson Sprint motor to 177.225 MPH and set a new land speed record on the Bonneville Salt Flats.[6]

1958 Expert Champion: Dick Mann

Dick Mann, the 1958 Champion at Sturgis, is one of the most outstanding competitors in the history of motorcycle racing. He was born in Salt Lake City on June 13, 1934 and grew up in Richmond, California, across the bay from San Francisco. His mother had moved to Richmond during World War II to work in Henry Kaiser's shipyards, cutting sheets of steel in the fabrication of the famous "Victory Ships".[1]

His first riding experience was gained on an old Cushman scooter that he used on his paper route. He later purchased a 125cc BSA Bantam and spent a lot of time "cow trailing" (trail riding) in the hills surrounding Richmond. At that time he grew to know Dick Dorrestyne, a cow trailing friend, who was described by Mann as a "truly natural motorcycle rider".[2]

Mann later purchased an old 350cc BSA and became excited about racing. He and his paper route buddies would meet at the high school running track and race, competing until the truck that delivered papers arrived at about 4:30am every morning.

When he started racing on real dirt tracks, he made a racing shoe out of a 1937 Hudson automobile bumper. The 350 wasn't fast enough, so he bought a shelled out BSA 500 single, paid 17 dollars for a cardboard Cromwell helmet and found an old set of leathers in the trash behind a motorcycle shop. His first real racing experiences began at Belmont, a local quarter-mile short track near his home. His bike wasn't competitive at the short track, so he saved his money and rode the 100 or so miles to Tulare, California where he raced on a borrowed BSA Star Twin.[3]

Prior to this first race at Tulare, Mann had found a job working for Hap Alzina (AMA Hall of Fame, 1998), an Oakland BSA dealer. After Tulare, he went to Hollister, the scene of the infamous Marlon Brando movie, "The Wild One", and experienced his first race on a soft or "cushion" dirt track. He did so well at Hollister that he was noticed by a BSA dealer from Cheyenne, Wyoming, who offered him a motorcycle and support in competing on the "Kansas Circuit" in the Midwest. Hap

Alzina would not let him go, and while he contemplated quitting his job, he entered a race at Bay Meadows where a BSA dealer, Ang Rossi lent him a stock street bike that had been hopped up for a customer. He won the Amateur event at Bay Meadows, wearing out the Hudson bumper shoe and his boot sole. A picture of Mann receiving the trophy with his left food clad only in a white stocking, was published in a motorcycle magazine, and he received a good deal of national publicity.

After this win, Mann was contacted by Louie Thomas, a noted BSA tuner from Los Angeles, who asked him to go east as Albert Gunter's racing partner. Alzina released him; Dick apologized to the Wyoming

Dick Mann, 1958 Expert Champion at Sturgis. (Courtesy of Ed Youngblood)

dealer and ended up taking a bus to Los Angeles after his car broke down.

Albert Gunter was one of Mann's heroes, and as a young racer, Mann was thrilled to be racing with him. They were supposed to head for Kansas, but Gunter decided to go to Sturgis instead. After completing a high-speed trip, they arrived in Sturgis on Friday night to race in the 3-Mile National at the 1954 Black Hills Motor Classic. Mann took first place in the Amateur feature race on Saturday and second in the National Championship Amateur final on Sunday. Gunter, of course, won the Expert final on Sunday.

Gunter and Mann continued as racing partners and worked the circuit together for the next several years. According to Ed Youngblood, everyone in racing found them to be "one of the oddest couples that could ever travel the circuit together." Youngblood went on to characterize Mann as a quiet, soft-spoken man who never said anything before carefully pondering his words. Gunter, according to Youngblood, never thought before speaking, and was "self absorbed, impetuous, abrupt, fastidious, opinionated and hot-headed" – quite the contrast to Mann's calm demeanor and unselfishness.[5]

After leaving Sturgis, the pair raced in Kansas and at the Springfield mile. Mann was noticed by Midwestern fans because he ran second behind Brad Andres until he bumped Andre's tire and fell. He was still able to recover and finish in sixth place.

Mann returned to Sturgis many times, winning the championship race a second time in 1966.

1958 Expert 2nd Place: George Roeder

George Roeder, who took second place in the Championship race at Sturgis in 1958, had an impressive career in the AMA Grand National Series (GNS) after competing in the 1958 Classic. Roeder's GNS ca-

George Roder, 1958 Expert 2nd Place at Sturgis. (Dave & Kathy Estep Collection)

reer spanned seven years, from 1963 to 1969, and he won a total of eight GNS races. Five of these victories were half-miles while the other three were mile wins.

His first victory was the Springfield Mile on August 18, 1963, and the second win was the five-mile AMA GNS half-mile at Freeport, Illinois on September 14. Roeder amassed enough in points in 1963 to finish in second place, one point behind Dick Mann. In 1964, he won the 15-mile, half-mile GNS event at Heidelberg, Pennsylvania in June and a seven-mile half at Kansas City, Kansas on July 25. In 1964, Roeder ended up in eighth place in the standings. In 1965 and 1966 he won one race, the 10-mile half at Columbus, Ohio. He placed fifth in points in 1965 but failed to make the top ten in 1966. Perhaps Roeder's best year was 1967, when he ended up in second place behind Gary Nixon after winning several podium finishes and the seven-mile AMA half-mile at San Jose, California and the 25-mile Sacramento mile.[1]

George Roeder was born on August 16, 1936 in Monroeville, Ohio. At age 17, Roeder lied about his age and won his first professional race in 1954. By 1956 he was a rookie expert. In 1957, the year before he come to Sturgis, he started the season on a brand new Harley Davidson and was sponsored by the Ohio Harley Davidson Dealer's Association. George had to pay a token $100 to take his bike off the floor. He considers his win at the Springfield mile in 1963 as his best race and 1963 as his best year. Although he never won first place in a road race, Roeder earned four podium finishes in the 1950s and took second place in the 1963 race at Laconia. He was also elected the AMA Most Popular Rider award in 1963 and 1965. He retired from racing in 1968 after breaking his arm, but came back to try in 1969 and 1974.[2]

In 1972 he opened a Harley Davidson dealership in Monroeville, which he continued until 1993 when he sold out to his oldest son, Will. Two of his younger sons, George II and Jess, have both won GNS events.[3]

George Roder passed away in the Spring of 2003. His funeral ceremony included a "last lap" at the local race track, where his casket was placed on a side-car rig and escorted around the track by his children and friends from the racing community. His wife Jessie continues to live near the motorcycle dealership, where George spent a good deal of time, tuning the racing bikes and traveling to races with George II and Jess.[4]

August 6-9, 1959

The 1959 program of events closely paralleled the 1958 format. The rally continued to be a four-day affair with a long tour on Thursday and a short morning tour and afternoon hill climb on Friday. Even the race purse, which had appeared to grow consistently from the rally's inception in 1938, remained at $2,400, the exact amount established for the 1958 Classic. The Friday night feed featured barbecued vension.[1]

On August 4, the *Sturgis Tribune* did a good job of explaining the AMA point accumulation process required for racers to move from Novice and Amateur to the Expert racer, or "White Plate," category:

> *During the year a record is kept on each rider and all the Races in the United States. Points are allowed for first, second and third places. When a rider has accumulated a given number of points he automatically graduates to the next higher class.*[2]

The *Tribune* also described the time trials/heat races selections.

> *Time trials are held to qualify riders in each class, and to properly place them in their heat race. Only 12 riders in each class can qualify at this race. Two heat races are held in each class and the three winners in each compete in the final event for that class. The finals each day pit the six fastest riders in their class, determined by the heat races.*[3]

As part of an ever-present effort to promote the value of the rally to local residents, the *Tribune* reported that a percentage of the rally's profit would be dedicated to the construction of a city swimming pool with an additional contribution to the Sturgis Fire

Men and machines leap from the starting line in late 1950s. (Pearl Hoel Collection)

Department. Of particular interest in 1959 was the City Council's war on outside privies, encouraging locals to hook up to the new city sewer system by banning outhouses.[4]

On August 7, the *Tribune* described the roar of motors as 152 motorcycles paraded down Main Street on their way out of town for the Gypsy Tour. The paper further noted that these riders had "virtually taken over the city park with their tents and trailers and that riders and passengers of all ages from children to grandparents were camping". It was further reported that a wide variety of motorcycles were represented in the tour and that brightly colored club costumes added to the excitement.[5]

Elements of increased public support can be clearly noted in Editor Bob Lee's positive editorial published on August 7, titled "A Different Attraction".

> *Sturgis is the focal point of enthusiasts of motorcycling this week as the 19th annual motorcycle races promoted by the businessmen of the community gets underway at the fairgrounds. This is the only event of its kind in the entire state and it will attract upwards of 500 cyclists from throughout the country. Speed will be the keynote of the annual event, but it will be restricted to the race track and not to the highways. Cyclists, unlike motorists, have a commendable safety record on the nation's highways. It requires more skill than most people think to handle a motorcycle at a high rate of speed, and the participants in the races here are experts in the field. The sponsors of the event are certainly to be commended for contributing a share of the profits to the Sturgis Fire Department and to the community swimming pool campaign. They have contributed generously in the past to the high school band, Boy and Girl Scouts and to the city recreation program. Attendance at the races will thus benefit the community as well as provide fast-moving entertainment. The community welcomes the participants and hopes they will enjoy their visit here.[6]*

Hoel reported a total of 545 registered Gypsy riders who would receive their AMA tour pins. Sandra Brubaker from Milwaukee, Wisconsin was selected Queen of the Rally for 1959. The winner over 19 other contestants, Sandra was presented a trophy and corsage by John Stingley, President of the Jackpine Gypsies. Hill climb winners included Norbert Hamling, Don Rice, Roger Satterlee of Rapid City, Al Nesshoffee of Mallard, Iowa, and Dan Deubler of Sioux Falls, South Dakota.[7]

Best dressed male and female rider prizes went to John Schnelzer of Cheyenne, Wyoming, and Margaret Stewart of Regina, Saskatchewan. The oldest rider, John Dahl, age 70 from Spirit Lake, Iowa was edged out, at the last minute, by Otto Bessman, age 77 of Riceville, Wisconsin. Mr. and Mrs. Dick Stanhope of Iola, Kansas won the oldest/longest-married-couple trophy.[8]

Racing Poster, The Sturgis Tribune, August 4, 1959.

Because of the increased participation by Canadian riders, a new award for longest distance from outside the United States was instituted and won by Bob Adams, who rode in from Toronto. The American distance trophy was awarded to Melburn Knight of Balsam, North Carolina and the Best Dressed Club Award went to the Tri-State Travelers from Sioux Falls, South Dakota.[9]

Races

A future Hall of Fame inductee, Darrel Dovel, did well in the Amateur class in 1959. Dovel won his heat race and then took second place in the Sunday Amateur final. Familiar names in the Expert class for both days of racing included Dick Klamfoth and Dick Mann, who were both winners at Sturgis in previous years. Klamfoth captured first in the Sunday Feature final and Mann placed third. A rider new to Sturgis, Dick Dorresteyn, took first in his heat race and then went on to capture second place behind Klamfoth. Dorresteyn, a childhood friend of Dick Mann, would go on to have an exceptional career at the national level and was inducted into the AMA Hall of Fame in 1998 for his many dirt track and TT wins.[10]

1959 might serve as a landmark year in the evolution of the Sturgis Classic and a sign of things to come. Rather than a supplement to the races, tour participation was becoming a dimension on its own, drawing riders to this small community in the Northern Black Hills of South Dakota.

1959 Expert Champion: Dick Klamfoth

Although a well loved and respected racer at Sturgis, Dick Klamfoth's real fame came from his wins at Daytona. His record three Daytona titles was not surpassed until 1998, after he was inducted into the AMA Motorcycle Hall of Fame. He was also initiated into the White Plate Flat Trackers Association as a Charter Member in 1982, and visitors will find his name and famous number 2 on the monument at Sturgis. Interestingly, this National Number 2 was assigned to him by the AMA when Johnny Spiegelhoff, the first Black Hills Classic Champion (1938, '39, '41 and '46), stopped racing.[1]

Races at Daytona until 1960 were run half on the sandy beach and half on a frontage road adjacent to the beach. In reflecting on his first win at Daytona, Klamfoth said that his Norton Manx, with its skinny tires, was a bit skittish in the sand, and he was often passed by the heavier Harley Davidson and Indian motorcycles. "But the Norton could really fly on the paved half of each lap, so I kept getting closer and closer to the front."[2]

After winning at Sturgis in 1949, Klamfoth continued his racing career in earnest. He had won the prestigious Langhorne, Pennsylvania 100 just prior to coming to Sturgis, and he went on to place second at Daytona in 1950. He also won the final on Saturday's racing at Sturgis in 1950 but lost to Chet Dykgraaf in the final event on Monday. He earned five podium finishes in 1950, but 1951 was his most successful season. During that year, he repeated his 1949 win at Daytona, won Nationals at Richmond, Virginia and Shreveport, Louisiana, and also won his first road race at Laconia.

In 1952 he realized his third win at Daytona.[3] According to Klamfoth, he nearly missed riding that day. On the day before, the racers had been informed that the race would be postponed for a day because of the wet conditions on the beach. He and some friends decided to go fishing. When they were in a restaurant purchasing sandwiches for their daylong excursion, a fan asked him about the race. Klamfoth informed the fan that the race had been postponed, whereupon the man showed him the morning paper, which indicated that the race was indeed being held. Klamfoth drove back to team headquarters, jumped on his racing bike and got to the track just in time to ride and win the race.[4]

Although he never won a Grand National Series Championship after its establishment by the AMA in 1954, he placed 4th in 1954, 9th in 1956, 3rd in 1957, 3rd in 1958 and 4th in 1959 — the same year he won his second championship race at Sturgis.[5] Klamfoth says his big problem was that he could never win a Grand National mile event. His lone mile win (in a non-national race) was at Du Quoin, Illinois where he rode the entire race in the soft dirt high above the groove. "I was doing so well at speed on the corners," he said, "that when I passed the flagman at the white flag (next to the last lap), I signaled to him that I was going to pass behind him at the finish line." Klamfoth did just that, passing to the grandstand side of the checkered flag.[6]

Dick Klamfoth went into retirement in 1962 but returned to Daytona in 1964 to try racing on the high-banked oval track and took 5th place. In all, Dick Klamfoth won 12 AMA nationals and one international race in Canada.

August 11-14, 1960

An interesting development prior to the 1960 classic was the problem of housing the visitors. As noted in 1959, the camping area at the City Park was filled to capacity, and by August 3, Hoel reported that most of the rooms were already reserved at local motels and hotels. The racing purse had grown to $2,700 and a new event, a Scrambles Race, was scheduled for Friday morning at a course located on the Hoel homestead near Bear Butte Lake. Hoel promised excitement and new experiences for riders and spectators alike. Identical to the program for the past three years, the Hill Climb event would be held after lunch on Friday.[1]

Because of the scrambles and hill climb events, the Jackpine Gypsies were able, in 1960, to save enough money from the spectator admissions to purchase five acres across the freeway from Sturgis and build a clubhouse. As the rally continued to grow in later years and the added events generated enough money, the Gypsies (with some help from a local banker) were able to build a new Short Track, a Scrambles course, and a Hill Climb venue, as well as provide bleachers for the short track.[2]

By August 3 Clarence Hoel indicated that things were really looking up for attendance. Many riders had registered earlier than ever in preparation for the Thursday Gypsy Tour.[3] Since no official routes were planned for Friday, it's safe to assume that some of these early visitors were beginning to tour on their own. This development, first noticed in 1959, was pivotal in the rally's growth to a seven-day format. As contemporary Sturgis residents can relate, riders actually begin visiting Sturgis and the Hills in earnest by the middle of July, two to three week before the official opening of the Classic. It is interesting to note this phenomenon, which probably began when veteran visitors started conducting their own Gypsy tours for those friends they could entice to join them at the Classic.*

---

* This was the author's first experience in 1977. Veteran riders encouraged him to "come along" and the rest is personal history.

Hoel also expressed excitement about the first visit to Sturgis by an AMA Official from the national, rather than just a regional, office. Mr. L. Kuchler, AMA National Secretary was planning to attend the 1960 rally.[4]

Another significant event occurred in July 1960 when the South Dakota State Highway Commission decided to connect state Highway 24, which entered Sturgis from the east, to a new highway: State Highway 34. Beginning on the South Dakota-Minnesota border and extending through Pierre to Sturgis, Highway 34 is the only State Highway that connects South Dakota from eastern border to western border.[6] Riders from Minnesota, Wisconsin and Michigan who opt for blue highways rather than the freeway often use this route in traveling to Sturgis.*

On Saturday night, Neil Hultman, AMA District 30 Referee and the Race Director, along with several other Jackpine Gypsies, escorted Mr. Kuchler, the visiting AMA officer to St. Onge for a steak dinner. Just as the steaks were served, Hultman received a call from his wife, who had suddenly gone into labor with their third child! Neil wrapped his steak in a napkin, threw it under the seat of his car and drove home to Sturgis. He picked up his wife and rushed her to the hospital in Rapid City where the new baby was born. At about 8:00am Sunday morning, Hultman found the cold steak and ate it as finger food on the way back to Sturgis, where he was to begin officiating race trials at 9:00am.[7]

Races

Sunday's half-mile racing program opened with a grand entry parade, led by the Motor Maids and Queen of the Classic, followed by the Jackpine Gypsies and members from other clubs riding antique motorcycles. The parade made a complete circle of the race track and then stopped in front of the grandstand, where everyone was introduced by the Mayor of Sturgis. The American flag was delivered by two skydivers who presented it to a squad of Sturgis veterans who performed the raising ceremony. Members of Company A, 100th Engineers of the Lead National Guard's Drill Team performed during the intermission on Sunday.[8]

---

* First time riders are to be forewarned, however. Highway 34, although scenic and breathtaking with its vistas and solitude, has essentially two gas stops after you leave Pierre, and these vendors are always closed on Sunday. Until recently, a sign reading "Next Services 134 Miles" was placed at the roadside 38 miles west of Pierre, and at the Highway 79 junction three miles east of Sturgis. The author's first motorcycle, a 1973 BMW with a small tank, could not safely make it from Sturgis to Pierre on Sunday after a weekend in the Hills. The solution was to carry a small two-quart container of gasoline and then top off the gas tank at the scenic overview along the Cheyenne River crossing. After much abuse from fellow riders, the author traded this bike for a 1974 Beemer with a larger tank.

Trying to keep it under control at the Hill Climb. (Pearl Hoel Collection)

For some reason, the *Sturgis Tribune* did not publish the results of the weekend's racing. They were, however, covered by the *Rapid City Journal*.

In preliminary reports, the Journal identified the 1960 race as a "National Half Mile Flat Track Motorcycle Classic." Although this was incorrect, it probably added hype about the rally for the *Journal's* readers. It was also interesting to note that the Hill Climb, scheduled for Friday afternoon, was branded the "South Dakota State Championship Hill Climb."[9]

By Friday it was noted that over 200 persons had participated in the Gypsy Tour and that over 400 motorcycles had arrived in Sturgis, filling hotels, motels and camping space to capacity. A "Donaker" crash was to be staged in the Saturday racing program, and Pappy Hoel's traditional burning wall crash was to be performed on Sunday.[10]

On Saturday, John Sanger of Tulsa, Oklahoma captured first in the Novice class and took prize money for posting the fastest time trial at 29.9 seconds. Marty Malchow of San Francisco, California won the Saturday Amateur class final, taking a prize of $60. He also posted the best time trial (28.45 seconds) for his class. The Expert final on Saturday was won by Larry Stone of Detroit, Michigan, followed by Bart Markel of Flint, Michigan, and Tom Cates from Evansville, Indiana. The Expert purse for Saturday's winner of the five-mile race was $135.[11]

On Sunday, Robert Strickler of Hutchinson, Kansas won the Novice time trial money and the Amateur money went to Marty Malchow. In the five-mile Novice finals, Charles Kelln of Barger, Texas placed first, taking a $60 purse. He was followed by Strickler and Donald Parker of Amarillo, Texas. The Amateur win and a $90 purse was repeated by Malchow, who had taken first place on Saturday. Larry Palmgren of Denver, Colorado and Francis Franklin of Kelso, Washington placed second and third. Bart Markel won the Expert and Championship final with a purse of $270. He was followed by Cates, Stone and a new young rider, Gary Nixon from Bethany, Oklahoma, who placed fourth.[12]

Two of the 1960 racers went on to distinguished careers. Bart Markel, the Expert winner, was inducted into the AMA Hall of Fame as a Charter Member in 1998. Markel was the AMA Grand National Champion in 1962, 1965 and 1966.[13] Nixon, who took Fourth place at Sturgis in 1960 was also a Charter Member of the AMA Hall of Fame. He was designated the AMA Grand National Champion in 1967 and again in 1968.[14] Nixon went on to win the feature race at Sturgis in 1961 and was inducted into the White Plate Flat Trackers group as a charter member in the early 1980s.

1960 Expert Champion: Bart Markel

A native of Flint, Michigan, Bart Markel was born on August 19, 1935 and became interested in racing when he was discharged from the Marine Corps in 1956. He started racing in scramble meets on an old JAWA and was unsuccessful until he paid $50 for an old B33 BSA. He entered his first flat track race in Wisconsin on the BSA, and by late 1958, he had earned his Expert license. When he competed in Sturgis that year, Markel was still racing in the Amateur class, winning both Saturday and Sunday championships. By 1959 he had won four top-ten places, including second place in the Springfield Mile. He got his first National win at the Peoria TT on August 28, 1960, two weeks after his second championship at Sturgis.[1]

As was the case with many of the racers at Sturgis, Markel went on to a stellar career at the national level. While at Sturgis in 1958, Markel enjoyed both the camaraderie and friendly treatment he received from the locals. One interesting story about his first visit to Sturgis had to do with visiting the Meade County Fair, which was running concurrently with the rally in 1958. Markel and two other racers, Bud Mays and Sammy Tanner, were watching the "Wild Man from Borneo" bite the heads off live chickens when Tanner threw a firecracker at the "Wild Man", who was chained to a post! The man promptly reached in his pocket, took out a key, unlocked his chains, and proceeded to chase Tanner all over the fairgrounds! The next day, Markel and some other riders saw the "Wild Man" in street clothes and in the Grandstand, cheering for Tanner in the Expert final.[2]

Bart Markel, 1960 Expert Champion at Sturgis. (Courtesy of Joann Markel)

During his career as a professional motorcycle racer, Bart Markel chalked up no less than 28 victories in Grand National Series (GNS) races. His best race was the half-mile, which accounted for 18 of these wins. He also won two miles, two short tracks, and six TTs. As noted above, his first GNS win was the TT at Peoria, Illinois. This win and other points earned in the 1960 season placed him third overall at the end of the year. In 1961 he slipped to fourth place, winning the Peoria TT for the second year in a row.[3]

Markel developed a reputation for being aggressive in the corners, and his fellow riders began referring to him as "Black Bart". His best season was 1962, during which he won six GNS races and earned the National Championship, including the coveted Number One Plate. The six races included the mile at Heidelberg, Pennsylvania on June 10, the half at Columbus, Ohio on June 24, the 50-lap mile at Springfield, Illinois on August 19 and a third consecutive TT at Peoria on August 26. Markel then closed the 1962 season by winning another half-mile at Lincoln, Illinois on September 16 and a second mile at Sacramento, California on September 30. Markel says that this was his all-time favorite victory. He and Ed Warren hauled his bike to California on an airplane. The motorcycle was equipped with aluminum forks, and when they arrived, "the California riders issued a protest, and we had to change the forks!" says Markel. "Consequently we did not get to practice, but we did win the race!"[4] The satisfaction of winning over the protesting competition made this an especially sweet victory for Markel.

In 1963, after coming off the number one spot, Markel failed to make the GNS top ten. He did win one GNS race that year, the lightweight TT at Peoria. In 1964, he was back in the GNS point standing at fourth place, winning half-miles at York, Pennsylvania; Hagerstown, Maryland and Columbus, Ohio. He was to win the Grand National title and the Number One Plate consecutively in 1965 and 1966. He was also voted the AMA Most Popular Rider of the Year in the 1966 season. During these two consecutive GNS title years, Markel won a total of five races including the York and Hagerstown half-miles and the Peoria TT in 1965, and another half and a short track at Hinsdale, Illinois in 1966.[5]

After winning two consecutive GNS Championships, Markel again failed to make the top ten in 1967. He did, however, win the half-mile at Louisville, Kentucky that year. In 1968 he was back in fourth place, having won half-miles at Richmond, Virginia, and Reading, Pennsylvania as well as the 20 lap TT at Peoria. He maintained fourth place status in 1969, winning half-mile races at Terre Haute, Indiana and Louisville. In 1970, although he did not make the top ten list, Markel had one GNS win, his second short track victory, at Hinsdale, Illinois.[6]

By 1969, Markel's racing career had begun to wind down. His last Grand National Series win was the half-mile at Columbus, Ohio in 1971. It was his 28th GNS race victory. His record of 28 wins lasted until 1982, and he is presently tied with Will Davis for seventh place overall in the GNS. His final Grand National Series appearance was at Atlanta in 1972, where he finished in 12th place. In all, Markel competed in 140 Grand National Series races. He was inducted as a Charter Member of the AMA Hall of Fame in 1998. He went to work for General Motors and retired in 1995. He lives in Flint, Michigan with his wife Jo Ann.[7]

Chapter Seven:
The Years of the Titans

During this five-year era, local coverage of the Classic was greatly overshadowed by the emergence of an outstanding Sturgis amateur baseball team, the "Titans". The Titans always seemed to be involved in a race for the South Dakota State Amateur Baseball Championship during most of the rally weekends in the early 1960s. As a result of this, coverage of the 1960-1965 rallies was quite limited in the Sturgis press.

Advertised for the first time as a three-day program, the 1961 rally included two new Friday attractions, a hill-climb and a scrambles race.

In 1962 the Championship final winner was Neil Keen, who went on to capture five feature race championships at Sturgis. In 1963, Jack Hoel and a friend climbed Bear Butte on small, 80cc Yamaha trail bikes, and the short track races were introduced to the Classic.

In 1964, a new practice, setting aside a section of Main Street exclusively reserved for motorcycle parking, was established. The number of visitors continued to grow, and the rally organizers attempted to get an accurate estimated count by requiring registration to qualify for awards and participation in Friday night's free "Feed." Also, chain link fencing was installed at the Meade County Fair Grounds in the interest of crowd control at the half-mile races.

In 1965, the Rally was officially designated as a five-day event with separate Gypsy tours held on both Wednesday and Thursday, leaving Friday open for racing. There were two Chamber of Commerce feeds, and the short track races were expanded to include both Thursday and Saturday evening events, all held at a new track constructed West of Interstate 90 on Jackpine Gypsy property. Housing visitors became a real problem in 1965, and some residents began renting rooms in their homes to the more familiar visitors. Also, a contingent of the Motor Maids organization came to Sturgis in 1965 to formulate plans for their National Convention in 1966, and Neil Keen set a new track record with a time trial of 25.94 seconds.

August 10-13, 1961

Apparently a new editorial policy, or a major shift in support of publicizing the rally, occurred in 1961. Whether this was a result of excitement about the local baseball team's success in summer league play or the attitude of the editor, the first page of the *Sturgis Tribune* in the months of July and August 1961 read like the sports page in earlier issues. The only coverage of the 1961 Classic is presented in one issue (August 16) and provides a report of the Gypsy Tour and a review of Friday's race statistics. The article did, however, characterize the 1961 Rally as both a financial and entertainment success.

While the rally had clearly grown into a four-day format in the mid 1950s, "official" rally planners had continued to promote it as a two-day event. 1961 was the first rally to be formally promoted as a three-day show, apparently giving official recognition of the Hill Climb and Scrambles races.

The Hill Climb event was divided into three categories, according to engine capacity of the motorcycles. The 250cc Class was won by Dan Deubler of Sioux Falls, South Dakota, and the 500cc and the 650cc Class events were won, respectively, by Lloyd Hicks of Mitchell, South Dakota and Dennis Adler also of Sioux Falls.[1] The

The first Northern Hills Gypsy tour assembles on Main Street Sturgis, 1961. (Pearl Hoel Collection)

The first Northern Hills Gypsy Tour assembled at Devils Tower in northeast Wyoming, 1961. (Pearl Hoel Collection)

Scrambles Race final, limited to 250cc machines, was won by Bill Mellenbrandt of Sioux Falls. Second place winner was Chuck Palmgren from Denver and Dick Strain of Rapid City captured third place.[2]

During the Friday night program, Polly Newcomb of Denver was selected the Queen of the 1961 Classic. The best-dressed female rider was Les Still of Sheridan, Wyoming and her male counterpart was Paul Reinike from Waterloo, Iowa. The oldest rider, Bill Wieland (age 70), was from Mitchell, South Dakota, and the longest married couple was Mr. and Mrs. Albert German (39 years) from Cozard, Nebraska. With regard to distance awards, the female award was given to Catherine McDowell, who rode in from Merced, California, and the male award went to Paul Ladd of Epping, New Hampshire. The final two distance awards went to Canadian riders. A couple from London, Ontario, Mr. and Mrs. Al Wolley captured the International two-up distance award and the International individual prize for distance went to Stan White of Oakville, Ontario.[3]

The Motor Maids, dressed in their colorful outfits and riding spotless motorcycles, opened the Saturday races by parading single file around the track. This was a repeat performance of the opening ceremony at the 1960 races. An interesting new dimension was apparent in reporting the results of the half-mile races. For the first time ever, the *Tribune* included the make of motorcycle used by each rider who placed first, second, or third in each of the races. There were 11 Harley Davidson's, 10 BSA's, two Triumphs, and a lone Maico in one of the Sportsman race heats. The number of nationally recognized riders was limited to just two: Babe DeMay of Moline, Illinois, and Gary Nixon from Oklahoma City.[4]

DeMay, who was elected to the AMA Hall of Fame in 2001, was described as a successful dirt tracker, the winner of the 1966 National Championship Races at Lincoln, Illinois, and a master motorcycle tuner. Nixon, inducted in 1998, went on to become the AMA Grand National Series Champion in both 1967 and 1968.[5]

DeMay won the Expert final in the Saturday program with Nixon placing second. Third place was taken by Dave Bostrom of San Francisco. On Sunday, the feature (Expert) race was won by Nixon. Second and third places were captured by Larry Stone of Farmington, Michigan, and Dave Bostrom.

In regard to the Harley Davidson riders, DeMay and Bostrom won two places (first and third) on Saturday, and the BSA riders, Nixon and Stone, took two places (first and second) in the Sunday feature race.[6] Nixon and DeMay were both inducted into the White Plate Flat Trackers Association as charter members.

1961 Expert Champion: Gary Nixon

In his high school years, Gary Nixon was a good athlete, lettering in wrestling. He was born on January 25, 1941 in Anadarko, Oklahoma and started racing in scrambles in 1957 at the age of 16. He began dirt track racing in 1958 after winning the Oklahoma State Scrambles Championship. He did not make much money that year, but by 1959 he was listed as an Amateur by the AMA and was sixth in the nation in point standings.[1]

In 1960 he began competing as an Expert at the Grand National Level. He earned a sixth place finish at the Springfield Mile and became a steady performer, qualifying in several National events.[2]

In 1961 Nixon received a good deal of recognition for winning the championship race at Sturgis. In August 1963 he won the AMA National Road Race at Windber, Pennsylvania and three weeks later he won first place at the Short Track National at Santa Fe Park, in Hinsdale, Illinois and was ranked sixth in the Grand National Series. Because of his versatility in dirt track, road racing and TT, by 1966 he was second in points, behind Bart Markel.[3]

In the early years of his career, Nixon developed a reputation as a moocher. He was always broke and sometimes had to borrow money from the other racers to pay for his entry fee. At first he only owned a trailer and talked other racers into towing it on the racing circuit, but he finally bought an old Lincoln from Everett Brashear to tow his trailer. Since this junker was always broke down, he continued begging tows. At one time, Dick Mann towed both the Lincoln and Nixon's Trailer to the next race. Once there, Mann told Nixon to park the Lincoln and towed only the trailer to the next two races, until Nixon had earned enough prize money to buy his own tow vehicle.[4]

In 1967, Nixon won the Daytona 100 on Saturday and then came back on Sunday to win the 200. For this and other points earned during

Gary Nixon, 1961 Expert Champion at Sturgis. (Courtesy of Gary Nixon)

the season, which included five other victories, Nixon was awarded the coveted Number One plate. He won it again in 1968. In 1969, Nixon crashed at the National Mile Race in Santa Rosa, California. For a time thereafter he raced with a stainless steel rod in his left leg and began to focus on road racing.[5]

Gary Nixon went on to become one of the world's best road racers, competing at the international level and representing the United States in the British-American Match Series. In 1976 he captured the World Prize Formula 750 Road Racing title, and was awarded the very first AMA pro athlete of the year award.

He retired in 1979 after 22 years of racing, and on June 12, 2003, Nixon was inducted into the Motorsports Hall of Fame. In total, he won 19 AMA National victories, riding for Triumph, Kawasaki, Suzuki and Yamaha. Nixon now lives in Maryland with his wife Mary. They have two grown children. He is actively involved in his business affairs and occasionally rides in "legend" and vintage events.

August 9-12, 1962

Coverage of the rally in 1962 was, as in the three previous years, quite limited. Unlike 1961, however, the *Tribune* did publish two items rather then just the one short article. Amateur baseball was still the hot topic in Sturgis during the summer months.

On Wednesday, August 8, the *Tribune* reported on the Thursday opening of the Gypsy Tour, followed by Friday's Scrambles Race and the Sportsman's Hill Climb, and the format for Saturday's and Sunday's half-mile races. A new twist in promoting the 1962 rally was the showing of a 16mm film, taken during the 1961 Gypsy Tour. It seems that the Jackpine Gypsy Club Members had been showing the film all over western South Dakota and eastern Wyoming during the winter months. The Friday evening program, which included the selection of a queen, a picnic, a street carnival and a Saturday night dance, followed the same pattern of previous years.[1]

Lee Still from Sheridan, Wyoming was selected the Queen of the Black Hills Classic on Friday night and presided over the Saturday and Sunday half-mile races. The longest distance motorcyclists (as described in the limited press coverage) were "three men from New Jersey and a mother and daughter from Lancaster, California".[2]

Neil Keen of Pasadena, California won Sunday's feature race. Second and third place were taken by Ronnie Rall of Mansfield, Ohio and Sammy Tanner from Bellflower, California. Darrel Dovel of Beaumont, California placed fourth.[3] Both Rall and Tanner went on to become significant racers in the motorcycle world. Tanner was inducted into the AMA Hall of Fame in 1999 and recognized for his contributions to motorcycle racing in general and as a regional motorcycle equipment distributor. Rall, inducted in 2001, was recognized by the AMA for his dirt track racing wins in the 1960's and 1970's. Rall also took third in the total number of AMA points earned in 1964, and won five AMA Grand National Series (GNS) races during his career.[4]

A truly interesting and impromptu event occurred on Sunday, August 12. During the races, the Expert riders had a conference and agreed to do a three-lap Trophy Dash. Race Officials came up with a trophy, and Sammy Tanner won the race. When he was awarded the Trophy, Tanner suggested that it be auctioned off to the highest bidder in the grandstand and that the money be given to George Thomas of Staten Island, New York, who had suffered a broken leg during the Saturday racing program. A motorcycle dealer from Denver won the trophy with a bid of $50. The racers then passed the hat and raised an additional $110 for Thomas.[5]

These early racers, working strictly for prize money and not for the major motorcycle companies as racers do today, were clearly a brotherhood.

Sammy Tanner (#7) leading Ronnie Rall in the Trophy Dash, 1962. (Dave and Kathy Estep Collection)

1962 Expert Champion: Neil Keen

Neil Keen, the all-time Champion of the Black Hills Motor Classic, actually won more races at Sturgis than any other rider. In all, Keen was to win five championship races, surpassing the record of Johnny Spiegelhoff who won four races in the early years of the rally (1938, '39, '41, and '46). Keen first came to race at Sturgis in 1957, and his racing participation spanned 13 years. His championship victories at the Expert level included 1962, '63, '68, '69, and '70. He also raced in final short-track events using a 250cc Yamaha.

The 1960s could almost be described as the "Keen Years" at Sturgis. When Neil did not take first place, he was still in the money and ended up on the podium at the finish. Keen, along with many Saturday wins,

Neil Keen, 1962 Expert Champion at Sturgis. (Mahony Racing Photos)

took second place in the Sunday feature races in 1965 and '66, and finished third in 1967. Keen also set several track records at Sturgis, including a time trial record in 1963 of 25.9 seconds that stood until 1975 when it was broken by Mike Kidd.

Keen was born in Lakeland, Florida on May 14, 1934 and grew up in Atlanta Georgia. He started riding motorcycles at age 14 and his first real motorcycle, after a series of scooters and motor bikes, was a Harley 125. In 1952 he moved to California and began riding for the Milne Brothers, a Los Angeles BSA dealership, where he also worked. He got involved in dirt-track racing in1954 at the age of 20, competing at Daytona and on the West Coast, mainly in Southern California. Keen's first race in Sturgis was in 1957 as an Expert. He was traveling with George Everett at the time.[1]

Keen says he always enjoyed coming to Sturgis to race, "Sturgis was always the Queen of the small town tracks." He said that the main reasons for this was the quality of track preparation and maintenance and better than average purses. He also enjoyed the beautiful Black Hills and says he could " see why the Dakota Sioux were ready to fight and die for them." Another major reason Keen enjoyed Sturgis was the kindness of the local people, especially the Hoel family, the Cecil Urban family and especially Neil Hultman.[2]

Keen also enjoyed the food. When Keen first came to Sturgis in 1957, "the largest beefsteaks were about $2.50 and hung over the edge of the serving platter". "Buffalo steaks and burgers were even cheaper," he said. "A buffalo steak that was larger than a dinner plate was about $2.00!"[3]

One of Keen's favorite racing stories at Sturgis had to do with his second-place finish in the 1965 final behind Babe DeMay, a traveling partner from Moline, Illinois. DeMay beat him by riding in the loose dirt between the groove and the infield grass — a "no-man's land where no sane professional rider would venture," according to Keen. DeMay was able to do this because he had drilled sheet metal screws into the knobs on the rear tire from the inside. "These screws greatly stiffened the knobs and made them dig!" Later in the race, as the ends of the knobs broke off, "the screws themselves did the dirty work." The AMA later initiated a rule stating that "No foreign object may be imbedded in the tire tread".[4]

In the early 1960s, Neil Keen's national reputation began to grow. He was identified early on by the press as a member of the "Original BSA Wrecking Crew", a group of BSA Goldstar "Mounted Marauders" who completely dominated Southern California's Ascot Park at Gardena, California for the first seven years of the 1960s. Ascot was a busy track hosting 29 races each season. The group included Keen, Albert Gunter, Jack O'Brien and Stuart Manley.[5]

Dick Mann describes Neil as the most dedicated professional racer he ever knew. "Neil Keen was truly the all-around professional competitor," said Mann. "He did not fall into the routine of limiting his competition to just the Nationals (GNS) during his career; he just kept competing in all the small-town races too! I bet that if a count was made, we would find that Neil raced in more professional races around this country than any other racer" Mann said.[6]

Neil Keen's career at the national level included many victories, including an outstanding and memorable GNS Championship race at Ascot Park in 1961. Keen was the pre-race favorite, but after gating well, another local racer, Don Hawley, set out to race only against Keen. He rooted Keen out and into the fence for three or four laps. Keen, to keep from crashing or worse, just slowed down for two or three laps. Hawley, who was focusing on Keen alone, slowed down also and the two riders found themselves in eighth place. When Hawley was suitably blocked, Keen proceeded to leave him, passing another rider each lap until he found himself in second place behind Carroll Resweber. "The National Champion, Resweber, was leading by a whole straight away and I took off like a man possessed to run him down—and did!" said Keen. Keen caught up to Resweber, who was at the limit of his Harley Davidson's speed, and made his move.

"We raced nose to tail for three laps and at the end of the backstretch, Resweber pointed inside; I shot past and was gone." Keen said he was already using the whole track and "even though there was room inside, I was reluctant to take a chance on knocking Resweber and going down." Keen decided to try and ride around the outside of his friend, a much more difficult task. Keen said, "I was damn glad he let me pass!" Keen then ran one lap at nearly full-throttle, letting go only when his bike started to get out of control. Once in the lead, he won by another straight-away length, "clearly in the fashion of my heroes Chuck Basney (Sturgis Champion 1948), Joe Leonard (Sturgis Champion 1953 and '57), Carroll Resweber, and Ricky Graham (Sturgis 1976), the real Supermen of our sport."[7]

Neil Keen was inducted into the AMA Hall of Fame in 2000 and was elected to Charter Membership in the White Plate Flat Trackers Association in 1980. According to Keen, his most prestigious honor was being taken into the Trail Blazers Hall of Fame in 1999. Membership in this

Neil Keen, Al Burke and Neil Hultman at Sturgis, 1992. Keen had just finished a lap on his restored BSA racer. (Neil Hultman Collection)

group is very special, says Keen, because the Trail Blazers group "honors race track people (mostly) and has for 60 years."[8]

Neil Keen retired from professional racing in 1974 after 21 seasons and became actively involved in the manufacturing of racing equipment. He also continued to serve on the AMA Competition Committee and was involved with vintage racing until 1998. For a time, Keen worked at the Milne BSA dealership. He later worked for Hudspeth Motors, a Harley Davidson shop, and John's Bike Shop, "the world's largest Schwinn bicycle dealership."[9]

Neil Keen attends the Sturgis rally whenever he can. His last visit was 1998, when he won all the vintage races at Rapid City. Keen and his wife, Kim, live in Wentzville, Missouri, a suburb of St. Louis. They have two children.

1962 Expert 2nd Place: Ronnie Rall

Ronnie Rall was born in Mansfield, Ohio on December 29, 1938 and grew up on a farm, beginning his riding career on a Cushman scooter. He later purchased a JAWA 250, soon followed by a 1957 Triumph Tiger Club and began competing in local enduro races, where he learned to broad slide in the corners. When he finally tried flat track, he really found his niche. He and his brother built an oval on the farm and took turns timing each other on laps. "That's where I really learned to ride," he said.[1]

Rall had a hard time getting his pro license. The AMA application form required a parental permission signature for any rider under age 21, and Rall's mom refused to sign. As a result, Ronnie had to wait until he was 21. In 1960, while looking for a sponsor, Rall was able to get a BSA Goldstar from a dealer at cost. Before entering his first professional race at Lawrenceburg, Indiana, Ron and his brother had to milk the cows, stop en-route to attend church and still get to the track for time trials by

9:00 a.m. He finished in the money ($29), paid for the trip expenses, and began his professional career. He turned Expert in 1962 and took three GNS podium finishes in his rookie year.[2]

In 1962, Rall traveled to Sturgis with his brother-in-law, Dave Estep. He won the Saturday final event ahead of Neil Keen and Sammy Tanner. On Sunday he slipped to second place, losing to Keen but beating Tanner and Darrel Dovel, who took fourth place. His traveling partner Estep took second in the Amateur final on Saturday and third on Sunday.[3]

Ronnie and Dave Estep had a pleasant outing at Sturgis in 1962, including several adventures. According to Estep:

> Ronnie Rall and I had decided early in 1962 that we wanted to go to Sturgis. I was working for A.D. Farrow Harley Davidson in Columbus, Ohio. Bobby Hill was doing the engine work on both of our engines and working a full time job. By the time it was time to make final plans for the trip, we realized that the Springfield mile would be shortly after Sturgis and Bobby would have little time to re-build both engines after we returned. We decided to let Bobby

Dave Estep (#99), Bobby Hill and Ronnie Rall (#52) at Darlington, North Carolina, 1962. (Dave and Kathy Estep Collection)

work on Ronnie's engine while we were gone and have Ronnie use my engine for Sturgis, which would have left me without an engine. I borrowed an engine from one of the other mechanics at Farrows. So with this as a plan, we loaded the two KR's and all our gear into my 1959 El Camino and headed for Sturgis. I thought we would never get through Iowa; it was endless cornfields, mile after mile. It was worth the trip when we finally got into the Badlands and on to the Black Hills.[4]

It was probably a good decision to hold back Rall's number one engine for a Bobby Hill overhaul. Two weeks after the Sturgis Rally, Rall was able to place second at the Springfield mile behind Bart Markel. Dave Estep won the Amateur race at Springfield using his own engine.

The two riders really enjoyed their trip to Sturgis. They toured the Badlands and the Black Hills and had a ball at the races. They were treated well by the local people and the race promoters. It was Estep's first opportunity to establish friendships with Darrel Dovel, Neil Keen and Gary Nixon. When Dave Estep had a problem with his forks, Clarence Hoel was more than willing to let him use his shop to make repairs. After taking second place in Saturday's Amateur final on a borrowed engine and damaged fork dampers, Estep returned and won first place on Sunday. Ronnie, who was a rookie Expert in 1962, placed second behind Neil Keen in the Championship race.[5]

One wonders if Rall would have won with his own engine. It was also interesting to note that Bobby Hill, the inveterate Indian racer and master mechanic, was tuning these two KR Harley Davidson motorcycles. Hill accompanied Rall and Estep to the GNS race at Heidelberg, Pennsylvania where Estep won the Amateur final.

The two riders returned from Sturgis via Milwaukee, where they were able to tour the Harley Davidson factory, and used some of their Sturgis prize money to stock up on parts. They also hauled Joe DeRuytter's Harley Davidson Sprint bike back to Ohio. DeRuytter had taken first place in the Novice Class at Sturgis in 1962.[6]

After placing second at Sturgis in 1962, Rall went on to an impressive career in the AMA Grand National Series (GNS). In total, Rall won five

*Ronnie Rall receives
the Red Phillips Award
in Columbus, Ohio,
1969. (Dave and Kathy
Estep Collection - Don
Pummel Photo)*

GNS races, including three half-miles, one short-track and one TT event between '63 and '69. Rall had his first GNS win, the 15-mile half-mile at Heidelberg, Pennsylvania in 1963. Later that year he won the 10-mile half at Columbus, Ohio and ended up in sixth place in the point totals. In 1964, Rall won the 14 lap TT at Peoria, Illinois and garnered enough podium finishes in additional races to place third in GNS points behind Roger Reiman and Dick Mann. Rall did not win or place again until 1968 when he won the half-mile at Livonia, Michigan. His last GNS win was the 25 lap short-track event at Houston, Texas in 1969. [7]

A strict Roman Catholic, Rall never missed church throughout his entire racing career. Traveling to races, he would always stop along the way for early morning mass. His mechanic and traveling companion, Edgar Fuhr, would sleep in the car while Ron was in church. "The church goers could not figure out what was going on," said Rall. "Here's this station wagon with a trailer of race bikes on the back with Fuhr asleep in the front seat!"[8]

The Harley Davidson factory approached Rall about racing for the factory team in 1964, but he told them that his responsibilities at the farm would preclude competing in some of the GNS races. As a result, he did not make the team. Farming always came first for Rall, but he continued to race in the Midwest in Ohio, Michigan and Indiana on the weekends, winning many races at county fairs. In his final GNS win at the Houston Astrodome, Rall's Bultaco racer seized a crankshaft during practice. His mechanic removed the jug from the racer and placed it on a stock bike. Rall ran the race and wasn't doing well until he accidentally shifted into a higher gear and found that the higher speed helped him go high in the corners and win. He took $2,750 for the first place finish and was awarded an additional $500 from Bultaco.[9]

In the early 1970's Rall became interested in flying. He would tear down his motorcycle, load it in his airplane, and fly to the races. He would then rent a car, load the bike in the trunk and go to the racetrack where he would reassemble the motorcycle and race. He completed in his last national in 1973 and continued to race locally for the rest of the decade.[10]

In the 1980s Ronnie Rall purchased a dairy farm in Engandine, Michigan. Rall and his wife, Allison, have seven children. He continues to ride in vintage races and still loves to fly his airplane. Of all the racers interviewed for this book, Rall was the only racer who had to finish milking his cows before he could speak with the author by phone!

1962 Expert 3rd Place: Sammy Tanner

Sammy Tanner, who finished in third place behind Neil Keen in the 1962 Classic Championship, had a stellar career, racing at the National level and competing against such distinguished riders as Albert Gunter, Neil Keen, Dick Mann, Bart Markel and George Roeder.

Tanner, affectionately characterized as the "Flying Flea" because of his size, first came to Sturgis in 1957 as an Amateur. Tanner won his heat races on both days, placed third in the final on Saturday, and won the Amateur championship on Sunday. Tanner returned to race in Sturgis in 1958 and 1962. In 1958, Tanner placed third in the Sunday Expert final. He repeated this third place finish in 1962.

Tanner was born in Houston, Texas. He started riding motorcycles in 1954 and began flat-tracking in 1956, sponsored by Stelter's Triumph of Houston. At this time, Tanner was competing in Texas, Oklahoma, Louisiana, Mississippi, and in the Kansas/Missouri circuit. Tanner's first trip to Sturgis was in 1957. He was 17 and broke, but he did have an old

Tanner (#7) after winning the Ascot Park National in Gardena, California, 1966. (Sammy Tanner Collection)

Plymouth station wagon and a trailer to carry his racer. To save money, he picked up two other racers in Springfield, Missouri to share expenses on the trip to Sturgis. After getting up the road about 150 miles, Tanner discovered that the other two riders were also broke and had no money for gas. He had to use his last few dollars to buy the last tank of gas, arriving in Sturgis late Friday evening with less than a quarter of a tank in the station wagon. None of the other racers had eaten anything since breakfast and were hungry and tired. One of the racers had heard about the "Buffalo Feed" at the City Park, so they headed out looking for a free meal. When they arrived at the park, they discovered that the cookout was finished and everyone was cleaning up! Two of the ladies took pity on the hungry riders and went to their pans and scraped up enough food to fill three plates. It was Tanner's first experience with Sturgis hospitality, and he has never forgotten their generosity! By the

Sammy Tanner at the Lincoln, Illinois National, 1956. (Sammy Tanner Collection - Photo by Jack Hall)

close of racing on Sunday, all three riders had won enough money for gas and food, so they piled in the station wagon to head south and compete in Kansas.

Tanner's second memory of Sturgis had to do with the Trophy Dash win in 1962. When George Thomas of Staten Island, New York broke his leg in the Saturday program, all of the racers knew that Thomas was flat broke and the discussion on Saturday night and Sunday morning centered on what the other racers could do to help out. Since many of them were also short on cash, Neil Keen came up with the idea of having a Trophy Dash. They figured that if they could find a trophy, they would stage a three-lap race and then auction the trophy off to the Grandstand crowd to raise some money for Thomas. Pappy Hoel found a trophy, and it was decided that the four riders with the best time trials would be involved in the Trophy Dash. These four included Tanner, George Everett, Neil Keen, and Ronnie Rall. In the original rider's meeting, they had decided that the four would stay in a close pack to give the crowd a real thrill. In the excitement of coming off his last race, Tanner forgot about the stratagem and took off like a shot. He was soon far ahead of the pack, and by the third turn he was thinking to himself, "Boy, I'm fast today!" It wasn't until near the end of the third lap that he remembered the original plan. He crossed the finish line, took the checkered flag, auctioned off his trophy and was embarrassed for the next several weeks. Tanner says that Neil Keen was really hard on him, teasing him about this race for the next several years.

In late 1957, Tanner began riding BSAs for Ray Hendershot, who had a shop in Kansas City, Kansas. Tanner's career on BSAs began to take off in 1958, the year after he first raced at Sturgis. Tanner's most significant win was at the AMA Grand National Series (GNS) mile race at Springfield in 1964.

Tanner's first inclusion in the Top Ten list of the Grand National Series was 1958. Tanner was sixth in GNS point standings and high point leader in flat-track at the end of the season. He was to repeat a sixth place standing in 1959 after winning the Grand National half-mile at Ascot Park in Gardena, California. He repeated this half-mile win at Ascot in

1964, the year he won the mile at Springfield. In all, Tanner won seven Grand National Series races, including four more half-miles, at Gardena (1965 and 1966) and at Heidelberg, Pennsylvania and Elkhorn, Wisconsin in 1966. The half was obviously Tanner's best race. He ended his career with 408 AMA sanctioned race victories, and he was five-time high point champion in flat-track.

Sammy Tanner retired from professional racing in 1972. He was inducted into the AMA Hall of Fame in 1999, the Dirt Track Hall of Fame in 2000, and the Trailblazers Hall of Fame in 2001. In 1965, Tanner started wholesaleing motorcycle-related products to dealerships in the off-season. When he retired from racing, his business, Sammy Tanner Distributing Company became his full-time occupation. He is presently moving his company to Fontana, California, which is only one block from the California Motor Speedway. "I just have to be near a racetrack," says Tanner. "Happiness is being close to racing, even if it has to be paved!" Tanner currently lives in Southern California and is a national distributor for ARAI helmets.

August 8-11, 1963

On July 31, 1963, the *Sturgis Tribune* reported plans for honoring early instigators of the half-mile racetrack. It seems that the track was originally established for horse racing and then later adapted for automobile racing.[1] A program organized by Clarence Hoel and the Jackpine Gypsies Motorcycle Club was to be held during Sunday's races, and six local men would be recognized, including:

- Dr. R.I. Woods, who raised $2,500 to convert the track
- Ed and Ron Cruickshauk, who worked in the early years as automobile race starters, judges, and timekeepers
- Frank Aukerman, one of the early racers who used a car with an airplane engine
- Ed Gronert, who revitalized the efforts to continue races after they began to lag in popularity
- King Riley, a popular driver and holder of the automobile track record of 30 seconds.

In an article published in *Road Rider* magazine, Clarence Hoel related a story regarding the evolution of Aukerman's airplane-engine powered racecar. It seems that the very first airplane to land in Sturgis was Aukerman's. As a youth, Pappy and his friends went to the Meade County Fairgrounds to see it land. After tinkering a bit with the engine, Frank Aukerman went into town for lunch and asked his brother Bert to watch the plane. Bert Aukerman, unable to stifle his curiosity, started the plane's engine and began to taxi it around the field. Much to the delight of Hoel and his friends, the plane took off. After wobbling around a bit, Bert attempted to land but unfortunately hooked the landing gear on a fence and crashed. Later, the Aukerman brothers salvaged the engine and mounted it on a propeller-driven sled. The next summer, they bolted the engine into a car chassis and raced it on the half-mile track. They named the racing car "Maybe", suggesting that "maybe it would finish the race and maybe it wouldn't."[2]

Coverage of the 1963 classic was again overshadowed by excitement regarding Sturgis' Titans baseball team. The Sturgis Tribune's coverage of the Classic, probably taken from the previous year's news item, outlined a program that was a carbon copy of the previous year's events. The 1964 rally again included a Thursday Gypsy Tour to the Southern Hills, a hill-climb and scrambles on Friday, and two days of half-mile motorcycle racing on Saturday and Sunday. Another short Gypsy tour of the Northern Hills was planned for Saturday morning. Pappy Hoel would again show a film in the open field by the big tent behind his motorcycle dealership on Thursday night and the awards program would be held in the City Park on Friday evening.[3]

According to Mrs. Carl Aga, reporter for the *Rushmore Ads*, visitors from nearly every state in the nation were in attendance by the weekend. She also reported a large contingent of riders from Canada and had even interviewed a racing fan from England, who said that he had read about Sturgis in the British motorcycle press. All of the visitors praised the scenery, the setting and the hospitality of the local people. Many of the regulars were back, and Don Vodden, one of the first Gypsies, returned with his wife to attend the 1963 rally.[4]

Nearly 250 motorcycles took part in the Gypsy Tour led by Fred Miller. He reported that many cycles were carrying two or more (hopefully by sidecar) persons. The Friday afternoon hill climb event was a success, and Dan Deubler of Sioux Falls, South Dakota, won the 250cc class. Another Sioux Falls rider, Bob Jansen, took the 500cc class title and Pat Brown from Rapid City won the Open class. The scrambles race winners included Bill Roder of Billings, Montana at 250cc; Don Hough of Cheyenne, Wyoming at 500 cc; and Tony Denius of Denver in the Open class. Don Vodden served as the announcer for these two events and Neil Hultmann was the Clerk of Course.[5]

The feed went off with out a hitch, and the visitors really enjoyed the program. One of the program's highlights was an entry by Lucy Huggin from Las Vegas, Nevada in the Queen competition, who turned out to be a male rider in drag. At the close of the program, Clearance Hoel was awarded a lifetime membership in the Jackpine Gypsies and was awarded a plaque for his 25 years of service to the rally. Awards of Black Hills Gold were given to the winners for distance, best costume, and best dressed club.[6] A Canadian lady, Mrs. Vera Cunningham of Georgetown, Ontario, was chosen Queen of the rally. Pat Green from Iowa and Bill Hutcheson, another Canadian, were chosen as best dressed riders. The distance award went to Ken Frezel of Wickford, Rhode Island, who traveled more than 2,500 miles to reach Sturgis. The Motor Maids distance prize – for 1,500 miles – was awarded to Lois Gutzwiller of Hamilton, Ohio, and the longest distance (1,742 miles) for a female rider was awarded to Sue Wissler of Landsville, Pennsylvania. The distance award for a married couple went to Mr. and Mrs. Paul Conaway of Costa Mesa, California, and the longest married pair (in years) was Mr. and Mrs. Albert German of Cozad, Nebraska. Julius Kegal of Freeport, Illinois, age 72, was the oldest rider. The best dressed club award went to the "White Spots" of Grand Island, Nebraska.[7]

The first Short-Track race at Sturgis, 1963. From left to right: Bob King, Don Rice, Norb Hamling, Jerry Karns, Geezer Emick, Jerry Cheney, Pat Brown, Clarence "Pappy" Hoel (standing). Bob Moore, who had organized this first race, had broken his arm and could not compete. (Pearl Hoel Collection)

Races

On Saturday, Sportsman races were held prior to the professional AMA-sanctioned classes, and Jack Hoel, riding a Yamaha for his dad's shop, won the Sportsman final. The Novice winner on Saturday was Ivan Aden of Lahambra, California, followed by Dan Pritten and Bob Wolf also from California. All three riders used Yamaha motorcycles. Mike Van Ness of Santa Monica, California took first place in the Amateur class. Second and third places were taken by Mike Moore from Cheyenne, Wyoming, and Tommy McCormick of Billings, Montana. Moore rode a Harley Davidson and the other two racers used BSAs. Neil Keen of Pasadena, California, won the Expert final, and second place went to Bill Erskig of Van Ness, California. Both of these riders used BSA singles. Third place went to Babe Demay of Moline, Illinois, riding on a Harley Davidson.[8]

On Sunday, Auden repeated a first place finish in the Novice Class, followed by Donald Butler of Linwood, California and Julian Arther from Seattle. Mike Moore, who took second place on Saturday, moved up to win the Amateur final on Sunday. Also placing were Dwight Ratcliff of Des Moines, Iowa, and Miles Eklund of Sioux Falls, South Dakota. Neil Keen again won the Expert class on Sunday, holding off Babe DeMay and Duane Shadley from Oscaloosa, Iowa. Jack Hoel lost his first place position in the Sportsman final to Denis Arens of Sioux Falls, South Dakota.[9]

Neil Keen who was to become a faithful contender at Sturgis, established a half-mile track record of 25.94 seconds in 1963, which lasted until 1975. Keen, a charter member of the White Plate Flat Trackers Association, was inducted into the AMA Hall of Fame in 2000. He was recognized as a 1960s and 1970s dirt track racer and as a member of the Original BSA Wrecking Crew.

Bob Moore

Bob Moore is a Charter Life Member of the American Motorcyclist Association, a Jackpine Gypsies Motorcycle Club Life Member and Charter Member of the White Plate Flat Trackers Association.

Bob fell in love with motorcycles in 1949 when he used to hitch a ride home from school with a neighborhood kid who had an Indian Scout. He began riding motorcycles in 1950 on an Indian Brave that belonged to a friend, and his first motorcycle was a Triumph Thunderbird. He belonged to the Black Hills Motorcycle Club of Rapid City and the Rapid Barons of Rapid City in the 1950s and joined the New Mexico Motorcycle Club of Albuquerque while serving in the Armed Services. Bob began competition racing in 1956, taking part in scrambles, dirt track, TTs, cross country events, hill climbs, observed trials and field meets.[1]

In the early 1960s, Moore began organizing and racing in short track events in Rapid City and Cheyenne and Casper, Wyoming. He invited members of the Gypsies to participate in the Rapid City short track races and several of the Sturgis area riders began to enjoy this form of racing. By 1962, he had convinced Clarence Hoel to start developing a short-track race at Sturgis and incorporating into the rally program. By the 1963 Classic, the track was completed and the first event was held. By 1968, Hoel had convinced Moore to join the Jackpine Gypsies.[2]

Moore served as president of the Gypsies from 1971 through 1975, and in 1993, after 25 years, he became a Life Member. Bob Moore designed most of the club's patches and pins and was also an excellent writer and cartoonist. Moore's well-constructed articles and written insights were included in nearly every piece of publicity about the Classic, beginning the early 1970's. His cartoons have been enjoyed by thousands of rally visitors in yearly supplements published by the local press. He served as the editor of the Jackpine Gypsy News, a club sponsored supplement sold to the visitors, from mid 1990s until 2001.

Bob was instrumental in helping Pappy Hoel and Al Burke organize the White Plate Flat Trackers Association in 1979 and served as its first president. He is a truly dedicated Gypsy and White Plate Flat Tracker, serving as a tireless worker and supporter of the Black Hills Motor Classic for nearly 40 years. He worked in sales throughout his professional career and moved from Rapid City to Sturgis in 1985. In 1984 he retired and built his dream home in Boulder Canyon, across the road from his good friend Neil Hultmann.

These days, Bob's priorities include the Jackpine Gypsies, whose goal has always been to promote Sturgis, the annual motorcycle rally, local motorcycle activities and more recently, the Sturgis Motorcycle Museum and Hall of Fame. Like the author, Bob is devoted to BMW motorcycles.

The Assault at Bear Butte

On a Saturday in May 1963, two riders, Jack Hoel and Bill Erickson, decided to climb Bear Butte on light Yamaha 80cc motorcycles. Whether the plan was to be the first to perform this feat as a publicity stunt or simply to test their riding skills is not clear. Perhaps they knew that plans were underway to include this landmark in the National Park Service as a National Monument, and they were determined to make the ride before vehicles of any kind were prohibited.

On the first day, after two hours of pushing and pulling their machines up the mountain, they decided to call it a day. They tied their bikes to a tree, hiked out and returned on Sunday.

Successful in their climb on Sunday afternoon, they arrived at the summit with Bob Early, a photographer who documented their feat. By the time they began an exciting descent, a crowd of local spectators had gathered to watch them through binoculars. These two little Yamahas are probably the only vehicles to ever reach the top of Bear Butte.

Jack Hoel (at right) and Bill Erickson congratulate one another after completing the assault on Bear Butte, 1963. (Jack Hoel Collection)

August 13-16, 1964

Improved coverage by the local media and four significant milestones related to the evolution of the Black Hills Motor Classic took place in 1964. The first development was the establishment of a new short track, west of Interstate 90 on Jackpine Gypsy property. This 1/5th mile track, open to non-professionals in 1964, was scheduled for "Sportsman" races on Saturday morning, before the opening of the traditional half-mile races at 1:30pm. To acquaint visiting riders with this exciting form of racing, Hoel, ever focused on publicity, moved the traditional Thursday night coffee and donut reception from his motorcycle shop to the short track.[1] Pearl Hoel, as dedicated as ever, now had to haul the food across town to the new site.

Moving back to Main Street, first tried in 1949, was the second milestone of the year. The City Council "as a gesture of welcome to the visiting cyclists" voted to reserve a section of Main Street exclusively for the free parking of motorcycles during the Classic.

The third development, designed to enhance the registration of visitors, was a series of significant door-prize drawings. Riders who registered would be eligible to win these prizes and be recognized on Sunday. Apparently more and more riders were coming and not bothering to register, causing problems for the rally leadership when it came to assessing an accurate total number of visitors.* In fact, local hotels, motels and campgrounds were already full by Wednesday, August 12, the day prior to the kick off of the Gypsy Tour.[2]

The 1964 Gypsy tour left Main Street at 9:00am on Wednesday for a tour of the Southern Hills and a Pearl Hoel picnic lunch at the State Game Lodge in Custer State Park. Competition on Friday included the hill climb, held five miles north of Sturgis in the morning, and a scrambles race held in the afternoon. The scrambles race, which had been held five miles north of town for the past three years, was moved back to Bear Butte Lake. For the first time, a one-dollar admission fee was charged at each of these events. Administrative costs must have been a mounting concern because of additional visitors and the expansion of rally activities. More financial concerns may have been behind the installation of new chain-link fencing at the fairgrounds, thereby limiting free access to the Saturday and Sunday half-mile racing events. Too many people were apparently getting in free.

---

* This problem continues today as rally officials continually strive, usually unsuccessfully, to get an accurate head-count. Because this effort began in 1964, it's safe to assume that growth in self-guided touring was becoming more commonly recognized. This recognition probably generated mixed feelings about any positive growth in numbers, as well as a serious concern for control, order, and safety.

Nothing was reported about the Queen selection, distance awards, oldest riders and other award presentations at the Friday night picnic and program. There was also nothing reported about the short track, hill-climb or scrambles events.

On Saturday and Sunday, the half-mile races were opened by the Queen of the Classic, escorted by a Motor Maid parade. Babe DeMay of Moline, Illinois won the expert final on Sunday afternoon, riding a Harley Davidson and collecting the $220 prize. Second place went to Tony Denius of Denver, riding a BSA and winning $180. Darrell Dovel of Waukegan, Illinois took $120 for third place on his KR750 Harley Davidson. Fourth place went to Larry Palmgren of Denver who also rode a Harley Davidson and collected $80 for his efforts. The first-ever record of a Japanese motorcycle win at Sturgis was posted in the Novice Pro-Class Final event, which was limited to 250cc machines. Eddie Hammond from Redondo Beach, California took first place on a Yamaha, and Bill Rodier from Billings, Montana placed fourth on a Honda. Hammond won $60 for the first, and Rodier won $14 for fourth place.[3]

With the introduction of the short track, the return of bike parking on Main Street, and the advent of significant door prizes for those who registered, 1964 was a pivotal year in the evolution of the Black Hills Motor Classic, clearly marking the signs of what was to come.

1964 Expert Champion: Babe DeMay

Cyriel "Babe" DeMay was born on March 11, 1938 in Moline, Illinois. As a teenager, he began hanging around Smitty's Tri-City Motorcycle Shop in Rock Island, and it was there that he met Bill Tuman, a National Champion racer riding out of Smitty's Indian dealership. DeMay first came to Sturgis as a protégé of Tuman in 1953 and rode one of Bill's Indian Scouts on this first visit. In Bill Tuman's own words:

> Babe started to ride for me on one of my Indian Scouts in 1953. When he was moved to the Amateur class, he was the hottest one on the track — no one took him for a racer because he looked like Ichabod Crane on a motorcycle, but at the drop of the flag he was gone. They all knew who Babe DeMay was then! At a 10-mile National at Richmond, Virginia, Babe got off dead last. When

> he got back to the starting line, he was leading and two guys were up at the tower entering protests. Babe won that Amateur race going away, but it seemed like we had to put zippers on his motor as he was torn down so many times. Most of the year went that way for him. When I quit going in circles, I gave Babe my racing gear (leathers), my BSA, and my number 51 and wished him all the luck he could find. A little side story, as you may have heard, the Babe stuttered real bad. At a track at Peckatonica, Illinois, it was real dusty so I told him "when you pass the finish line count to three and turn left." His reply was,"Yyyoooooouuuuu wwwwaaaannnnttt mmmmeeee tttooo ggggeeett kkkiillled?"[1]

A few years after the demise of Indian, DeMay was racing on BSAs and still using Smitty's shop as headquarters. He continued to develop his skills as a racer and also gained a reputation for being a master mechanic and motorcycle tuner.

In DeMay's consecutive Sunday championships at Sturgis in 1964 and 1965, he was riding a KR750 Harley Davidson motorcycle. He

The author interviews Babe DeMay in Springfield, Illinois, 2002. (Author Photo)

continued competing at Sturgis over the next 14 years. His fondest memories of Sturgis include the honesty of the racing officials, the good food and the support he received from Clarence and Pearl Hoel. According to De May, Pappy always sent him expense money, if needed, and enough money to get home if he failed to take a good purse.

In *Circle Track Magazine,* Joe Scalzo described DeMay as winning more second and third places than any other racer during the years 1961 to 1967. At Sturgis, he took second in the Expert final in 1961 and 1967, and he won consecutive West Coast Regional Championships in 1964 and 1965. DeMay generally raced in Cambridge, Illinois on the Friday of rally week and then hurried to Sturgis to compete, generally arriving by noon Saturday to begin time trials. Perhaps DeMay's most outstanding career win was the Grand National half-mile at Lincoln, Illinois in 1966.

DeMay retired from motorcycle racing in 1967 and started racing stock cars. He did well during the 1968 season, winning many local half-mile dirt-track events. In 1969 he returned to the motorcycle racing circuit as a mechanic and tuner. He was asked to join the Harley Davidson racing team and tuned for several riders including Dave Sehle, Rex Beauchamp, Mark Brelsford, Mert Lawwill and Cal Rayborn.

At age 65, DeMay is still tuning on the national circuit and is the owner of DeMay Racing, which is in the process of moving from Pottstown, Pennsylvania to Collierville, Tennessee, where De May will begin tuning for J. R. Schnabel in 2003. DeMay's life has been devoted to motorcycle racing. His weekly schedule on the national circuit consists of spending Monday through Friday in the shop and then traveling Friday afternoon through Sunday night supporting his racers in national competition efforts.

Babe DeMay was inducted into the AMA Hall of Fame in 2001, and was chosen as a Charter Member in the White Plate Flat Tracker's Association in 1982.

August 11-15, 1965

Officially expanded to a five-day format in 1965, the Black Hills Motor Classic began on Wednesday, August 11, with a 150-mile Northern Tour through the Bear Lodge Mountains to Devils Tower in Wyoming, where the riders ate lunch. After touring Devils Tower National Monument, the tour returned to Belle Fourche, where the Chamber of Commerce served afternoon refreshments. The riders then returned to Sturgis and the new Bear Butte State Park for a dinner sponsored by the Sturgis Chamber of Commerce.

On Thursday, the program included a typical Gypsy Tour to the Southern Hills and ended with evening short track races held across the interstate highway from Sturgis. Apparently this was still a "Sportsmans" race. Friday's activities included the hill climb and the scrambles races, both held at the site five miles north of Sturgis. The hill-climb was set up to include three categories, including 250cc, 500cc and an Open Class for motorcycles larger than 500cc.[1] A second Chamber of Commerce "feed" was scheduled for 5:30pm in the City Park, at which time Kay Thomas from Fort Dodge, Iowa was crowned the Queen of the 1965 Black Hills Motor Classic. Saturday morning began with a short tour of the Northern Hills. With such a busy schedule and a growing interest in the rally, it is no surprise that housing became an even greater problem in 1965. A few residents actually began renting rooms in their own houses to visitors because of the huge crowd.

Races

Racers were allowed on the track at 9:00am on Saturday for practice. The annual flag raising ceremony, conducted by the local Boy Scouts of America Troop, was begun at 1:45, just prior to the official time trials.[2]

Apparently there were enough racers to create three solid classes of dirt trackers, including Novice riders with green plates, Amateurs with yellow plates, and Experts with the coveted white plates. Additional short-track races were scheduled for Saturday evening. The Saturday and Sunday half-mile races were AMA sanctioned.

Thursday night's short track races were divided into two sections (or classes), both limited to 250cc machines. The Class A event was won by Norbert Hambling of Rapid City. Hambling used a Ducati motorcycle to beat out Jim Pengram on a Harley Davidson. Geezer Emick placed third in this event on a Maico. In the Class B race, the winner was Tom Tolinger of Greeley, Colorado. Second place went to Al Chapman from Wolf Point, Montana and third went to Tom Benson of Williston, North Dakota. Tolinger and Chapman both used Ducatis and Benson was riding a Honda.[3]

Early scrambles races west of Sturgis prior to the construction of Interstate 90. (Eva Satterlee Collection)

Friday's scrambles, or motorcross, was divided into three sections. The 175cc Class race was won by Al Davis from Pueblo, Colorado. Davis used a Montessa motorcycle to defeat Barry Horn on a Kawasaki and Larry Sheldon of Mitchell, South Dakota on a Honda. The 100cc class was broken down into Class A and Class B sections. The Class A Scrambles was taken by Dan Duebler of Sioux Falls, South Dakota. Second and third place were taken by Cleo Corkill and Bill Gikling. Corkill rode a Yamaha, and Gikling raced on a Honda. The Class B 100cc section was won by Jack Oler form Casper, Wyoming. Second and third place were won by Mike Murphy of LaCrosse, Wisconsin and Dick Strain of Rapid City. All three of these racers used Yamaha motorcycles.[4]

Queen Kay Thomas and a Motor Maids Parade opened the Saturday and Sunday feature half-mile races. The Motor Maids, incidentally, had chosen Sturgis as the site for their 1966 National Convention. Although Neil Keen of Pasadena, California was the top money winner and had set the new track record the previous year, he ended up in second place in Sunday's Expert Final. Babe DeMay of Moline, Illinois, who also won in 1964, took the 1965 final championship.[5]

A large number of Japanese motorcycles were entered in the 1965 half-mile race, including three Yamahas who placed 1-2-4 in the Novice Finals. Charlie Dawson from Omaha, Nebraska placed first followed by Jack Hoel in second. Fourth place went to Jim Messing, also from Omaha. Leon Beshard of Denver took third place riding a Bultaco.[6]

1965, like 1964, was another significant year in the growth of the Classic. The establishment of a five-day format, the scheduling of two separate "short track" races and the actual onset of renting rooms in family homes to visitors are all evidence of enhanced interest, support, and expansion. After the dust had settled in 1965, the editor of the *Sturgis Tribune* provided a rather detailed and positive response to the 1965 Classic under the heading "Highly Successful":

> *The annual Black Hills Motor Classic which ended here Sunday was truly an outstanding event. It brought cyclists from long distances to our community and we believe they had a good time here. At least, we didn't hear any complaints from any of them. Rather, they were complimentary about the reception they received here and about the fine arrangements that had been made for their comfort and pleasure.*
>
> *Fears that the Classic would be taken over by hoodlums this year proved to be groundless – as we earlier predicted they would be. Chief of Police Merlin Ehlers reports that his force experienced absolutely no difficulty with the cyclists. In fact, he doubts that any other group of comparable size could be any better behaved.*
>
> *The department was prepared for trouble, but it simply did not develop. That it did not is a credit to the cyclists and the sport that is their avocation. It demonstrated once again that cyclists are merely normal people who have a fondness for riding free as the wind, and not beatniks as some people believe.*
>
> *The sponsors of the Classic are certainly to be commended for their hard work in arranging an active program for the visiting cyclists, many of the cyclists make their trip here their annual vacation and they want to see as much of our famous Black Hills as possible while here. The Gypsy tours arranged by the local club provide this desired opportunity.*
>
> *There is no question about the Classic being a good thing for the community. Some of our citizens don't like the noise of the motorcycles, but the temporary annoyance is a small price to pay for the privilege – and that's what it is – of hosting so many visitors. The cyclists spend money while here and it gives the business community an economic boost of considerable import. They also provide some good entertainment as they compete in the hill climbs and races.*
>
> *The efforts of many local people went into making this year's Classic such an outstanding success. They serve without compensation and their only reward is the*

satisfaction of knowing that they have helped their community. We can all be thankful for their unselfish service.

Next year Sturgis will be host to the national convention of the Motor Maids of America, Inc. an organization of women cyclists. This is one outgrowth of the town's reputation for doing such a good job of handling the Classic over the years. Already plans are underway to make their convention here a memorable one.

The annual Classic is history again for another year. It will be difficult, indeed, to top this year's event. But you can bet the effort will be made to do it! The event deserves the support and active assistance of many of our townspeople.[7]

Babe DeMay

One of Neil Keen's favorite stories about Sturgis is losing the 1965 Championship to Babe De May, who was Keen's traveling partner to Sturgis that year.

According to Keen, Babe won the race by passing him inside the groove — the loose dirt between the track and the grass, "a no-mans land where no professional rider would venture." To make matters worse, riding inside the groove sprayed gravel trash all over the smooth surface of the upper track, forcing other riders to proceed with caution, and as a result, lose speed in the turns. At the end of the race, Keen examined DeMay's racer and discovered that he had used metal screws on the left outside tread of his rear tire.[*] Keen gave DeMay a bad time about it, and DeMay responded by relating some of the creative things Keen had done in the past. They both had a good laugh about it, went on traveling together as pals and remain lifelong friends.[1]

Jack Hoel, however, tells an even more interesting story about DeMay. Apparently the Babe had something of a stuttering problem. In the early days of his racing career, DeMay asked one of the old-timers about how to increase his speed in the corners. This older racer told De May

---

[*] Apparently someone else reported this or some other similar situation to the AMA and the practice was banned in the next year of racing.

that when he started into a corner, he always listened to the other engines in the pack. When the other racers backed off on the throttle, he would quickly count "one-two-three" and then back off on his own throttle, insuring a bit of an edge in speed while entering the turn. DeMay took this advice and in the first race entered the corner too fast. After he high-sided his bike and lost the race, DeMay confronted his erstwhile mentor, berating him for bad advice. In further heated conversation between these two racers, DeMay admitted that he had counted "o-o-o-ne, t-t-t-two, th-th-th-three" and was going much too fast to make the turn! "Aha!" exclaimed the old racer, "For you Babe, you probably better stick to o-o-o-one!" According to Jack Hoel, Babe DeMay often told this story on himself and maintained that, for him, a count of o-o-o-one always worked just fine.[2]

Phil Town

One of the most significant events to happen in the town of Sturgis during the summer of 1965 was the opening of Phil Town. For the times, this super modern truck stop facility, located near the new I-90 exit at the south edge of Sturgis, provided nearly all the amenities available to truck stop/convenience store customers of today.

The Phil Town exit on I-90 has always served as a landmark to riders approaching Sturgis from the south and continues to provide service to visitors and veteran riders as a meeting place. The restaurant has been the scene of many rally-related banquets and dinners.

Chapter Eight:
Law Enforcement and the Keen Years

From 1966 to 1970, the rally continued to grow and press coverage returned. Nationally-ranked racers came to compete and housing the ever-increasing number of visitors continued to be a problem.

One-week prior to the 1966 rally, Sturgis hosted the 26th Annual Motor Maids Convention. This group of female motorcyclists had been visiting Sturgis for several years, and in 1966 they established the practice of riding in the parade at Sunday's featured half-mile Championship. While the format of the 1966 rally remained largely unchanged from 1965, the short track races were held later in the evening because of newly-installed floodlights at the Gypsy track. On a down note, vandals savaged the new Gypsy Clubroom, destroying furniture and club records.

Additional involvement and support by community groups was key in 1967. The Jaycees, the Lions Club and even the Titans Baseball team started assisting with the show. 1967 also marked the first public reports regarding the rally's economic impact in Sturgis – over $150,000 in 1967 alone.

In 1968, motorcycles started arriving on Monday in anticipation of the official Wednesday opening. The Classic committee established "True Western Friendship" as the year's motto and a search for additional housing was on. Saturday's races were canceled due to rain, but a crowd of over 3,000 watched a program including 24 Amateurs and 25 Experts compete on Sunday. Neil Keen, winner in 1962 and '63 won his third Championship race in 1968. Some rowdy behavior occurred in the City Park camping area, and a few riders were caught pouring and igniting gasoline strips on the highway between Ft. Meade and Sturgis.

As a result of problems in 1968, law enforcement was reorganized and improved in 1969. Meetings involving local police, state Highway Patrol leaders, and Sheriff Deputies from both Sturgis and Deadwood (Lawrence County) were held prior to the rally, which resulted in a peaceful rally. Neil Keen won his fourth championship at Sturgis on Sunday.

By Tuesday night prior to the official opening of the 1970 rally, the City Park was filled to capacity with campers. Law enforcement procedures had been further enhanced, and record crowds were in attendance at the races. Although scattered thunderstorms limited the number of Gypsy tour riders during the rally's first two days, Saturday and Sunday were bright and clear for racing. 1970 also marked the emergence of Japanese racing motorcycles at Sturgis. By 1977, out of 95 motorcycles in competition, 45 were made in Japan. Neil Keen took his fifth championship on Sunday, forever marking the late 1960s in Sturgis as the Keen Years.

Motor Maids National Convention: July 7-10, 1966

Not limited to just the rally, Sturgis residents had a slightly different motorcycling experience in 1966. In July the Motor Maids of America descended on Sturgis for their 26th Annual Convention — a four-day affair beginning on July 7 and ending on July 10.

The history of this national female riding group began in the late 1930s when Linda Dugeau, of Providence, Rhode Island, came up with the idea. Dugeau contacted riding clubs, motorcycle dealers and manufacturers to determine if there were enough female riders to form a group. As a result, the Motor Maids organization was chartered in 1940 with 51 members. In 1941, the group was recognized by the AMA and issued Club Charter 509. The first National Convention was held in Columbus, Ohio in 1944 and annually thereafter in July or August.[1] Dot Robinson of Detroit, Michigan was the first President, an office she maintained for the next 25 years. Robinson was replaced by Doreen Hamilton of Wichita, Kansas in 1966, the year of the National Convention in Sturgis.[2]

Membership in the Motor Maids was limited to women who either owned or operated their own motorcycle or a bike belonging to a member of the immediate family. Women who attended rallies as motorcycle passengers or traveled by car could only participate as "visitors". Parading at charity and motorcycle events was a tradition established early in the club's history, and white gloves became the defining characteristic of Motor Maid's parade uniform.

For the 1966 convention, Motor Maid officials arrived in Sturgis a few days prior to the convention to be sure that everything was in place. Registration began on Wednesday night, July 6, and on Thursday ladies were taken on a Four-Wheel Tour conducted and guided by National Forest Service personnel. The vehicles were provided by the Sturgis Four-Wheel Club.[3]

The convention's General Session was held at 5:30pm on Thursday night and the "Maids" were greeted by Mayor Francis Langin. After dinner the women traveled by car to the Black Hills Passion Play and were escorted by units of the South Dakota Highway Patrol. On Friday, members of the Jackpine Gypsies escorted the group (finally riding on motorcycles) on a typical Gypsy Tour, taking in the usual Southern Black Hills attractions. They returned to Sturgis for a Friday night "light lunch" and entertainment provided by the Sturgis High School Music Department.[4]

Breakfast, provided by Yamaha International (through the local Hoel dealership), was served in the city auditorium on Saturday. After a morning lecture about Bear Butte, the group elected officers for 1967 and then rode out to Bear Butte, where the Chamber of Commerce, Tri-State Milling and both Sturgis banks hosted a luncheon. At 5:00 pm the Motor Maids organized a parade on Main Street for the Sturgis residents, and the Annual Banquet was held after the parade at the Phil Town Inn. On Sunday, not to be out done by Clarence Hoel and Yamaha, the Rapid City Motorcycle Dealership treated them to breakfast courtesy of "The Harley Davidson Company."[5]

Local support for Motor Maids 1966 Annual Convention was clearly echoed in a *Sturgis Tribune* editorial in July of 1966:

Welcome, Motor Maids

It isn't often that a national convention comes to Sturgis. In fact the 26th convention of the Motor Maids of America, now underway here, is the very first. This organization, formed 26 years ago in Columbus, Ohio to promote better motorcycling and companion-

ship between women of like interests, has selected Sturgis for its convention this year for a very good reason. Many of its members were impressed with the hospitality shown to cyclists who come here every August for the Black Hills Motor Classic — a popular and traditional event for motorcycle fans from all over the country.

The Chamber of Commerce, in cooperation with Clarence Hoel and other Classic workers, lined up a busy schedule of interesting events for the visiting cyclists. We are confident they will return to their respective homes with renewed admiration for the attractions here and with kindly thoughts about the friendly people they will meet here during the next few days.

These women take their cycling very seriously and it's as much a hobby to them as golf, riding, bridge and other less spectacular recreation is to other housewives. They love the wind in their faces as they discover the many fascinating features of the countryside, and they are expert riders. They have an enviable safety record too.

It is with sincere pride that we welcome the visiting Motor Maids and thank them for traveling great distances to convene here. We'd like to see them back for the Classic in August too, and we suspect some of them will return for that annual event. Sturgis isn't a very big town, compared to the places where they have convened in the past, but we believe the visiting Motor Maids will like it here. It is a privilege to have them here and we are pleased to open the chute of western hospitality to them.

Come see us again girls![6]

August 10-15, 1966

The 1966 Classic started out on a sour note for the Jackpine Gypsies Motorcycle Club. A person or persons unknown vandalized their new clubhouse, located at the new short track/scrambles facility west of the I-90 Interstate Highway. The burglary was perpetrated in July, about a month prior to the opening of the rally. The vandals broke three windows and ripped up two American flags and the club's AMA safety award banner. They also slashed furniture, smashed the clock, disabled the pop machine and then poured coffee grounds and chili over everything. The biggest loss was damage to Jackpine Gypsy Club records. Dating back to 1936, these records were scattered about and, in some instances, damaged beyond recovery. Interestingly enough, the perpetuators opened the back of the television, removed all of the small tubes except for the picture tube but did not otherwise damage the set.[1] The Gypsies posted a $100 reward for information leading to an arrest, but according to Neil Hultman, no one was ever caught.[2]

Apparently, the five-day format begun in 1965 worked out well because the 1966 rally was organized on a similar basis. Now touted as a "Family Affair" by the *Sturgis Tribune*, the Classic began on Wednesday, August 10 with a day-long Gypsy Tour through the Bear Lodge Mountains to Devils Tower* in Wyoming.[3] Nearly 140 motorcycles participated in the Wednesday Tour, returning to Belle Fourche in the late afternoon where they were treated to refreshments by the "Belle" Chamber of Commerce.[4] Thursday's riders took in the traditional Mt. Rushmore and Southern Hills Tour. Thursday evening's short track races were held on the new track, west of the I-90 freeway on Jackpine Gypsy Property, and newly-installed lights helped these races continue after dark.[5]

Friday began with the Sportsman's hill climb at 9:00am on Pappy Hoel's property near Bear Butte, east of Sturgis. The scrambles races (motocross) were scheduled for Friday afternoon on a new course established on leased land just south of the new short track. The traditional Chamber of Commerce "Feed" was held Friday evening and, for the first time, was open to racers, tour participants, contestants, and the local citizens of Sturgis. The Chamber had apparently figured out the logistics for feeding everyone. Friday ended with a program, the presentation of trophies and awards, and the election of the Queen, but none of the results were reported.[6]

To fill out the events on Saturday, a short tour was scheduled, including a tour of Homestake Mine in Lead and a visit to downtown "Historic Deadwood." Those riders not taking this tour were encouraged to visit the half-mile track in the morning and

---

* Devils Tower, a loccolith like Bear Butte, is a geological phenomenon resulting from the eruption of a hot mass of igneous rock (granite) in prehistoric times. Both of these loccoliths are actually tiny mountains and outlying versions of the Black Hills formation. The central core of the Black Hills, although much larger than either Devils Tower or Bear Butte, is just another version of an igneous rock eruption ringed by limestone hills, which are actually chunks of bedrock that fractured as the hot mass of granite rose to the surface.

Devils Tower in nearby Wyoming. (Author Photo)

watch the racers practice. The AMA-sanctioned races began at noon with time trials, and the heat races started 1:00pm. Finals were held on Sunday.[7]

Dick Mann, now listing Honolulu, Hawaii as his home, was the top purse winner ($537), taking both his heat race and the Expert final on Sunday. Babe De May placed second, and Neil Keen of Pasadena, California (the track's time-trials record holder) was third. On Sunday, Mann won both races with De May and Keen swapping second and third places from Saturday's racing. Ken Bright of Ponca City, Oklahoma and Johnny Isaacs of Cheyenne, Wyoming won the Novice and Amateur finals.[8]

Although no specific effort was made to assess total attendance for the five day event, it was reported to be the largest attendance ever, and the grandstand was filled to overflowing for both Saturday and Sunday's races. The involvement of the Belle Fourche Chamber of Commerce in the Devils Tower Gypsy Tour is also a clear indication of growing support for the rally in nearby communities which also stood to benefit from the annual event.

Dick Mann's National Career: Part One

After winning his first race in Sturgis in 1954, Mann's professional career took off. He turned Expert in 1955 in time to compete in the Daytona 200, where he took a notable 7th place. During the next three years his name became more and more familiar to racing fans, and by 1957, he was ranked in the Top 10 in Grand National Series standings. In the years following 1957, Mann won 24 Grand National Series races: a mile and a

From left to right: Bart Markel (1960 Expert Champion at Sturgis), Sammy Tanner (1962 Expert 3rd Place at Sturgis), and Dick Mann (1958 and 1966 Expert Champion at Sturgis). (Mahony Racing Photos)

short track event, two half-mile races, eight TTs and 12 road races. The mile and short track races were at Chicago, Illinois in 1972 and Hinsdale, Illinois in 1969. Both of the half-miles were won in the 1960s. The first victory was Heidelberg, Pennsylvania at a distance of 15 miles, and Mann's second win at the half-mile (12 miles) was at Reading, Pennsylvania in 1967 — the year after his second championship at Sturgis.[1]

Mann's experiences as a youth, cow trailing in the hills around Richmond, paid off greatly in the TT category. He was able to win a total of eight Grand National TTs, five of which (1959, '64, '67, '69, and '72) were at the difficult track at Peoria, Illinois. The other TT championships included Gardena, California in 1963, and Castle Rock, Washington and Houston, Texas in 1971. Mann's most successful Grand National category, however, was road racing. He began by winning the 100 at Laconia, New Hampshire in 1960 and '62. 1964, in turn, proved to be one of his three best road-racing seasons. Mann earned three victories including Windber, Pennsylvania (50 miles), Indianola, Iowa (175 miles), and Carpentersville, Illinois (150 miles). He repeated this triple in 1965, winning at 120 miles at Wentzville, Missouri; 80 miles at Nelson Ledges, Ohio; and repeated his 1954 150-mile Carpentersville victory. Mann won the coveted Daytona 200 back to back in 1970 and 1971, and finished his career with two hundred-mile races at Kent, Washington and Mt. Pocono, Pennsylvania to complete this third triple in this event.[2]

In all, Mann's career in the Grand National Series ratings spanned a total of 16 years. He was the first rider to ride and win in all five events in this series and was ranked in the top ten in 13 of these 16 years. He was ranked tenth in 1973, eighth in 1958 and '68, sixth in 1957, '69, and '72, fifth in 1960, fourth in 1970 and third in 1959, '61, and '62. In 1964, Mann was ranked second behind Roger Reeman, and in 1965 he missed the top honor again, taking second place behind Bart Markel. He captured the coveted Number One position twice, the first in 1963, beating out George Roeder by one point. He took his second Number One ranking by a comfortable margin of 133 points over Gene Romero in 1971.[3]

Although he was devoted to BSAs, Mann competed in the Daytona 200 a total of 15 times on six different makes of motorcycles. His Daytona experiences began in 1955, when the track was laid out on the beach and road course. He continued to compete on this track until the new-banked concrete course was completed in 1961. He did take second place twice. In 1970, however, Mann won the coveted 200 on a 7th marque, the new CB750 Honda. As this was Honda's first win at an AMA Grand National event, Mann and his victory received considerable additional publicity. Mann returned to BSA for the second Daytona Championship in 1971. He was awarded the AMA's Most Popular Rider Award in that year and continued to place in the top ten for two more years. He retired from the National circuit in 1974, having competed in over 230 AMA nationals and many other AMA-sanctioned races. At the time of his retirement, he was ranked second in the number of Grand National wins.[4]

In 1975, Mann qualified for the US Six-day Trials Team and competed on the Isle of Man competition where he took a bronze medal for his efforts. It must have been exciting for local fans to hear his name called over the public address system at this event. Mann was also awarded the AMA "Dud Perkins" Award in 1995 for his contributions to the sport of motorcycle racing.[5]

August 9-13, 1967

The five days of the 1967 Black Hills Motorcycle Classic closely paralleled the format of the previous year. Touted by Clarence Hoel to be the biggest and best ever, the 1967 rally would include several new attractions, involving traditional as well as new sponsors. Continuing a practice begun in the mid-1950s, the Chamber of Commerce sponsored a carnival starting on Monday and coinciding with the opening days of motorcycling activity. The Saturday night dance at the City Auditorium was resurrected, sponsored by the local Jaycees – a new local rally supporter. And the Sturgis Lion's Club was brave enough to purchase and raffle off a new motorcycle. A final public relations coup was the involvement of the Titans Baseball Team. While the team had competed with the rally for summer publicity since the late 1950s, they were scheduled to man the Grandstand concessions for the Saturday and Sunday AMA-sanctioned half-mile races.[1]

In the interest of improving crowd control, the Gypsies contributed $800 to expand the chain-link fence at the half-mile track area. They were also matching a Sturgis Chamber of Commerce contribution to paint the wooden advertising fence on the back straight-of-way. Hoel, now characterized by the *Tribune* as the "Grandaddy of the Event", reported that all of the town's motel rooms had been reserved by July, and he urged local citizens to consider providing rooms or camping space for the visitors. Rally registration was moved to the City Auditorium, and Harold Lauer, a Gypsy Club member, assumed Pappy Hoel's responsibilities for organizing and supervising the three Gypsy Tours. These tours followed the same pattern from 1966, beginning with a Wednesday Tour which traveled through the Bear Lodge Mountains to Devils Tower and returned through the Northern Hills. The Thursday Gypsy Tour followed the traditional route through the Southern Hills with stops at Sylvan Lake, the Needles Highway, Mt. Rushmore, Custer, Hot Springs, and the State Game Lodge. The third tour was a short Saturday morning ride to Lead-Deadwood with visits to the Homestake gold mine and Deadwood's historic Main Street.[2]

Navigating the scrambles course, 1960s. (Eva Satterlee Collection)

Short-track racing would begin on Thursday evening, and the Hill Climb and Sportsman's Scrambles were scheduled for Friday on the Gypsy property west of the I-90 freeway. Hoel reported that 18 additional acres of leased property had now been purchased and that both the Scrambles and the Hill Climb would be held entirely on Jackpine Gypsy Club property.[3] The Friday night feed and program, now characterized as a banquet, was to be held in the City Auditorium but was changed back to the City Park by race week. Neil Hultman, who was in charge of the overall racing program, reported the track ready for the AMA-sanctioned half-mile races, which were to be held Saturday and Sunday.

One interesting public relations move was scheduled during the second day of racing. Sunday's event was designated as "Mayor's Day", and chief city officials from all over the Black Hills were invited to participate and be honored in the ceremonies.[4] The Wednesday, August 9 edition of the *Sturgis Tribune* included an interview with Jim Tagaris from the Denver AMA office. Tagaris commented that "Sturgis has the only real Gypsy Tour in the United States and this is one of the reasons that makes the Classic one of the greatest attractions in the states." He went on to say that, "the Classic has grown in such popularity that it is thought of in the same terms as Daytona and is known as the 'Motorcycle Indianapolis'."[5]

The *Tribune* also took a new twist in covering the weekend races, focusing on the Classic's economic impact in Sturgis. By their best assessment, the *Tribune* asserted that visitors to the 1967 Classic had pumped over $150,000 into the local economy.[6]

Races

Bill Leibig of Rapid City won Thursday evening's 100cc short track final, and second and third were taken by Harry Taylor of Athina, Oregon and Mike Kaplin of Denver. In the 175cc final, the winner was Roger Richards from St. Paul, MN with second and third going to Jeff Holthuof of LaCrescent, Minnesota and Howard Johnson of Bismark, North Dakota.[7]

The Friday morning Hill Climb results were also reported for the first time in 1967. Paul Montgomery of Pueblo, Colorado took the 100cc climb, reaching a distance of 70 feet. Roger Sandoff of Minneapolis went 75 feet to win the 175cc class, and Jerry Miner of Casper, Wyoming, won the 250cc class at 106 feet. The 500cc class was taken by Bill Fuller of Oklahoma City at 116 feet. In the Open Class (bikes greater than 500cc), Larry Ehrnes, a local from Lead, reached 119 feet. More and more riders from outside the Black Hills area were starting to compete and win in the "Sportsman" events.[8]

On Friday afternoon, the 100cc Sportsman's Scrambles class was won by Daryl Gade of Pine Bluffs, Arkansas. The 250cc and 500cc classes were taken by Steve Collins (address unknown) and Dick Weeks of Greeley, Colorado. The Open Class winner was Orien Heideerink of Sioux Falls.[9]

Sunday's half-mile Expert final ended with a surprise when John Isaacs of Riverside, California passed both Babe De May and Neil Keen in the final lap to win the race. According to Pappy Hoel, "any rider that can pass De May and Keen on a curve is really doing something!"[10]

The 1967 rally, although generally similar in format to the 1966 Classic, did provide new dimensions of community involvement and support. The new group participants, including the Jaycees, the Lion's Club and especially the Titan's Baseball Team, along with the Mayor's Day activities, all provided evidence of continued interest among members of the Sturgis community.

1967 Expert Champion: Johnny Isaacs

Johnny Isaacs was born in Cody, Wyoming in 1948. When he was 14, he talked his mom into buying him a mini-bike, which he rode around town during the summer of 1962. In 1963 he bought a 55cc Yamaguchi that was promptly destroyed when his school counselor ran a stop sign and hit Isaacs. That summer he used the insurance money from the accident and money earned in a cotton candy stand to buy another Yamaguchi.

Following the influence of Bert Smith, the district Yamaha sales representative, Johnny became interested in racing. He journeyed with Smith and won his first race at age 15 in Billings, Montana — unbeknownst to his mom. Later in the summer he went to Sturgis with Smith and entered his first "big race". When Smith was promoted to national sales manager for Yamaha and moved to California, Isaacs moved with him, took a part-time job with Yamaha and applied for a Novice license. That year he was able to win number 1 as the Novice of the Year.

In 1966, Isaacs become friends with Kenny Johnson and Norm McDonald, who owned several BSA dealerships and manufactured the famous KN Air Filters. They sponsored him as a racer on a BSA Goldstar and took him to Sturgis, where he won the Amateur Final. In 1967 he

Johnny Isaacs, 1967 Expert Champion at Sturgis. (Johnny Isaacs Collection)

returned as an Expert. On the night before the Sunday final, a racing friend from California took him out to walk the track. They both determined that the track watering had dampened the dirt just outside of the groove, which could mean more speed in the corners. The water in the groove had either run off or dried up, so Isaacs resolved to run just outside of the groove for traction in the turns. He returned to his bike and cut notches in his tires for greater gripping power.

After a bad start, Isaacs realized that he was passing everyone and that he had elected a good strategy. After passing Neil Keen in second place, he was able to pass Babe DeMay and win the race. He was a pretty excited 19 year-old to beat out these two nationally-ranked racers.

In 1968, Isaacs entered the Army and could not return to Sturgis for racing. In 1971, he moved to Oklahoma to work for KN Motorcycles.

Isaacs started the Vintage Dirt Track Racers Association in 1988 and was active in this organization until 1998. At present, he owns a motorcycle shop that caters to British bikes. At 54, Johnny Isaacs still competes in Vintage and modern dirt track races.

Johnny Isaacs' legacy at Sturgis spanned five years, starting at age 15. In 1963 and 64 he raced as a Sportsman, in 1965 as a Novice, in 1966 as an Amateur, and took the Feature Race in 1967 at age 19 as a White Plate Expert. He still has a soft spot in his heart for the rally and has returned several times in the 1990s to serve as Race Referee. He has not, however, visited the rally in recent years, commenting that it has become entirely too big. He and his wife generally come a week early instead, picking up new patches and T-shirts and visiting their old friends in the Jackpine Gypsies.

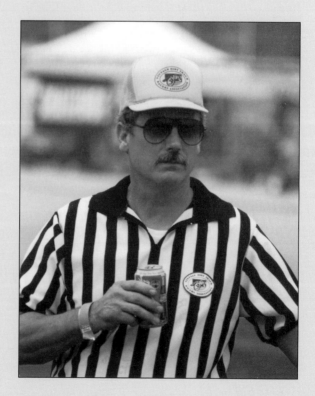

Johnny Isaacs, AMA Referee. (Johnny Isaacs Collection)

August 7-11, 1968

Even before the 1968 Classic was underway, it was clear to rally organizers that they would be busy. A week prior to the opening of the 1968 Classic, Chamber President Wayne Baker made a plea for an additional 20 community volunteers to assist with rally events. Baker also needed someone to drive to Hayes Corner, 140 miles east of Sturgis, to repair the sign on Highway 34, which had blown down. Since this stretch across western South Dakota provided a 70-mile shortcut to riders arriving through Minnesota and Wisconsin, Baker was concerned that new riders might miss the junction and end up on the longer route via Rapid City. He also applauded local residents Gunner Early and Hank Aaberg for erecting a new sign just south of Phil Town that welcomed riders arriving via Interstate 90.[1]

The Chamber's need for more help was clearly confirmed on the following Monday (August 5) when large groups of motorcyclists started arriving, two days prior to Wednesday's official opening of the rally. To get a handle on the ever-elusive "count", the Black Hills Motorcycle Classic Board opened for registration at the City Hall headquarters on Tuesday and displayed rally trophies and awards in the windows of the *Tribune* and The Joint, a local rider hangout, hoping to entice some of these early arrivals to sign the registration book.[2]

Sturgis was now being officially characterized in the *Sturgis Tribune* as "Cycle City." The typical schedule of events was slated, beginning with the Northern Hills/Devils Tower Tour on Wednesday, the Southern Hills Tour on Thursday, and a short optional tour scheduled for Lead-Deadwood and Spearfish Canyon, designed for riders not wanting to participate in the all-day ride. Thursday evening Sportsman Short Track races were followed up with a Friday morning Hill Climb and an afternoon Scrambles race. On Friday evening, the traditional feed and program was held in the City Park.[3]

The Tribune reported only two program winners from Friday night. The award for shortest marriage went to Mr. and Mrs. Mickey Hennessey of Stillwater, Minnesota, who had been married the previous Saturday and were attending the Classic for their honeymoon. The other award went to the Tri-State Travelers of Sioux Falls, who captured their seventh prize (in eight visits) as the best-dressed motorcycle club. Selecting the rally queen was also changed slightly in 1968. Rather than involve the traditional panel of judges, applause determined the winner of "Miss Congeniality", which went to Mrs. Jessie Griffin of Minnetonka Beach, Minnesota.[4]

Neil Keen rounds the corner at the Sturgis half mile, 1968. (Mahony Racing Photos)

The 1968 Classic also turned to an official rally slogan, "True Western Friendship," which had been used informally among riders since the mid-1960s. The new slogan clearly reflected the opinion of many motorcyclists who were having a good time in a community that treated them with respect.

Races

Saturday's racing program was to include the regular half-mile event in the afternoon and the evening short track races, limited only to professional riders. As it turned out, rain cancelled the afternoon half-mile races, but heat races were held on Saturday evening at the short track. Neil Keen of Decatur, Illinois won the Expert class race while second place went to Darrel Dovel of Georgia and third to Billy May of Coeur d'Alene, Idaho. Keen also won the half-mile final on Sunday. No stranger to the Black Hills Motorcycle Classic, Keen had won the Expert half-mile in 1962, set the track record in time trials in 1963, won the professional short track final in 1965, and placed second and third in the Expert half-mile in both 1966 and 1967 respectively. Riding a BSA in the half-mile, Keen liked to come from behind in the last lap and surprise the leader, which he did in 1968, passing Pat Gosch of Omaha on the last turn.[5]

The 1968 Classic saw the largest number of competitors to date with 112 riders registered for racing. They included 25 at the Expert Level, 24 each in the Novice and Amateur classes, and 49 Sportsmen. As a result, fans and racers alike were disappointed by the Saturday rainout. Sunday's Grandstand Crowd of more 3000 spectators, however, established a new one-day attendance record.[6]

Dick Mann's National Career: Part Two

Dick Mann's professional motorcycling career was not limited to racing. The contributions he made to the sport of motorcycle racing in general are unmatched by any other rider in his generation.

In 1956 in the interest of improving the sport, a group called the Motorcycle Riders Incorporated (MRI) was organized. Prior to this time, racers were at the mercy of owners, promoters and the AMA Competition Committee. MRI provided a vehicle for speaking out and against inadequate safety precautions and unfair treatment of those taking the greatest risk. Mann's fellow riders elected him as one of the MRI rider representatives. His duties were to act in the best interest of the riders, and in 1958 when a promoter refused to re-surface a dangerous track and further to arbitrarily reduce the amounts promised for the purse, Mann and another rider, Donnie Smith, organized a boycott. The AMA, siding with the promoter suspended their licenses. At this point Mann realized that earning recognition for his fellow riders would necessitate a quieter and more deliberate approach.[1]

An interesting story related to the development of such an approach occurred a bit later. Mann, Neil Keen, and Albert Gunter decided to dress up in suits and ties and appear before the AMA Competition Committee to voice concerns. When Keen and Gunter started laughing at Mann in this get-up he asked what was going on. It seems that the only T-shirts Mann owned had large BSA logo's on the front and these logos were visible through his white shirt. It was Mann's turn to laugh when he looked at the two others and said "...you look just the same!" The riders all had to turn their T-shirts inside out to avoid the obvious. The three riders were able to establish the first recorded rider/management dialogue that day, but later, after the three representatives had departed, the AMA Committee voted 26 to 1 to ban Mann's G50 Matchless racing bike.[2]

As time went on, Mann continued to work the system to improve conditions for the racers. In time he helped to overcome the inconsistencies and confusion and to generally improve the sport. Areas that were adjusted included unified training for race officials, improving the rules for safety and providing adequate warning to the riders regarding equipment prohibitions. One of the best things coming out of these deliberations had to do with the Amateur riders. These young and inexperienced riders, using large 750cc motorcycles were having entirely too many accidents. The MRI leadership was able to convince the AMA to limit Amateur Racers to 250cc machines.[3]

Mann continued to work tirelessly to improve conditions during his career and the organizational and leadership skills he developed in the process served him well in retirement, when Mann became heavily involved in the early years of the American Historic Racing Motorcycle Association (AHRMA). He contributed by serving on the rules committee prior to the establishment of the AHRMA and then was appointed to the Board of Trustees, serving in this capacity for over 10 years.[4]

To The Reader:

Dick Mann's stellar career as motorcycle racer, frame tuner and contributor to the integrity of, and rules of safety for, the sport of professional motorcycle racing have been well documented in two very well written biographies. The first, Motorcycle Ace: The Dick Mann Story, written by Mann and co-authored by motorcycle writer Joe Scalzo was published in 1971, near the end of Mann's active career as a racer. This book is out-of-print, but is probably available at your local library or via inter-library loan. The second biography, Mann of His Time, by Ed Youngblood is currently available and well worth purchasing. It should be available in your local bookstore or from Amazon.com.

August 6-10, 1969

The Sturgis Titans Baseball team was back in a pennant race in 1969, and as a result, *Tribune* coverage of the Black Hills Motorcycle Classic was limited to a full page article on opening day, August 6, and post-rally race results on August 13. A new twist, a half-mile, AMA-sanctioned sixth day of racing, was scheduled for Tuesday, August 12 at the Black Hills Speedway in Rapid City — two days after the Sunday close of motorcycling activities at Sturgis. It was becoming clear that the popularity of the Classic, along with larger and larger crowds in the Black Hills, had substantial economic benefits for the entire region.

The five-day program in Sturgis was similar to previous years with the Northern Hills Gypsy Tour to Devils Tower on Wednesday and a new Sportsmen Short track Race in the evening. Thursday's events included the traditional Southern Hills tour and the regular Thursday night Sportsman's short-track event. Friday consisted of a morning Hill Climb and an afternoon Scrambles Race. The traditional Friday night "Feed and Awards" program was again held in the City Park. On Saturday morning, a short tour through Lead and Deadwood and back to Sturgis via the breath-taking Spearfish canyon was scheduled for those visitors not wanting to watch practice at the half-mile track. The professional half-mile races, starting at noon at the fairgrounds, were followed by a 6:30 series of short-track races limited to professional riders. Sunday afternoon included the half-mile championship, and visitors and racers were encouraged to stay over until Tuesday for the AMA-sanctioned races in Rapid City.[1]

Growing concern about the rowdy behavior of some riders, along with ever-increasing attendance, was again an issue in planning for the 1968 Classic. Law enforcement officials, including Sheriff John Egger and Chief of Police Eldon Van Dyke, supported by Mayor Joe Egger and State's Attorney William Coacher, were able to organize a law enforcement team that included Meade County Deputies, Sturgis Policemen, auxiliary police volunteers from the Black Hills Four-Wheelers Club and Military Air Police (APs) from Ellsworth Air Force Base in Rapid City. The Sheriff also deputized 15 volunteers to help keep order in the two city parks open to camping.[2]

As a sign of the times, Sheriff Eggers referred to those few undesirables who appeared in Sturgis the previous year as "Hippie-Type Cyclists".* A group of roughly 20 "Hippie-Types" were riding machines near Deadwood that were in clear violation of South Dakota State Motor Vehicle Code and not wearing legal helmets. Met by a

---

* It would be interesting to hear what motorcycle gang members would say if they had known that they were being characterized as hippies.

1969 Rally Poster. The Sturgis Tribune, August 1969.

contingent of South Dakota State Troopers, Lawrence County Sheriff's Deputies and Meade County (Sturgis) personnel, the motorcyclists were asked to leave the state. They apparently complied but were later arrested in Nebraska.[3]

Peace was ultimately maintained during the five-day event, and Mayor Joe Egger, in describing the record number of motorcyclists attending the rally, stated at the August 11 city council meeting that, "we experienced absolutely no trouble with them, principally because our people were well-prepared to deal with any trouble makers." The mayor went on to praise the conduct of the large numbers of visitors and noted that many of the riders expressed their appreciation of the law and order atmosphere that prevailed during the week's events. He also commended the local law enforcement participants, the volunteers, and asked the council for permission to draft a letter of thanks to the Commander of Ellsworth Air Force Base in Rapid City for the support from the Air Police contingent.[4]

These early efforts to plan and organize, in anticipation of the influx of thousands and thousands of riders that were to come in the 1970s and later, was a very positive move. If trouble had erupted into riot-like behavior in 1968-69, it probably would have seriously affected future attendance at the Classic. Most riders would probably hesitate to travel thousands of miles to attend a riot or try to enjoy themselves in a threatening environment. Without such planning and vigilance, the rally could have easily succumbed to a natural death due to non-participation.

Competition

The results of the Friday morning hill climb event were posted in "feet covered" for the two smaller displacement categories (100cc and 175cc) and in "time elapsed" for the three larger classes. (Apparently most of the cycles with larger engines were making it all the way to the top of the hill.) The 100 and 175cc classes were won by Al Davis of Pueblo, Colorado and Jack Oler of Casper, Wyoming. Davis reached 111.5 feet on his 100cc Hodaka, and Oler registered 111.0 feet on his 175cc Yamaha. Dan Krebs of Rapid City took the 250cc class on a Ducati with a time of 7.5 seconds. The 500cc and open class climbs were won by Clint Ellis of Boulder, Colorado and Bob Donohue from Wisconsin Rapids, Wisconsin. Ellis, riding a Triumph, posted a time of 5.1 seconds and Donohue pushed his Indian to the top in 4.7 seconds.[5]

There were five classes in the Friday afternoon Scrambles. The 100 and 125cc classes were won by Bill Liebig of Rapid City using a Bridgestone, and Gene Scherschlight riding a Kawasaki. The 175cc class and 250cc races were won by Randy Leutjens on a Honda and Jerry Cheney on a Yamaha. Both riders were from Sioux

Neil Keen sits out the short track final after losing his chain, 1969. (Mahony Racing Photos)

Falls, South Dakota. Roger Richerts of Wayzata, Minnesota won the 500cc class on a Maico. No short track results were reported.[6]

The AMA half-mile racers were hampered by hot dry winds on Saturday, and times were slow. On Sunday, the weather was calm and cooler and a record crowd of spectators experienced an exciting afternoon of racing.

Mike Van Bibber of Albuquerque, New Mexico took the Amateur class final on Sunday on a Honda. Second and third place went to Bob Haynes of Redwood City, California and Dan Deubler of Sioux Falls, a charter member of the White Plate Flat Trackers Association. Haynes rode a Harley Davidson and Deubler's third was taken on a Triumph.[7] Neil Keen of Decatur, Illinois and his trusty BSA took the Expert final on Sunday. Second and third places were won by Grant Brown of National City, California on a Triumph and Jack Forrester of La Fayette, Illinois, riding a Harley Davidson.[8]

With careful attention to the importance of law enforcement and crowd control, the 1969 Black Hills Motor Class marked yet another significant milestone in the growth of the rally. The development of interagency cooperation and planning effectively established an organized and successful deterrent format that was to become key in the success and continued growth of the rally through the 1970s and 1980s.

Jack Hoel

The only son of Clarence and Pearl Hoel, Jack Hoel is an ideal example of a young rider who experienced, firsthand, the evolution of American motorcycle racing's acceptance of Japanese marques (like Honda, Yamaha, and Kawasaki) in competition with the beloved Harleys and Indians. He also personifies the changes in dirt-track racing that occurred after the demise of Indian motorcycles. As a young man, growing up in a legendary motorcycling family, he began riding at an early age. In this environment and as a result of love for his parents as they agonized through the difficult years of the 1950s*, Jack discovered that he wanted to help out.

His first adult dream was to complete a degree in mechanical engineering and work in the world of motorcycle design. After completing two years of college at the South Dakota School of Mines and Technology, Jack succumbed to calculus, dropped out of school and joined the Army. While stationed in Germany, he discovered the immense amount of motorcycle activity in Europe and became involved in racing venues — many of them new to him and unpracticed in the U.S. Through Pappy's efforts, Jack acquired a Matchless G80CS and a Royal Enfield Indian 500cc single, and he began racing in the 500cc class circuit. Unfortunately, Jack wasn't too successful, losing many races to the Maico factory team in moto-cross.[1]

The Grass Track races, however, provided him with a new challenge. Generally held in German or French soccer stadiums, these races lasted the entire day. By 1957, Jack Hoel was the ADAC (the AMA's European equivalent) Grass Track Champion for Germany.[2]

Returning to Sturgis in 1959, Jack was soon exposed to the Yamaha bikes at his father's dealership. While these early Yamahas were little 50cc units, he was very impressed with their maneuverability and stamina. After riding the new Yamaha twins in the early 1960s, Jack approached the district sales manager for Yamaha about a job. In a new position as sales manager for Yamaha, Jack visited the Yamaha Headquarters in California and became more intimately involved with the company. Because of the Hoel name, his experience in the Sturgis races, his friendship with a myriad of riders, and his mechanical ability, Jack was immediately asked to visit over 100 upper-midwest Yamaha Dealers as a Regional Sales Manager. From this job, he became the Assistant Service Manager for Yamaha in the U.S. and moved to California.[3]

After about six months into this new job, Jack began collecting data for Yamaha's newly formed Technical Research Department. He would become an instrumental player in the development of newer and bigger Yamahas for moto-cross competition and dirt-track racing. Faithful to his father's passion for "hopping up" bikes for racing, Jack Hoel in-

Jack Hoel receives a congratulatory handshake and wreath after being named the German ADAC Grass Track Champion. (Pearl Hoel Collection)

sisted upon the inclusion of a GYT-KIT (Genuine Yamaha Tuning Kit) for those customers who might want to race.[4]

From that time forward, Jack Hoel became more and more intimately involved as a "Test Pilot" for nearly every new Yamaha prototype, traveling back and forth between his home in California and the Yamaha factories in Japan. He was deeply involved in documenting strengths and weaknesses in engine development, frame-related maneuverability and acceleration. Since early Yamahas were all 2-stroke machines, Jack encouraged the company to design a 4-stroke twin for the American touring market and larger displacement competitions. The final result was Yamaha's first 4-stroke motorcycle: the XS-1 650cc Roadster.[5]

Introduced in the American market in 1969, the XS-1 had great appeal and sold well. At first glance, the motorcycle, more than any of the early Japanese models, resembled a classic image of many of the British 650's available at the time. In the early 1980s this motorcycle became the XS 650 Heritage Special and total sales in the U.S. exceeded the six-figure mark by 1983.[6]

The young man from Sturgis, South Dakota had incidentally realized his dream of designing better motorcycles. He later became involved in the Team Yamaha program as a racing consultant, traveling to all of the major races where Yamaha was competing. In this capacity, he assisted the racers, mechanics, and pit crews and reported back to the Yamaha management team.[7]

Too young to be thoroughly committed to the older traditions of Harley Davidson, Indian and "American only," Jack Hoel personifies the motorcycle enthusiast of his generation and experienced, first-hand, the changes that led to the world of American motorcycling today.

August 5-9, 1970

Branded as the 30th annual event, the 1970 Black Hills Motor Classic was to again break records for attendance and interest.* Continued growth in participation was evidenced by both the limited amount of camping space available and the impressive number of riders registered for and participating in the tours and other events. One day prior to the official opening, the *Sturgis Tribune* reported that the city campgrounds were filled to capacity. On Wednesday, August 5, over 300 motorcycles participated in the Northern Tour, traveling to Spearfish in South Dakota and to Beulah, Sundance, Devils Tower, and Hulett, Wyoming before re-entering South Dakota at Belle Fourche for the return to Sturgis.[1] The traditional Friday night "Feed" served over 2,600 persons, and rally officials estimated that more than 3,000 motorcycles attended the five-day event.[2]

The rally format again duplicated previous years with the Wednesday Northern Hills Tour and Sportsman's short-track races, a Southern Hills Tour on Thursday with evening professional short-track heat races, a Friday Hill Climb and Scrambles Race (now characterized as motocross) and the evening "Feed and Awards" program. Black Hills trail rides were available to those riders not interested in attending the Thursday evening Short Track event. The Saturday and Sunday racing format included AMA sanctioned half-mile races during the day and the Professional short-track finals Saturday evening.[3]

On Monday, August 3, a special meeting was held to plan for law enforcement policies and procedures in anticipation of the five-day classic. Persons involved in planning did "not anticipate any trouble as most of the cyclists attracted to the Classic are good citizens and reputable people."[4] States Attorney William Coacher and Meade County Sheriff John Egger went on to indicate that, based on the limited problems and successful vigilance experienced in 1968 and 1969, preparations were still necessary to handle any potential troublemakers. A representative from the South Dakota Attorney General's office was present to clarify apprehension and arrest policies and provide liaison for the various law enforcement entities involved. It was also determined that a large number of volunteers would be deputized to assist and enhance the number of regular officers.[5] Such planning, which had begun in 1969, had proven

---

* As part of gathering historical information concerning the evolution of the "Black Hills Motor Classic," it is interesting to note the difficulties in establishing an actual sequence in numbering. While the 1970 Classic was identified as the 30th annual event, careful analysis of the actual sequence reveals that 1970 should actually be characterized as the 29th annual event, but only if a person starts with the first official AMA-sponsored races in 1938. If a person counts from 1937 (the first unofficial meet organized by Hoel and the Jackpine Gypsies), then 1970 is clearly the 30th Annual Black Hills Motor Classic

effective in preventing trouble and assuring the safety of the "good" motorcycling visitors. Sheriff Egger and Meade County State's Attorney Coacher summarized the planning session, indicating that everyone just wanted the visitors to "have fun" during their stay in Sturgis.

Having delegated his responsibility in leading the tours to veteran Gypsy Club members, Pappy Hoel gave a welcoming speech at the beginning of both the Wednesday and Thursday tours. And with the large number of tour participants involved by this time, Pearl Hoel had stopped providing the noon lunches but still served as hostess to the dozens of riders who camped in the big circus tent pitched behind the Hoel's motorcycle shop. Weather on Wednesday and Thursday was a bit dicey, with scattered thundershowers, but everything cleared up on Friday for three sunny days of racing.[6]

During the Friday night program, the longest distance male and female trophies were awarded to Alec Bossmerry from Florida and Katherine Ralph from Covina, California. The longest distance Motor Maid trophy was given to Vivian Galley from Michigan. Best-dressed rider awards went to Deanna Whipple of Rochester, Minnesota and Dillard Akros of Paso Robles, California. The Black Toppers from Denver won the Best Dressed Club Award. There was no information regarding the election of a "Classic Queen."[7]

The oldest rider in attendance in 1970 was Julius Kegal from Freeport, Illinois. Kegal, age 78, had recently been featured in a German newspaper as being the oldest active motorcycle rider in the United States. He rode a 1970 BMW motorcycle, incorrectly characterized by the *Tribune* as made by the "Berlin Motor Works."[*] According to Kegal, he had ridden his first cycle in 1910, and 1970 marked his 26th trip to the Classic. On his first visit in 1941, Kegal saw a sign south of town stating, "The 3,600 Citizens of Sturgis Welcome You." He concluded that nothing had changed and he still felt very welcome whenever he visited the Classic![8]

Races

Thursday evening's Sportsman Short Track Races included four classes: 100cc, 125cc, 175cc, and 250cc. The winners included Steve Nichols of Riverside, California in both the 100cc and 125cc classes; Larry Phillippe of Cedar Rapids, Iowa at 175cc, and Garry Scott of Riverside, California at 250cc. To Pappy Hoel's delight, three of the

---

*As a long-time BMW rider, the author often had a bit of fun during the 1970s and early 1980s responding to questions about the BMW marque. In those days, when BMW bikes were uncommon in the Upper Midwest, the author and riding companions would often tell people that BMW stood for "Big Montgomery Ward".

four classes were won on Yamahas. Chuck Palmgren of Freehold, New Jersey won the Professional short-track final, followed by Larry Mace and Mike Mathews. Palmgren also placed 4th in the Saturday half-mile final.[9] Winners of the Hill Climb and Motorcross were not reported.

The Saturday Expert final was taken by Dick Mann of Richmond, California on a BSA. Second and third place were won by Keith Johnson of Seattle, Washington on a Norton and Neil Keen of St. Louis, Missouri on a Yamaha. Sunday's Expert final winner was Neil Keen, who also took the largest purse ($615). Second place and the second highest money ($543) was awarded to Dick Mann on his trusty BSA. Third and fourth place went to Squire Tomasie of Tacoma, Washington riding a Triumph, and Seattle's Keith Johnson riding a Norton.[10] It is interesting to note that there were so many races on Sunday that the half-mile "Sportsman" events continued into Sunday evening.

Of further interest in 1970 was the major shift to Japanese motorcycles – a total of 45 Japanese machines spread among the racing field. With regard to separate marques, Yamaha led the way with 37 racers, followed by Bultaco (18), BSA (15) and Triumph (13). There were six Suzukis, three Harley Davidsons, two Kawasaki's, one Norton and one Husquevarna.[11]

Chapter Nine:
Expanding Numbers and Problems

T he early 1970s brought tremendous growth in rally attendance, due in large part to continued recognition of the Classic in national motorcycle publications. A five-minute special about Sturgis and the Gypsy Tour, which aired on CBS television and was hosted by Roger Mudd, only added more fuel to the proverbial attendance fire.

Merchants and business people throughout the region also began to recognize the dramatic economic impact of the rally on Sturgis and the Northern Black Hills. At an estimated $30 per person per day spending rate, merchants quickly determined that each one thousand visitors could spend over $100,000 in a three to four day period.

One particular rally milestone in 1971 was the sale of Hoel's Motorcycle Shop. After 33 years in the business, Clarence Hoel sold out to a Rapid City businessman. In 1972, the rally was extended to six days (running Tuesday through Sunday), and visiting riders actually began arriving in Sturgis on Friday, three days prior to the official opening. The City Park camping spaces were sold out by late Monday afternoon.

By 1973, the Classic Committee had again negotiated an AMA Regional Championship sanction for the half-mile event. This Pacific Coast Regional Championship race encompassed all states west of the Mississippi River. Although not as significant as a "National," it proved key in attracting the best riders from the West Coast, including many riders from California, a hotbed of dirt track racing. In addition, growth in Gypsy Tour participation became nearly unmanageable. The train of riders on both the Southern and Northern tours extended almost eight miles in length.

In 1974, after 34 years of "separation," the two "sponsors" of the rally (the Black Hills Motor Classic Committee and the Jackpine Gypsies) finally established a joint committee comprising representatives of both groups. As a means of shortening the lengthy train of bikes, the 1974 Gypsy tours were broken into two days of touring with 12 different groups.

The rally was extended to its present seven-day format in 1975, and Youth Night, an event for 9 to 11 year-old racers was introduced. Clearly signaling the tremendous growth of the rally, nearly 5,000 persons participated in the 1975 free "Feed" on Friday evening.

August 11-15, 1971

In an address to the Sturgis Rotary Club on July 28, Clarence Hoel commented that 33 years had passed since the first rally in 1938 and that it might be appropriate to trace the rally's history and clear up confusion about rally sponsors and committee responsibilities.[1]

According to Hoel, the 1938 rally had begun because of the interest of several downtown businessmen who raised a racing purse of $500. In cooperation with the Jackpine Gypsies Motorcycle Club, this group of businessmen formed a loose organization that worked together to oversee the 1938, 1939 and 1940 rallies. In December 1940, the businessmen formed the Black Hills Motor Classic (BHMC) and essentially took over administration of the event. The BHMC was to have an original term of incorporation of 25 years and life memberships were sold for $2.00 per person. Membership provided shareholders with a share certificate and the privilege of working, free of charge, on rally events. There were no dividends as all money raised was returned to the BHMC treasury to fund the ensuing year's expenses.

Committees from the membership were assigned separate tasks to prepare for each year's rally. Initially, only business owners could belong to the BHMC, which is why Hoel, as a motorcycle dealer, was eligible for membership. (As time progressed, so many Jackpine Gypsies were involved in the BHMC committee work that many of them were allowed to join as well.)[2] While some Gypsy members belonged to the BHMC and worked separately on BHMC committees, the BHMC committee was legally in charge of the rally and half-mile races.

With regard to the 1971 Classic, Hoel informed the Rotary members that BHMC's projected pre-rally expenses would total $6,000 and was broken down as follows:

Prizes for the Racers	$3000
Expenses for the Race Officials	$1100
Expenses for the Friday Night Feed	$800
Track Preparation	$700
Contingencies	$400

Hoel then justified the expenses by stressing the economic impact Sturgis could anticipate with 2,000 projected visitors. If each visitor spent about $150 over the five days of the rally, the total economic impact on Sturgis and the surrounding area could be as much as $300,000.

He then explained that the Gypsies were independently responsible for the Gypsy Tours, the short-track races, the hill climb, and the scrambles or moto-cross races. Money invested and earned in these events was pumped back into the facilities or shared with community groups like the volunteer fire department, the hospital, the high school band and scouting troops.[3]

A week prior to the opening of the rally, the local city fathers expressed concern about making the visiting riders feel welcome. Grass in the City Park had dried up from lack of rain, and as a result, they decided that the city should rent a portable pump to take water from Bear Butte Creek, flooding the park to "spruce up the area before the cyclists arrive next week."[4]

By the first day of the Classic on Wednesday, August 11, the *Sturgis Tribune* reported over 500 persons on 274 motorcycles had departed Sturgis for the Northern Tour to Devils Tower, Wyoming. An equal or larger number had remained in town to "hang out" until the 6:30pm Short Track Races began.[5]

CBS News was on hand to tape the Thursday tour to the Southern Black Hills for broadcast on Sunday night in a nationally-televised program hosted by Roger Mudd. Gunner Early, proprietor of Gunner's Lounge on Main Street and President of the Jackpine Gypsies, was ecstatic after seeing the program on Sunday evening — the final day of the rally. He characterized the five-minute video segment as a "first" for Sturgis. The cameraman had taped the 457 persons on 377 motorcycles leaving town on the Southern Hills Gypsy Tour and then followed them, filming via helicopter.[6]

At the Friday night "Feed" and program, Early presented Neil Hultmann and Bruce Walker with recognition awards for their dedicated service to the Classic.[7] A young couple from Anchorage, Alaska, took the prize for longest distance ridden (Larry Ungerecht) and longest passenger (Kathy Ungerecht). The Ungerechts were on their honeymoon and had traveled nearly 8,000 miles from Anchorage through Mexico and the American Southwest before arriving in Sturgis. According to Kathy Ungerecht, the only fearful experience she had was in Arizona when a pick-up truck full of cowboys pulled along side their Harley Davidson 74. Both of the Ungerechts were wondering what to expect until one of the cowboys popped a can of cold beer and handed it to Kathy. The couple planned to log another 4,000 miles before returning to Anchorage.[8]

Other awards included International distance awards to Ed Fennell of Toronto, Ontario and Evelyn Noble of Edmonton, Alberta. The Motor Maid distance award went to Illa Settle of Zanesville, Ohio. Best Dressed Male and Female Riders were

Lowell James of Vallejo, California and Joan Writhe of Denver, Colorado. The Westminster California Motorcycle Club took the Best Dressed Club Trophy.[9]

Racing

The Hill Climb, held on Friday, had been expanded to seven classes. The winners included:

Size	Winner	Hometown	Cycle
100cc	Ron Anton	Minneapolis, MN	Motobeta
125cc	Dan Bernph	Omaha, NE	Bultaco
175cc	Robert Martis	Humboldt, IA	Bultaco
250cc	Dave Dahl	Custer, SD	Yamaha
350cc	Lawrence Ehner	Lead, SD	Harley Davidson
500cc	Charles Henry	Breckinridge, MN	Honda
Open	Harold Odegaard	Harwood, ND	Custom[10]

In the Scrambles event, now characterized as Moto-Cross, the winners were:

Size	Winner	Hometown	Cycle
100cc	Brian Mundle	Ft. Dodge, IA	Kawaski
125cc	Mike Myers	Riverside, CA	Yamaha
175cc	Dennis Wolfe	Scranton, IA	Ossa
250cc	Jim Pomeroy	Yakima, WA	Bultaco
350cc	Larry Schultz	Ft. Dodge, IA	Maico[11]

Because Jim Pomeroy would become the first American to win a Grand Prix Motocross Race in Europe, his 1971 win in Sturgis added yet another level of excitement and prestige to the 1971 Classic. Prior to 1971, only nationally-rated dirt track racers had participated at Sturgis.

In the professional short-track races, the winner was Charles Seale of Lantana, Florida riding a Bultaco motorcycle. Delbert "Chubby" Armor of Denver placed second followed by Michael Caves of Galesburg, Illinois; both riders were mounted on Yamahas. In the consolation race short-track event, first and second place were taken by Daniel Blacco of Portola, California and Richard Waller of Bothell, Washington.

Charles Seale was the big money rider and winner in Sunday's Expert Pacific Coast Regional Half Mile Championship. Seale also won heat races on both days as well as the Saturday afternoon half-mile final and the evening short track. Second and third place in the championship race went to Darrel Dovel of Daravelle, Georgia and Lewis "Sonny" Burres of Portland, Oregon. Seale rode a BSA, while Dovel and Burres both rode Triumphs. Fourth place went to Larry Palmgren of Freehold, New Jersey, on a BSA. Dovel and Palmgren were both elected to the White Plate Flat Trackers Association in the mid-1980's. Other half-mile winners included Amateur Michael Collins of Albuquerque, New Mexico and Novice Steven Nichols. Collins rode a BSA and Nichols a Yamaha.[13]

According to Sturgis Police Chief Ted Dickson, the potential for serious problems in 1971 had been averted through the assistance of the State Troopers, the Sheriff's Office and special policemen hired and used during the peak hours of activity. In Dickson's opinion, these special officers developed a genuine rapport with the visitors. The only major problem during the week was the theft of three motorcycles, two in Sturgis and one in Lawrence County. A fourth cycle theft was reported by the Pennington County Sheriff's Office which reported finding the faring and fenders of a motorcycle near Mystic. They assumed that the engine and the frame were taken and the rest of the bike left in the forest.

By Saturday, the attendance had reached more than 3,000 machines, far exceeding Pappy Hoel's prediction to the Rotary Club of 2,000 riders. At $150 per rider, the seven-day economic impact of the Black Hills Motor Classic was quickly approaching half a million dollars. With an ever-increasing number of visitors and the national publicity from the CBS television coverage, 1972 was sure to be an even bigger experience.

1971 Expert Champion: Charles Seale

Born on November 5, 1943 in Montego Bay, Jamaica, Charles Seale grew up in Florida after his parents moved when he was three years old. At age 14 he got his first motorcycle — a Triumph Terrier. He later acquired a Parilla Grand sport and became involved in road racing. In 1959, when he was 16, Seale modified the Parilla and began short-track racing at Dade City, Florida. Later in 1962 he toured the Midwest and competed as a Novice. After competing in more than 15 races on a Harley Davidson Sprint bike, Seale was approached by the Harley Davidson factory representative who offered support. Seale returned to Florida and closed his motorcycle shop in preparation for the 1963 season.

He moved to the Midwest and raced for Harley Davidson as an Amateur, soon moving to Expert and winning races. In 1969 he began racing on BSAs and by 1970 was awarded white plate #47, finishing high in overall point standings for Experts. In 1971, the year he was Pacific Coast Regional Champion at Sturgis, he earned recognition as the highest point Expert overall. It's important to note that this recognition was for all AMA-sanctioned races and not merely the Grand National Series, which only recognized points earned in National events.[1]

At Sturgis in 1971, Seale was described as the "Big Money Winner" because he won both of his heat races, the feature Expert race on Saturday, the Short track on Saturday night, and the Pacific Coast Regional Championship on Sunday. It was only his third year as a professional.[2]

In 1972, Seale took fourth place in the final at Sturgis and ended up in second place in points overall in the AMA Expert division. Seale did not

Charlie Seale, 1971 Expert Champion at Sturgis. (Seale Collection)

often compete in the Grand National Series, preferring to enter most of the other AMA sanctioned races. During his career he placed 15 times in the top ten in total points and was in the top five a total of six times. He won many state and regional championships, competing in over 250 feature races during his career. He described Ascot in Gardena, California as the toughest track to win. [3]

Seale enjoyed his trips to Sturgis and described the weekend as being really fun, due in large part to the community's hospitality, which "was second to none." As for racing at Sturgis, Seale said it, "was not an easy place to win. It was always dry and slippery, requiring a good start and some finesse sliding with the motorcycle straight vertical to maximize traction." Before his win in 1971, Seale found an old racing horseshoe in the infield. He took this to be a good omen and went on to win most of the state and county fair circuit races after his win at Sturgis.[4]

One of Seale's more exciting racing experiences was on the 1971 county fair circuit. Sonny Burres, Seale's top competition, kept pinching Seals into the wall. One time, Seales leaned over, tapped Burres' shoulder to make room, and startled Burres, who cut back on his throttle, letting Seale win by a bike length. Several spectators approached him after the race and asked if he had turned off the other rider's throttle.[5]

Seales retired from AMA racing in 1975 but did well in the Canadian Circuit in 1976, ending up in third place overall. He came out of retirement in 1979, competing in match races for a promoter in Australia. It would be his last year in competition and his 17th year as a professional racer.

After ending his racing career, Seale began to pursue a career in business. He presently owns and operates *Camera Cars of Florida* and is still actively involved with motorcycles. In his business, Seale uses motorcycle sidecar rigs as camera platforms for television and movie production. He most recently worked under contract to Universal Studios, busily involved in the filming of *2 Fast 2 Furious*, a Miami-based sequel to the recent box-office success *The Fast and the Furious*, a hot-rod movie filmed in Los Angeles. Seale is married and lives with Mary Jo, his wife of 18 years, in Lake Worth, Florida.

August 8-13, 1972

The 32nd Black Hills Motor Classic began on Tuesday, August 8, marking the rally's growth from a five to six-day format. As fate would have it, a small crisis had developed in the preceding week because a project to repave Main Street was running a bit late. According to the *Sturgis Tribune*, paving was completed by noon on Monday, August 7th in a "photo finish" as many riders had already descended on "Cycle City" that morning. Despite flood damage in some of the camping areas, the city park was completely filled by Tuesday evening.[1]

Rally events began with an Amateur hill-climb at 1:30 Tuesday afternoon. A Black Hills and Devils Tower Gypsy Tour made up the day program on Wednesday and was capped off with Amateur short-track races at 8:30pm at the Gypsy Park. Thursday started off with the traditional Southern Hills Tour. An alternative activity scheduled for those not taking the Gypsy Tour was an "Escorted Trail Ride" followed by a second evening of Amateur short-track. Friday afternoon activities included an Amateur motocross event on the Gypsy Club grounds at 1:30pm. This was followed by the annual Chamber of Commerce "Feed" and a colorful program staged by the Gypsies. Over 300 riders participated in both days of touring.[2]

On Saturday, the AMA-sanctioned half-mile races were scheduled for the Fair Grounds Track, followed by the Professional short-track event at 6:00pm on the club grounds west of town. The purse for the half-mile was set at $1,500, and $1,200 had been committed for the Professional short-track event. Short-track was apparently becoming more respectable to the professionals! A $2,100 purse was up for grabs at Sunday's half-mile feature races.[3] One new event – a dinner honoring the "Retreads" (a club for riders over the age of 40) – was held on Saturday night at the Veterans Club and hosted by the American Moto Guzzi Owners' Club.[4]

Races

The winners of the Tuesday night Amateur hill climb included:

Size	Winner	Hometown	Cycle
100cc	Bill Thorpe	Jefferson, IA	Bultaco
125cc	Steve Kastner	Yale, IA	Bultaco
175cc	Maris Masingill	Pawson, IA	Bultaco
250cc	Michael Fertig	Fort Dodge, IA	Kawasaki
500cc	Frank Prohaska	Plattsmouth, NE	Honda
Open	Joseph Toman	Nebraska	Triumph

On Saturday, the Expert final was taken by Charles Seale of Lantona, Florida with second and third place going to Neil Keen of St. Louis, Missouri and Paul Pressgrove from Tecumseh, Kansas. All three riders rode BSA motorcycles. The Junior and Novice Finals were won by Chubby Armour of Denver on a Harley Davidson, and Randy Cleek of Shawnee, Oklahoma riding a Yamaha. In the Saturday evening short-track event, Randy Cleek took first place, followed by Art Larson of Yukon, Oklahoma on a Bultaco and Vern Johnson of Albuquerque, New Mexico on a Yamaha. [5]

Sunday's feature race was won by Paul Pressgrove, who finished a quarter lap ahead of second place winner Paul Ely. Both riders were mounted on BSA Gold Stars. Carl Patrick of Culver City, California took third place on a Triumph. Neil Keen, the track record holder at 23.94 seconds, did not place in the Sunday race. Merlyn Plumlee of Colorado Springs and Vern Johnson of Albuquerque, New Mexico won the Junior and Novice finals.[6]

1972 Expert Champion: Paul Pressgrove

Born in Tecumseh, Kansas in 1949, Paul Pressgrove and his older brother Kenny used motorcycles instead of horses to work cattle and ride fence lines. Kenny started racing and was so successful that younger brother Paul followed in his footsteps soon after. (Tragically, Ken Pressgrove was killed in an on-track pile-up early in his career while filming "A Race of Champions" which was to appear on the ABC television's Wide World of Sports.) After about three years of racing, Paul began to win races. By the time he raced at Sturgis for the first time, he was 23 years old — a savvy and seasoned Expert.

On the Saturday night before his 1972 championship, Pressgrove walked the track after a day of racing in the hot sun. He quickly realized that the evening watering had failed to soften up the dirt in the turns. In fact, the track was too dry and hard in the corners to allow a rider to complete a fast three-point broadside turn.

Even though the track had been heavily watered earlier in the evening for the Sunday Championship races, Pressgrove realized that it was not going to go well for him. At that point he hit upon a solution. After rolling over one of the many bales of hay, placed in the corners as a safety precaution for a high side crash, he discovered that the soil underneath, sheltered from Saturday's hot sun, was moist and soft. Pressgrove took the time to move each bale out about four to six feet. Then during the Sunday races, Pressgrove went very high in the turns, used the soft soil as a superior riding surface, and won the 1972 championship.*

Pressgrove went on to win and place at Sturgis for the next three years. In 1973 he won the professional short track and placed third in 1974. By 1975, the Alloy XR750 Harley Davidsons were beginning to dominate the half-mile dirt-track racing scene, and his faithful BSAs couldn't keep up. Pressgrove was contacted by a Harley Davidson dealer from Virginia Beach, Virginia, and showed up in Sturgis with a new XR750. That year he took first place in the Saturday Final and a third place on Sunday.

During his career, Paul Pressgrove won a total of 125 main events, including State Championships in Illinois, Oklahoma, Florida and New Mexico along with several county fair races in Kansas, Minnesota and elsewhere in the Midwest. His win at Lincoln, Illinois was probably the most important to Paul. One of his greatest ambitions was to compete in the Springfield Mile. Since the "Mile" was not held at all during the years of his professional racing career, Pressgrove never got to compete in this classic event. Lincoln, the site of the Illinois Championships at that time, is located about 30 miles north of Springfield, Illinois.

After winning eight races in the 1976 season, Paul was involved in a crash that ended his professional racing career. At the Lakeside Speedway in Kansas City on July 29, just 10 days prior the opening of the 36th

---

* Dirt tracks are extremely difficult to maintain adequately. In fact, the proper preparation of the racing surface is a scientifically calculated process that is always subject to the whim of the local climate. Dirt track maintenance can frankly become a genuine nightmare for race planners and officials. Work on a track begins weeks before fans ever see the opening ceremonies and includes grading, watering, packing and adding calcium chloride to both prevent dust and pull moisture from the air. The dirt itself is a mixture of clay, sand and salt, and the quality of the local soil typology is crucial to providing a viable racing surface. Corners are crucial. The soil has to be firm enough to prevent ruts and soft enough to allow for the foot-down, American style of dirt-track racing.

Classic, Pressgrove high sided in his time trial. When he woke up, he told his wife to get him up and out of the hospital so he could race at Sturgis. It was September 22, and he had been comatose for 55 days.

Paul Pressgrove currently spends his winters in Costa Rica and his summers at his New Mexico ranch, where he still uses dirt bikes instead of horses. He is a pretty regular spectator and visits most of the major motorcycle races. He returns to Sturgis yearly to visit old friends, see the races and admits that the vicarious experience of watching others race is a limited substitute for the joy he felt while racing motorcycles.

Paul's fondest memories of Sturgis include the warm welcome he received every year from both of the Hoel's, race officials, and local citizens. Of particular note, however, is a story from his first year at the Classic. It seems Pressgrove and another racer were having fun taking hose showers with some of the pit area females on Saturday during the races. Since this activity was viewable in the grandstand, the mayor ap-

Paul Pressgrove, 1972 Expert Champion at Sturgis (Courtesy of Paul Pressgrove)

Paul Pressgrove at Pearl Hoel's "Retreads" Breakfast, 2002. (Author Photo)

proached Clarence Hoel asking him to make them stop. As a trade-off, it was determined that the City Pool woul be made available to racers from that day on, free of charge.

Harley Davidson XR750

In 1952, Harley Davidson introduced a factory-produced racing motor-cycle, the KR750. This side-valve design held its own for over a decade, competing against technically-superior English racers like BSA, Match-less, Norton and Triumph. (The KR raced against these smaller engine bikes because the AMA classified the 750cc displacement of the KR as equivalent to the 500cc overhead cam engines from England.) By the late 1960s, however, the KR's competitive edge was beginning to wane. In 1970, the AMA Grand National rules were changed, and classifica-tions were finally defined by actual engine displacement and not "equiva-lencies". As a result, English bike builders started building racing engines with larger displacements, and the days of the KR were numbered.[1]

From 1967 to 1971, Harley Davidson riders at Sturgis won once while racers on Triumphs and BSAs took the other four titles.

In 1970, Harley Davidson introduced the first XR750. This first example of the XR, based on the production Sportster engine, had a cast-iron cylinder configuration and overhead cams. It held its own for two years while the Harley Davidson engineers developed a new alloy-based racing engine. Available in 1972, the "Alloy XR" motorcycle began dominating dirt track racing when Mark Brelsford won the Grand National Championship. This racing bike quickly overtook the racing scene, and racers riding the XR won 20 national championships in the next 27 years. If the reader gets to watch a dirt-track race today, chances are the winner will be riding an XR750.[2]

The Harley Davidson XR750 (Courtesy of Steve Matz)

August 7-12, 1973

Touted as the longest and largest motorcycle rally in America by the *Sturgis Tribune*, the 1973 rally was expected to draw riders and visitors from all 50 states and include riders from Europe and Canada. In addition, Sturgis would again host the AMA Pacific Coast Regional Three Mile Championship for half-mile dirt track. (The Pacific

Coast region comprised 15 states, essentially the western half of the United States.) A crowd of 8,000 motorcycle enthusiasts was expected for the six-day event, and several top racers were registered, including 1972 Champion Paul Pressgrove; Neil Keen, the champion in 1968, '69 and 1970; Sonny Burres who placed third in 1971; Dick Mann, the 1966 winner; and Chuck Palmgren, the fifth-ranked racer of 1972.[1]

The *Tribune* also noted that the Black Hills Motor Classic had been characterized by the AMA as the rally with "the only true road tours in the United States". Because the 1972 Gypsy Tours had produced trains of riders nearly eight miles long, a new format was developed in 1973. Three groups would leave Sturgis for the Northern Hills Tour on both Tuesday and Wednesday. A similar approach was employed for the Southern Hills touring. As a result, there were six groups leaving town each day for a total of 12 tour groups.[2]

The typical schedule of events was planned, beginning with the two Gypsy Tour routes and groups, the short track races on Wednesday, Thursday and Saturday evening, a Friday hill climb and "Feed" and three days of half-mile racing. The Amateur half-mile heat races were moved to Thursday afternoon and the Expert races were featured in the Saturday-Sunday slots. Total purse for the three weekend events was $6,600. (There was no mention of a motocross competition.)[3]

By Wednesday, August 8, the *Tribune* reported that Julius Kegel, now 81 years of age, had again traveled to Sturgis on his BMW from Freeport, Illinois. Kegel, a Sturgis regular and the oldest rider at the rally, reported that he clocked an average of 30 to 40,000 miles a year, touring in the United States and Europe. His most recent trek, including his arrival at Sturgis, had included 1,700 miles of touring, completing 688 miles in his best day![4]

In the same issue, the Mayor of Sturgis issued a proclamation, recognizing the importance of the rally in both economic and recreational terms, and declared August 7th through the 13th as "Sturgis Motorcycle Days". The Sturgis Lions Club had expanded their raffle efforts, using two motorcycles to raise funds for the South Dakota Sight and Service Foundation. Pappy Hoel had arranged to donate a dirt bike, supplied by the Yamaha Corporation, and the Honda Company, through Jim LaMar's Lamar Motor Sports Cycle Shop, had matched his donation.[6]

Competition

The very first hill-climber to reach the top on Friday was Maria Masengill of Dawson, Iowa, who took second place in the 175cc class with a time of 5.45 seconds. She was the only registered female rider in the event, and, unfortunately, no other hill climb event outcomes were reported. On Friday night, the Midwest Motorcycle Club from

1973 Rally Poster. The Sturgis Tribune, August 1973.

J.C. "Pappy" Hoel Short Track, dedicated in 1973. (Author Photo)

Bloomington, Minnesota took the award for the best dressed riding club, and Donna Whippel of Rochester, Minnesota was selected Queen and led the Motor Maids in parade around the half-mile track at Sunday's races. Paul Jeffries, age 71, of Salt Lake City, Utah was awarded the "Old Timers" award by the Retread's Club.[7] Apparently Julius Kegel, at age 81, was not a member of the Retreads organization.

Edward Daley of Sapulpa, Oklahoma won Saturday's half-mile Novice race and Donald Palmgren of Colorado Springs took the Junior (Amateur) event. The Expert final went to Charles Joyner of Oregon City, Oregon. The Saturday evening professional short track event was won by Paul Pressgrove, the 1972 half-mile champion. Second and third place were taken by Neil Keen (half-mile winner in 1968, '69, '70) and Charles Joyner. Pressgrove used a Bultaco, Keen a Yamaha, and Joyner rode a Kawasaki in the short-track event.[8]

Sunday's Pacific Coast Regional Championship races provided a great deal of color and excitement. The stands were packed to capacity, and people seated in automobiles ringed the track. The nationally recognized field of racers was individually introduced to the grandstand crowd and the Jackpine Gypsies Motorcycle Club and visiting Motor Maids made parade circuits of the track between races.

Charles Jordan of Howell, Ohio won Sunday's Novice half-mile event, and the Junior final was taken by Vernon Johnson, of Tulsa, Oklahoma. Louis "Sonny" Burres of Portland, Oregon was the Expert winner.

Community acceptance of the Classic continued to grow during the 1973 rally. There were no reported law-enforcement problems, and the expanded participation by the Lions Club, coupled with the Mayor's proclamation, are both indicative of expanding community support. One subtle indicator of what was to come was clearly evident on Main Street. For the first time, parked motorcycles dominated main street parking, almost continuously, during all six days of the event. It would eventually become an officially sanctioned policy.

1973 Pacific Coast Regional Half-Mile Champion: Sonny Burres

Sonny Burres was born on November 21, 1935 in Portland, Oregon, grew up in the Portland area, and started riding motorcycles in high school. After a discharge from the Navy in 1958 in San Diego, Burres purchased a 650 Triumph motorcycle and had a ball riding the streets. But in a week, the bike's engine failed. Burres rebuilt the engine and started to use it in drag racing. Once back in Oregon, Burres ran into an old Navy buddy and became involved in "Hare and Hound" races in Eastern Oregon. In 1959 he entered the state championship race in Newbery, Oregon and won.

In 1960 Burres purchased a 1959 BSA Spitfire and began dirt track racing in Oregon on local tracks and became a regular at Boise, Idaho. He soon decided to devote his life to motorcycle racing and spent the next five years watching other racers and learning how to do better. His fellow racers characterized him as a "snoop" because he was always quizzing them about engine tuning and frame modifications. He also developed a reputation, like Albert Gunter, for playing mind games with the other riders at the starting line. He often would pull up to the starting line last or first and then back out, wave his hand, stare at the other riders, adjust his gloves and so forth.

Burres began to compete at the national level in 1966 on sponsored Triumph motorcycles. His first race under sponsorship was the Springfield Mile, and Everett Brashear (the 1952 Sturgis Champion) was his racing manager. Northwest (Oregon and Washington) racers were nationally recognized as TT specialists, and naturally, Burres was one of these riders. He was good at TT, winning two Grand National Series Championships in TT at Castlerock, Washington in 1971 and Peoria, Illinois in 1975. His real love, however, was flat track racing.

Burres first came to Sturgis in 1971 and took third place in the Pacific Coast Regional Championship race behind Charles Seale and Darrel Dovel. He won this race in 1973 and placed second in 1974. Burres

Sonny Burres, 1973 Pacific Coast Regional Half-Mile Champion. (Mahony Racing Photos)

was still competing at Sturgis in 1978 and lent his Triumph racer to Terry Poovey, so he could compete on Saturday. On Sunday Poovey's Harley Davidson was repaired, and he went on to win the Classic final in 1978.

Burres carried the national number 69 until he retired in 1979. He came back in 1981 and earned enough points to reclaim this number for one more year.

Sonny Burres still lives in the Portland area where he owns Burres Specialties and provides mechanic services for cars and motorcycles. He still competes occasionally in Vintage TT racing.

The Gypsy Tour

By 1972, the Gypsy Tours were becoming quite well organized. Now officially characterized as "The Northern Tour" (to Devils Tower, Wyoming) and "The Southern Tour" (via Sylvan Lake, the Needles Highway, Mount Rushmore and the State Game Lodge), each tour had South Dakota State Trooper escorts, many Gypsy Club leader guides, radio communication, first aid support and a pick-up service for disabled bikes. All state and national park fees were included in the ticket, and the riders received a free catered picnic at noontime — all for the minimal fee of $4.00 per person.

Each motorcycle was provided with a Tour Instructions Packet that included tour tickets, a rally decal, a rally program, and a flag or ribbon to be tied to the handlebars of the motorcycle. Packets were color coded for each tour — the Northern Tour, for instance, used a brown envelope and green and yellow flags and tickets.

With over 30 years of experience in leading these Tours, the Gypsies had established some very basic rules that everyone had to follow. For instance, riders were instructed to "Gas Up" (there were to be no stops for 160 miles), "Stay in Place" (Gypsy Club members were posted to

The Gypsy Tour pauses at Lake Pactola Reservoir during a Southern Hills Tour, early 1970s. (Eve Satterlee Collection)

ride at every 10th or 12th bike interval), and to "Ride Safely and be Considerate of Others". Riders were additionally required to maintain a riding interval of no more than 14 and no less than 10 bike lengths between each machine. This rule was particularly important because the train of riders was rarely less than five miles long, and at times it could stretch as much as eight miles in length.

August 6-11, 1974

1974 was a signal year with regard to organization and management of the rally. As the reader may recall, The Black Hills Motor Classic (BHMC), an organized sub-committee of the Sturgis Chamber of Commerce, and the Jackpine Gypsies Motorcycle Club (JPGMC) were, officially, separate entities and were responsible for different elements of the rally. The BHMC crew managed the half-mile races, the prize money, the Friday Night Feed, and rental and leasing rights in the downtown area. The purview of the Gypsies included the various Gypsy Tours, the hill climbs, the scrambles (or motocross), and the short-track events. In the early days, membership in the BHMC was exclusively restricted to proprietors of a business, one of whom was Clarence Hoel. Through his membership in both groups, Hoel provided a constant liaison between the BHMC and the Gypsies. As the years passed and individual Gypsy members continued to provide most of the labor and support for the BHMC, several of them joined this "semi-exclusive" organization.

According to Neil Hultman, however, the BHMC ultimately became a victim of its own success. By 1974 the local business owners were completely overwhelmed by the size of the rally crowd. The work in planning and implementing the half-mile races as well as related problems like law enforcement, expanding campground space, and arrangements with local home owners for lodging, began to fall more and more and more heavily on all of the Gypsies. These club members also had to serve as referees, race officials, and general staff for the half-mile races. In other words, the major work of the rally was simply demanding too much of the merchants (the core of the BHMC), who could no longer devote time away from their own main street businesses during the rally. At the same time, the Gypsies, also under pressure because of the success and growth of the rally, were feeling a great deal of tension. The separation of the two organizations and the continual informal crossover and responsibilities also provided a great deal of confusion that remains evident to this day. In an attempt to resolve some of the confusion, the two groups merged in 1974, creating a joint committee comprising members of both entities. This committee was, therefore, charged with the responsibility of running the half-mile events. The BHMC provided the purse money, and the Gypsies volunteered their time and labor, but the BHMC treasurer still retained any profits.[1]

It would seem that the agreement to cooperate was more focused on economic than social interaction. According to George Hayes in an article in the Fall issue of *Rider* magazine, the new BHMC/JPGMC "working group" included 15 members, but the Gypsies still supervised the Gypsy Tours and all other non-half mile events exclusive of the committee.[2]

On August 7, 1974, the *Tribune* again characterized Sturgis as "Cycle City" and the "Largest and Longest Motorcycle Rally in America." Space for the multitude of visitors continued to be a problem. By Monday night, the city park and Boulder Canyon Park were both filled to capacity and people were pitching tents along the highways leading into town. Gunner Early, the BHMC/JPGMC Committee President and owner of Gunner's Lounge, a main street landmark, reported that getting an accurate visitor count remained a problem. One ploy underway in 1974 offered free tickets to the Friday night "Feed" for those who registered. This was also an obvious effort to determine the amount of food necessary for the annual event.[3]

Race officials (the BHMC/JPGMC committee) were in constant fear of over-estimating the number of visitors. Because the numbers had grown steadily each year, a policy of increasing services and similar dimensions had prevailed. Organizers, however, were always concerned about what might happen if the numbers started to decline. Since the rally was essentially organized as a "bare bones" non-profit effort, there was always ongoing concern about depleting the financially limited treasury. By Wednesday afternoon, officials rapidly grew concerned about a slight drop in the number of Gypsy Tour participants leaving Sturgis on Tuesday and Wednesday morning.[*] Concerns, however, were alleviated when someone noted a $500 increase in City Park camping fee revenue. The people were clearly there, and some speculated that many return visitors were probably touring the Black Hills on their own, leaving the Gypsy Tours to the newcomers.[4]

With so many Novice half-milers coming every year to the races, the professional Novice half-mile races were scheduled for Thursday instead of Saturday. As it turned out, the planning was on the mark as 121 Novice riders showed up for practice. The *Tribune* reported that 15 heat races (a new record) were held to sort this group out but failed to report the final results. The rest of the week's schedule followed the typical format with Sportsman's short track races on Wednesday and Thursday and the hill climb and "Feed and Program" on Friday. The total purse for all events amounted to $6,975, with $3,000 earmarked for the Sunday Championship series.[5]

Sunday's final event was again the AMA-sponsored Pacific Coast Regional Championship race. Because of this regional endorsement, many racers from Oregon and Washington joined the ranks of California racers coming to compete. Race officials, pleased with the number registered, were excited about some of the big name "Expert" riders who were planning to attend. Top on the list was Randy Skiver of Everett, Washington and the 1973 Pacific Coast Champion. Skiver was one of the top 100 professional racers in the nation and held National White Plate number 35. His chief competitor in the Pacific Coast finals, Sonny Burres of Portland, Oregon (National number 69),who had won the previous year's Pacific Coast Regional held at Sturgis, was also registered. Two more racers, Pat Mariniacci from Seattle, ranked number 19 by the AMA, and Chuck Joiner of Oregon City, Oregon (ranked 14), were also coming. Many nationally-ranked Juniors were also registered, including Don Smith of Salem, Oregon and Darrell Hendricksen of Seattle, who were ranked second and third respectively. Tammy Session of Bellevue, Washington – a promising Novice and the first professional female racer to compete in Sturgis – was also registered! [6]

---

[*] The counts were not that bad. 437 tour participants were present on Tuesday, and another 276 left for the Southern Hills Tour on Wednesday morning.

254

Races

Rain caused a delay in the half-mile racing event on Saturday afternoon. After using trucks and other heavy equipment to pack the race-track, the races began at 3:00pm. This created a problem for the Saturday night Short Track Races, which had to be postponed until Sunday.

Interestingly enough, the Pacific Coast riders touted so heavily in the August 8 edition of the *Sturgis Tribune* did not do all that well. In the Junior Final, Chuck Jordan of Powell, Ohio captured first. He was followed by Dan Cartright, (no address available), Joe Valentine of Cheyenne, Wyoming and Chuck Dawkins of Kansas City, Missouri. In Saturday's Expert final event, Steve Droste of Waterloo, Iowa placed first, followed by Richard Wascher of Seattle. Droste raced on a Harley Davidson and Wascher on a Triumph. Third place went to Chubby Armour of Denver, while Skiver, the West Coast Champion, ended up in fourth place.[7]

To compensate for the late afternoon short track finals on Sunday, the half-mile championship racing began at 11:00am, an hour earlier than planned, and the typical entertainment events took place. Mayor Francis Langin crowned Kathy Anderson of Bloomington, Minnesota as Queen of the rally to preside over the races. Steve Droste, the Saturday feature race winner, placed first in the Expert final on his Harley Davidson. He was followed by Sonny Burres of Portland, Oregon on a Triumph. Randy Skiver, the Pacific Coast Champion in 1973, placed third, followed by Bill Dusenberry from Wichita, Kansas in fourth.

In the rescheduled short track races, Henry Hapke of Collinsville, Illinois took first. Skiver placed second and Paul Pressgrove of Tecumseh, Kansas – now a Sturgis regular – placed third.

1974 Pacific Coast Regional Half-Mile Champion: Steve Droste

Steve Droste, the 1974 champion at Sturgis, almost missed the race. During the preceding week, he had been racing in the Kansas circuit. When the last day of racing at Belvedere was cancelled due to rain, he decided to head for South Dakota. Driving in a torrential down pour, Droste was involved in an accident and his van was rendered undriveable.

Luckily, another racer picked him up. The two racers crammed all their bikes into the friend's van and continued on to Sturgis. Droste ended up winning the feature Expert race on Saturday and took the championship on Sunday.

Steve Droste was born in Waterloo, Iowa, in 1953 into a motorsports family. His father was a successful stock-car racer, and Steven's first race at age 13 was on a 100cc Yamaha. During practice, the chain came off and damaged the bike. His father had just purchased a new Yamaha 250 DT1 and had taken it to the race for a break in. While he tried to fix Steve's 100cc bike, his father let Steve practice on the new 250 DT1. Droste ended up riding the 250 in the race and took second place.

When Steve was 15, he rode in his first half-mile dirt track race, taking second place on a Maico. Because Droste had to wait until he was 18 to get his AMA professional license, he raced locally for about two years, first on a 750 BSA and later on a 750 KR Harley Davidson. Steve

Steve Droste, Pacific Coast Regional Half-Mile Champion at Sturgis, 1974 (Steve Droste Collection)

also performed a jump act during intermission at the dirt track events, one time clearing seven parked cars.

By the time Steve was 18, Yamaha began sponsoring the jump act and provided him with financial support. He began racing as a Novice, and at the end of 1971, Droste decided to quit jumping and concentrate on racing. During 1972 he raced mainly in the Midwest, and entered a few nationals, placing between fifth and tenth place in most of these more competitive venues. In 1972 at age 19, Droste won the Junior (Amateur) Half-Mile National at Colorado Springs, Colorado.

Droste retired from racing in 1979 at age 28. He still lives in Waterloo and works as a sales manager for Ranger Blade Manufacturing, a company that supplies industrial blades for the food processing industry. Steve and his wife Roxanne enjoy touring on their Harley Davidson and generally take a long road-trip vacation every year. Their six-year-old son Tyler is active in BMX racing and is just getting started in go-kart racing.

August 4-10, 1975

Identified in the *Sturgis Tribune* as the 35th rally, the 1975 Classic had grown into a seven-day (full week) format, beginning on Monday afternoon with three classes of motocross held at the Jackpine Gypsies Track west of Interstate 90. Tuesday's new attraction – young racers on minibikes – culminated in a "Youth Nite" under the lights at the short track and included four categories: 0-65cc, 66-75cc, 76-85cc and 86-105cc. The Amateur short track races started on Wednesday and continued at 8pm on Thursday evening. Amateur half-mile races were held in the afternoon on Thursday. By Friday, the format assumed the traditional pattern with an afternoon hill climb and the evening's traditional Feed and Program. Saturday and Sunday were devoted to professional racing.[1]

The weekend racing program, culminating in the feature event on Sunday, was again sanctioned by the AMA as the Pacific Coast Regional Championship Race for the third year in a row. National AMA Professional Competition manager Mel Parkhurst was in Sturgis early in the week and reported that over 100 racers had pre-registered for the 15-state regional championship. He indicated that the race was not limited to just the Western States riders and was drawing racers from the Midwest and Atlantic regions as well. Parkhurst reported that five of the 99 riders holding national White Plate numbers had pre-registered, including number 35, Randy Skiver of Everett, Washington; number 67, Pat Marinacci of Seattle; number 69, Sonny Burres the 1973 winner at Sturgis from Portland; number 74, Paul Pressgrove, the 1972 winner at Sturgis from Virginia Beach, Virginia; and number 92, Steve Droste, the 1974 winner who had apparently moved from Waterloo, Iowa, to Flint, Michigan.[2]

Several promising Juniors were also expected, including Brad Hurst from Eugene, Oregon, Steve Eklund from San Jose, California, and Mark Smith from Dublin, California. Also registered at the Novice level were Rick Graham, Rick Waters, and Vince Mead, ranked 2nd, 3rd and 5th nationally. A total purse of $8,100 was established for the weekend of racing with $2,000 earmarked for the Saturday half-mile event, $2,600 for the Saturday evening short track, and $3,500 for the Sunday Championships.[3] By Wednesday, August 6, Gunner Early, President of the Black Hills Motor Classic Committee, predicted over 200 racers in the three professional categories: Novice, Junior (Amateur) and Expert.

On Friday two fatal motorcycle related accidents were reported. The first one occurred when two machines collided three miles south of Deadwood on Highway 385. One of the riders was severely injured and the other, Kirk Langel of Norfolk, Nebraska, died in the Deadwood Hospital. The second accident occurred in the dangerous Rainbow curve on the Boulder Canyon Highway between Sturgis and Deadwood, when Bruce Vandriel of Hills, Minnesota crashed into a stone wall. Vandriel was not wearing a helmet.[4]

Races

The winners of the Friday Hill Climb for the eight classes were reported as follows:

Size	Winner	Hometown	Cycle
100cc	Steve Hopkins	Newton, KS	Kawasaki
125cc	Galin McGraw	Plattsmouth, NE	Bultaco
175cc	Steve Hopkins	Newton, KS	Kawasaki
250cc	George McGraw	Plattsmouth, NE	Bultaco
350cc	Robert Hopkins	Newton, IA	Kawasaki
351-500 cc	George McGraw	Plattsmouth, NE	Bultaco
501-750 cc	Don Jauhlin	Mankato, MN	Honda
OPEN	David Klase	Fargo, ND	Harley Davidson

It would seem that the Hopkins and McGraw families dominated this event in 1975![5]

On Saturday's half-mile preliminary races, Michael Farmer of Colorado Springs won the Novice race on a Honda, and Bill Miller of Bellevue, Nebraska took the Junior race final. The Expert final was won by Paul Pressgrove of Virginia Beach, Virginia. Number 74 nationally, Pressgrove was the 1972 Champion at Sturgis. Second and third places on Saturday were taken by Chubby Armour of Denver and Rickie Campbell of Millford, Ohio. All three racers rode the new Harley Davidson XR750 racers. In the Saturday night professional short-track finals, Robert Smith of Tulsa, Oklahoma beat out Don Palmgren of Lakewood, Colorado and Rick Graham of Pacific Grove, California, who placed second and third respectively.[6] Graham went on to become the Grand National Champion in 1982, 1984, and 1993 and was inducted into the AMA Hall of Fame in 1998.[7]

In the Pacific Coast Regional Championship on Sunday, Vince Mead of Garden Grove, California won the Novice final and Steve Eklund of San Jose, California was the Junior race winner. Both of these California racers had been highly touted as likely winners earlier in the week by the *Sturgis Tribune*. The Expert riders noted by the *Tribune*, however, did not do as well in the Championship races. Mike Kidd of Fort Worth, Texas took first, followed by Mike Collins of Albuquerque, New Mexico in second and Paul Pressgrove, the 1972 champion and Saturday's preliminary winner, in third. All three were riding new Harley Davidsons, as was Rick Campbell of Milford, Ohio, who set a new track lap record of 25.27 seconds in the Sunday time trials, eclipsing the 12 year record of 25.94 seconds established by Neil Keen in 1963.[8]

Steve Eklund, who won the Junior Final on Sunday, went on to become the AMA Grand National Champion in 1979. Mike Kidd, the Expert Champion, became the AMA and National Champion in 1981. Both of these racers were inducted into the AMA Hall of Fame in 1988.[9]

Community support for the Classic continued to grow in 1975. In the midweek edition of the *Tribune*, the Editor, in solid support of the rally concept, congratulated the efforts of Classic officials and the Jackpine Gypsies, and encouraged the community at large to support the rally. In an editorial entitled "Welcome Cyclists" he stated:

> *You have to see it to believe it! We're referring, of course to the number of cyclists who have turned up in Sturgis for the 35th annual Black Hills Motor Classic and Rally. It's simply amazing how many cycling enthusiasts the event draws every year. It didn't seem possible that last year's record crowd would be surpassed this year. But there's every indication that's what's happening. This is the first year we've seen so many cyclists taking part in the traditional road tours. Although it's impossible to get an exact count of the number of cyclists in town because some of*

them don't bother to register, it's a certainty that last year's record turnout is at least equaled. And the events scheduled for the remainder of this week will very likely push the number of participants to a new high.

The people of the Sturgis area, naturally, are delighted to have all these motorcycle buffs in the community. We welcome them and extend our best wishes for a most delightful stay. There's much to see, especially of historical interest, in the Sturgis area and we hope the visiting cyclists will avail themselves of the opportunity to become better acquainted with the region while here. If they do, we are confident they will want to return in future years.

Congratulations are certainly in order to the officials of the Classic and the Jack Pine Gypsies, the host club, for the outstanding arrangements they have made to assure a good time and lots of action (on the tracks) for the visiting cyclists. They have worked extremely hard to handle such large crowds with efficiency, and the community should commend them for it. The townspeople can show their appreciation by giving them all the support they need, whether it's volunteer help or paid attendance at the Rally events.

Townspeople should also get downtown to look over the wide variety of motorcycles now in the community. It's truly remarkable how innovative and imaginative so many of the cyclists have been in creating their unusual bikes. But above all else, greet the visiting cyclists and make them feel welcome in the true tradition of western hospitality. If you do, next year will be bigger than even this year — and that will really be something![10]

1975 Pacific Coast Regional Half-Mile Champion: Mike Kidd

Mike Kidd was born in Fort Worth, Texas in 1953 and grew up in the Dallas/Fort Worth area in a family of motor racing enthusiasts. His dad, Don Kidd, often promoted races and a younger brother also raced. Don purchased a quarter-midget in 1958 and took Mike to his first race that same year. At Mike's first race, Don knew he had something special as Mike began making passes on the inside and outside at the halfway flags. With one lap to go, Mike took the lead and then headed out the pit gate, crashing into several racecars in the pit area. When Don ran over and asked ask why he pulled off, Mike explained that the throttle was stuck wide open, and he headed to the pit area to look for his dad. Mike went on to win the National Championship in Quarter Midgets (QMA) in Phoenix, Arizona in 1961 at the age of 9.

In 1964 Kidd became interested in motorcycles when a friend of the family opened a Yamaha shop. His first racing bike was a Yamaha 80cc with a full race get-kit and his initial competitive efforts included a short track and TT race.[1] It was not uncommon to see Kidd racing in dirt track, enduro, motocross and cross-country as an amateur throughout the U.S. At the age of 13, Kidd received his first sponsorship from Bultaco motorcycles. He turned professional in 1970 and moved from Novice to Expert

Mike Kidd (#72), 1975 Pacific Coast Regional Half-Mile Champion. (Mike Kidd Collection)

in 1971 and 1972. The first national of 1972 saw three rookies on the pole for the short-track National at the Houston Astrodome with Kenny Roberts, Mike Kidd and Gary Scott. All three riders would go on to become AMA Grand National Champions.[2]

In 1974, while riding for the Triumph factory, Kidd was third in the National Championship points but went down hard at the annual Santa Fe Short Track National, breaking his leg, only to break it again in January of 1975 while training. This kept Kidd out of the championship series until August.

While sitting out for almost a year, Kidd began making plans to return to the 1975 National Championship Series on a new XR750 Harley-Davidson. His first stop was the Pacific Coast Regional Championship races held in Sturgis. Kidd unloaded his new Harley-Davidson to take the win, giving him confidence to pick-up on the Grand National Series tour the next weekend in Terre Haute, Indiana. "The Sturgis win was something special that year. Having broke my leg twice while never racing a Harley, I needed a win against some strong riders before returning to the Grand National series," Kidd said. "To take a win at Sturgis was exactly the boost I needed to get my racing career going strong again," he added.[3]

Kidd unloaded the same Harley-Davidson he used at Sturgis to win the Terre Haute Grand National on the very next weekend. Terre Haute, incidentally, was also the first Grand National to have all main event riders competing on Harley-Davidson motorcycles, beginning the Harley Davidson dominance that remains today with XR750 dirt trackers.

Kidd's best memories of his 1975 win at Sturgis include a conversation with Phil Darcy. Kidd had noticed a Carlisle tire on the front of Darcy's bike. "He told me how good it worked, so I put one on my bike. That same Carlisle tire helped give me the win at Sturgis and Terre Haute," Kidd said. He also related an interesting event that had to do with Sandra, his wife. The Kidds had just married the year before in 1973. "In addition to taking on the task of being a wife, Sandra also took on the responsibility of taking care of me while I was injured. She was a real trooper, willing to do what ever it took to keep us both together," said Kidd. "While traveling up to Sturgis, we did what most other racers did back in the 70's

— live out of a van. We had been on the road for a couple days on the way to Sturgis, so after the win, she politely asked if we could finally get a motel room." Kidd said, "Of course," knowing full well "that everything in town was full!"[4]

Mike Kidd had a spectacular career, winning no less than 12 Grand National races, six of which came on half-mile dirt tracks like Sturgis. In 1974, before he came to race at Sturgis, he won the 10-mile Grand National half-mile at Columbus, Ohio and earned fifth place in the Grand National Series standings. This was his only victory riding a Triumph. For the rest of his races, Kidd used Harley Davidsons. In 1975, one week after winning the Pacific Coast Regional Championship at Sturgis, Kidd won the Grand National half-mile at Terre Haute, Indiana but missed out on a top-10 placement in the 1975 standings. In 1976 he won the 25-mile race at Indianapolis. Kidd's greatest number of Grand National race victories occurred in 1977 and '79, winning three races each year. The 1977 season included victories at Columbus, Ohio; San Jose, California; and Middletown, New York, and he placed seventh in the national standings. In 1978 he did not win a national race but still accumulated enough points to make the top 10 list. 1979 included mile victories at Sacramento and Indianapolis and the half at Topeka, Kansas, ending fifth place in points. His one win in 1980, the TT at Gardena, California, and points in total placed him fifth for the second time. Kidd's best year for overall total points was 1981. He won two Nationals, the TT at Gardena and the mile at Du Quoin, Illinois and enough points to receive the coveted Number One plate.[5]

Kidd's professional racing career spanned 12 years. Although he initially raced Triumphs, he finished his career riding Harley Davidsons. In 1979 and 1980, Kidd was sponsored by the U.S. Army with support from the Harley Davidson Motor Company. He was a factory rider for Honda in 1982 and '83 and retired from professional competition in 1983 at the age of 30 to pursue a career in the motorcycle industry as a promoter of amateur and professional events.

In 1984, his first year as a promoter, Mike Kidd was named Promoter of the Year by the AMA. Kidd put together the National Arenacross Series in 1984, which is now second only to Supercross in national spectator attendance. He is currently a Vice President of Clear Channel Motor Sports, directing over 100 annual arenacross, dirt track and road race events throughout the U.S.[6]

He lives in Fort Worth, Texas with his wife, Sandra, and will celebrate 30 years of marriage in 2003. They have a son, Randy, 25, a daughter, Tammy, 22, and a brand-new baby granddaughter, Bailee.

Chapter Ten:
The Real Party Begins

Over 18,000 visitors were expected to attend the 1976 classic, and race officials noted that over 90 racers were pre-registered by July 28. Also, the impact of "Sturgis" to tourism in the State of South Dakota was evidenced by the appearance of the Governor at the Sunday's ceremony prior to the races. By the second day of the 1976 rally, riders from every state except New Hampshire and Vermont, had registered at Rally headquarters.

Trouble did emerge, however, late in the week. A few undesirables, camping in the City Park, began staging sex shows behind back-lit canvas and another group poured gasoline across highway 34 between Ft. Meade and Sturgis. These actions ultimately led to increased planning for improved security and crowd control the following year.

In 1977, several milestones occurred that would change the rally forever. In an effort to resolve problems experienced during the 1976 rally, the City Park was leased to a private businessman for the duration of the rally, which resulted in better supervision and crowd control at the site.* A creative way of solving the crowd control problem via law enforcement was also initiated in late 1976. Letters were mailed to every law enforcement agency in the state, soliciting part-time help. Certified officers who were interested in working for the City of Sturgis and/or the Meade County Sheriff's Office were asked to apply. Selected officers served eight-hour shifts on duty, earning some extra money, while their families were, in most cases, able to enjoy a family outing in the Black Hills. This plan proved quite effective and remains to this day. Officers wear their normal uniforms, and visitors to the rally meet county deputies from throughout South Dakota along with police officers from Sioux Falls, Aberdeen or Brookings. 1977's third milestone was the appearance of novice female racers. While none of these ladies placed in any of the time trials or heat races, they did provide

---

* This approach, while workable during its first few years, failed to resolve all problems, and the City Park was finally closed to camping during the rally by 1983.

some additional excitement for the racing fans. By 1977, the rally's economic impact on Sturgis was estimated at over $1.8 million, not including money spent in Rapid City and other Black Hills communities.

Keeping with the now well-established schedule and seven-day format, the 1978 Classic saw additional attendance following the release of Steven Spielberg's *Close Encounters of the Third Kind*, which was filmed at nearby Devils Tower. The National Convention of ABATE was also held in Sturgis for the first time in 1978. The year also marks the first significant interaction between visitors and local church groups. Several congregations began serving breakfast to the riders in church basements as a moneymaking activity.

Proving to be one of the "calm" years, the 1980 rally included even more visitors, as evidenced by nearly 1,900 registered campers in the City Park and the establishment and growth of several additional private campgrounds adjacent to the community. Both of the City's banks reported over $800,000 in deposits by closing on Friday afternoon, and three full blocks of Main Street were filled with parked motorcycles for all seven days of the rally.

As the rally quickly approached the 1980s, getting an actual attendance count became more and more difficult. Many visitors on motorcycles never bother to register, and the thousands who come by car to participate and soak up the karma feel that it is improper. According to one Sturgis resident, getting an actual attendance figure is like counting the snowflakes in a South Dakota prairie blizzard. This simile is apt when one considers the coming and going of the crowd as well as the speed of the changing population. Some blow away to the next drift, while others leave drifts upwind and settle for a short time before moving on. Sturgis continues to be a carnival, a celebration, a bash, a racing event, a rally, and many other things to thousands who flock annually to this small, quiet community in the Black Hills of South Dakota.

August 9-15, 1976

According to the *Sturgis Tribune*, over 18,000 cyclists were expected to attend the 1976 Classic. David Despain, a Public Relations specialist with the AMA, reported that 91 professional racers had registered as of July 28, including Mike Collins from Albuquerque (1975 Second Place), Paul Pressgrove (1972 Winner), Merlyn Plumlee from Colorado Springs, and Michael Willett from Sanford, Colorado.[1] Nationally recognized merchandisers, including Bates Leathers, Cycle News Magazine and KRW Helmets, had donated contingency prizes for Sunday's half-mile program in addition to the already established $3,500 purse. It would be the fourth time the Pacific Coast Regional Championship Races were held at Sturgis.

Sturgis Mayor Kelley reported that the city park, damaged by a flood in June, had been reconditioned and more space and additional shower/bathroom facilities had been installed. The schedule of events for the seven day rally duplicated the program from 1975, beginning with an Amateur motocross on Monday and culminating in the regional championship race on Sunday August 15.[2]

On Wednesday, August 11, the Sturgis Tribune reported that Governor Richard Kneip and Miss South Dakota USA, Nadine Oppoid, would be present for the opening of the Sunday Championship Races. Bob Moore, an artistically talented Jackpine Gypsy member, had designed a liquor bottle and had made 2,800 copies of the bottle as a fund-raiser. The Governor was scheduled to break the mold as part of the opening ceremonies. The opening ceremonies would also include two skydivers from Spearfish who would "attempt a landing on the fairgrounds to signal the start of the races."[3]

Monday's motocross, now sanctioned by the AMA as a Regional CAN-AM Amateur Qualifying Race, would represent a six-state region comprising North and South Dakota, Colorado, Nebraska, Montana and Wyoming. The highest point winners would qualify for a Pacific Regional Semi-Final Race in Plymouth, California on September 12, and if successful there, move on to the National Amateur Motocross Championship Races at Carlsbad, California on October 10.[4] The Wednesday edition of the *Rushmore News* reported the results as follows:

Size	Place Winner	Hometown	Cycle
125 cc	1st – Jay Rice	Aurora, CO	Suzuki
	2nd – Mike Loeffler	Denver, CO	Suzuki
	3rd – Dave Kahler	Rapid City, SD	Honda
250 cc	1st – David Bergeron	Rapid City, SD	Husquevarna
	2nd – Jack Todd	Littleton, CO	Suzuki
	3rd – Steve Elgard	Littleton, CO	Bultaco
Open Class	1st – Randy Leutjens	Sioux Falls, SD	Maico
	2nd – Keith Parmely	Casper, WY	Maico
	3rd – Mark Borgman	Littleton, CO	Maico[5]

On Tuesday afternoon, rally visitors were treated to a good old Northern plains hail storm. Someone commented that it was a good thing South Dakota had a helmet law as the half hour storm included golf ball sized hailstones. The City Park tent city was in shambles and local residents, after losing their flowerbeds and gardens, had to dig out their snow shovels to clear sidewalks. Most of the riders took the storm in good spirit, involving themselves in snowball fights. Two riders, Bruce Caldwell of Thunder Bay, Ontario and Mike Lodahl from Edina, Minnesota, erected a curvaceous snow girl on one of the main street sidewalks.[6]

The awards program for visiting riders was conducted on Tuesday evening. The award for "Best Dressed Motorcycle" was a blue Harley Davidson with a trailer owned by Norman and Beverly Taylor of Hastings, Nebraska. In the "Best Bike" category, a black and chrome three-wheeler owned by David Iversen of Aberdeen, South Dakota, was selected. The "Best Chopper" award was given to "The Red Barn", a Honda owned by Tom Blessing of Sturgis and R. D. White of Boulder, Colorado was awarded the "Best Side Car" trophy for his 1950 Indian rig.[7]

Because the hail was followed by an evening rain, the Youth Mini-Bike races, scheduled for Tuesday evening at Short Track Park, were postponed until Wednesday noon. Gypsy Tours started on Tuesday and Wednesday, and nearly 600 riders took part in six separate tours.[8]

Cycles and riders line main street Sturgis by Rally Headquarters, mid 1970s. (Author Photo)

On Wednesday, Bob Lee, the Editor of the *Sturgis Tribune,* again wrote an extremely supportive editorial concerning the Classic's positive impact in the community. After commenting on the public amazement about the continued growth of the rally, he repeated verbatim the same text he had used in his 1975 editorial regarding community support and praise for the hard work of the Black Hills Motor Classic/ Jackpine Gypsy joint committee. He also lauded the city workers for their prompt action in getting the city park ready for campers.[9]

On Friday night, sometime after the "Free Feed," things got out of hand in the city park. While most of the visiting campers were the family-oriented type of motorcyclists, a few were obviously not. Amidst a party atmosphere, including bonfires and probably too much beer, several incidents occurred involving nudity and similar sexually related behavior. The most outlandish incident included a back-lit curtain, which afforded a view of male and female silhouettes performing sexual acts. In addition, a group of riders began pouring lines of gasoline across Highway 34 between Sturgis and Ft. Meade, lighting the gasoline and then challenging riders to cross the strip of fire. According to Ramona Hultman, the motorcyclists showed no fear riding through the fire, but automobile drivers were hesitant, which created a line of backed-up cars and an ensuing traffic problem. The police gained control of both situations in a short time, but the reactions of the "good" campers and concerned Sturgis residents created an atmosphere of anger and disgust, which was readily apparent at a City Council meeting on Monday night following the rally.[10]

Races

By Saturday, several professional racers were on-hand for the first day of half-mile competition, vying for the $2,000 in prize money. One of the more interesting entrants was a Novice, Margo Kind – a professional racer who was determined to earn enough points to become an Expert in two years. In the end, Eddie Lawson of Ontario, California won the Novice division winner on a Bultaco.* The Junior winner was Don Goss of Hartland, Michigan. Walter Hundt of Dallas, Oregon took Saturday's feature half-mile race for the Experts, and second place went to Sonny Burres of Portland. Both of these racers rode Triumph motorcycles. Third place was taken by Mike Eaves, of Galesburg, Illinois, who was riding an XR750 Harley Davidson.[12]

---

* Eddie Lawson, racing in Sturgis as a Novice in 1976 went on to win a large number of racing honors. Lawson was the 500 cc World Racing Champion in 1984, 1986, 1988, and 1989. In 1982 he was the AMA Superbike Champion, and in 1984 he was voted AMA Pro Athlete of the Year. Lawson was inducted into the AMA Hall of Fame in 1999.[11]

During Saturday evening's professional short track races, spectators were treated to an exhibition of motorized unicycles, or monocycles (as characterized by the *Tribune*). The riders demonstrated their skill by circling the short track circuit several times on these single-wheeled, motorized machines. In the two-wheeled racing, the Novice title was taken by Lance Jones of Gadsden, Alabama riding a Yamaha. Junior and Expert were combined for the championship final and Mike Eaves of Albuquerque, New Mexico, took first place on his Bultaco. Second and third place were won by two riders from Texas — Randy Carthell of Amarillo placed second, and James Rawls of Euless ended up in third. Carthell rode a Penton motorcycle and Rawls a Kawasaki.[13]

On Sunday, Sturgis Mayor Harold Kelley presented the Black Hills Motor Classic Queen trophy to Betty Grant during the opening ceremonies of the Pacific Coast Regional Championships. In the Novice division a young racer, Randy Mamola, took an early lead and held it throughout the race. He and his Yamaha motorcycle were severely challenged in the final lap by Eddie Lawson, Saturday's winner and future AMA Hall of Fame candidate. Lawson had been able to come from seventh place to challenge his fellow Californian from Santa Clara. In the Junior Division, Randy Goss of Hartland, Michigan used his Harley Davidson to repeat his Saturday win. The Expert Pacific Coast Regional Champion was Mike Collins of Albuquerque, New Mexico. Second place was taken by Chubby Armour of Denver. Vern Johnson of Albuquerque, New Mexico took third. All three of these Expert racers rode Harley Davidsons.[14]

The Aftermath

As mentioned earlier, the Friday night incidents in both the park and on Highway 34 became the subject of much heated discussion at the following week's Sturgis City Council meeting. In addressing the council, one local resident asked about eliminating the Classic altogether and contended that "the motorcycle races are a financial and safety burden on the City without returning anything to it". Not surprisingly, his remarks were challenged by a member of the Jackpine Gypsies, who indicated that the nearly 18,000 visitors had brought at least $900,000 into the community during the previous week. Bruce Walker, a former Sturgis Mayor, commented that the rally was the community's one major event and the Friday night happenings were only the second instance of trouble in 36 years. Another resident questioned the value in ruining the entire rally for thousands of people when only a few people were to blame. Police Chief Russell Hilton indicated that the Friday-night troublemakers were small groups of two of three people – far different from the large packs or groups that had caused trouble in previous years. Bill Coacher, the Meade County States Attorney, reinforced Hilton's opinion, pointing out that more than half of those arrested were first-time visitors and unaware of the rally's largely peaceful nature. Coacher urged the council and the BHMC/JPGMC joint committee to work together toward a solution.[15]

Protests about the rally were also evident in letters to the editor of the Sturgis Tribune. One resident, who indicated that he was not against the rally, asked for "fair play" for "Country Days", the high school rodeo, and fixing up the arena at the fair grounds instead of pouring money into the city park. He further bemoaned the loss of revenue from main street parking meters and asked the city to support the citizens of Sturgis who spend the "other 51 weeks of the year" living here. Another resident referred to the Classic as a week-long nightmare focused on merchant greed. She complained about inflated prices in the stores and restaurants, garbage dumps in the City Park and the harassment of the local citizens. While she did admit that most of the visitors were neat and clean and agreed with her about what was occurring, she pointed out that the merchants' regular customers – who were supposed to support the downtown businessmen through the year – "were not profiting from the rally".[16]

In Tribune Editor Bob Lee's second reaction to rally week, he undoubtedly found himself in a quandary about what to say.

You don't throw the baby out with the bath water! That ancient axiom summarized our reaction to the suggestion that the annual Black Hills Motor Classic be discontinued because of the trouble experienced here last Friday night with the visiting cyclists. This year's event, the 36th in the history of the Classic, attracted a record number of cyclists. It is a credit to the law enforcement agencies involved that there wasn't more trouble than there actually was, considering the unprecedented number of cyclists here for the Classic.

As is usually the case whenever large numbers of people are congregated, the troublemakers represented only a small minority of the visitors. Unfortunately, they gave the entire group a poor image. It has been our observation over a period of years that the vast majority of the cyclists who come here each year is composed of decent, hard-working and responsible people. Their avocation is motorcycles and they are just as avid about it as other groups are about their hobbies. Some people have an aversion to motorcycles, mostly because they are noisy, and we suspect part of the criticism we've heard since last Friday is based more on a general dislike of the machines than on the trouble that developed at City Park last Friday night.

In any event, the trouble at the Park was quickly quelled by the law enforcement force rallied to the scene. An unprecedented number of arrests was made and the disturbance ended. There wasn't any further trouble on Saturday and Sunday when the week - long Classic came to an end. By the time the troublemakers knew that the Classic sponsors meant business when they advised the visiting cyclists upon arrival that, "We're keeping this event clean; misconduct or actions which tend to soil our event will be promptly handled by law enforcement officers." And so they were!

It is significant, we believe, that the trouble didn't break out until late in the week when there wasn't any organized activity on the Classic program following the free dinner and awards program at the park. Undoubtedly some of the cyclists became bored and started looking for some excitement. It was this situation that led to the trouble. It is a problem that the Classic sponsors will undoubtedly consider when they schedule activities next year.

Local law enforcement agencies always gear up for the extra policing required during Classic week, but the lawmen can't be everywhere all the time. They did, in our judgment, do a good job of maintaining order and responding to the trouble spots last week. In our opinion, the Classic has been a good thing for the community over the years even though their has been some trouble connected with it in some years. We endorse proposals for greater preparations for crowd control at future Classics, but we do not subscribe to the contention that the event should be eliminated. The problems can be handled. They have been in the past and we feel assured they can be in the future too. Let's not panic and throw out the baby with the dirty water![17]

It would seem that 1976 marks another major milestone in the evolution of the rally. The continual growth, and the evolution of an infrastructure capable of dealing with the large numbers of riders, continued to be a problem. Although many Sturgis and Black Hills residents strongly disapproved of the turmoil and swift-paced activity created by the influx of visitors, it was evident that the power structure, including the merchants, law enforcement officials, the local riding club and the *Sturgis Tribune*, all supported the continuation of the Black Hills Motor Classic. They may have been unable stop it anyway.

1976 Pacific Coast Regional Half-Mile Amateur Champion: Randy Goss

Born in Flint, Michigan on January 12, 1956, Randy Goss developed an early interest in motorcycles, which was readily supported by his parents. When honored at the inaugural induction into the Dirt Track Hall of Fame in 1998 as one of the 24 past champions at the Springfield Mile, Goss said that he felt proud and honored to be there and that his memory was enriched by the fact that his "mom and dad worked two jobs to buy him a motorcycle."[1]

After winning at Sturgis in 1976, Goss went on to distinguish himself at the national level. During his Grand National Series (GNS) racing career (1977-1986), Goss won a total of 16 Grand National races. His best venue was the half-mile, where he captured nine victories. He also won three short tracks, two TTs and a pair of mile races. Goss currently ranks number 17 in the all-time Grand National Series record book.[2] Randy's first GNS wins were in 1979 and included half-miles at Middletown, New York; Des Moines, Iowa; and Gardena, California. In point totals for the year, he ended in third place behind Steve Eklund and Jay Springsteen. In 1980, he won the mile at San Jose and ended up Number One in point standings. Goss slipped back to third in 1981 behind Mike Kidd (Sturgis Champion 1975) and Gary Scott from Springfield, Ohio. His victories in 1981 included two half-mile Grand Nationals at Gardena, California. Goss retained his third place position in 1982 after winning the TT at Peoria and the half-mile at Gardena. In 1983 he won the mile at Indianapolis and the half-mile at Hagerstown, Maryland. By the end of year, Goss was back in the Number One spot.[3]

In 1984 after winning four Grand National Series races, Goss finished the season in third place for the third time. His wins that year included two short-track victories at Houston and St Louis, a half at Hagerstown and the TT at Hinsdale, Illinois. He did not place in the top-ten in 1985 and '86 but won a Grand National each year, including the short track at Houston in 1985, and the half-mile at Gardena, California in 1986 [4]

In January 1992, Goss began working for Roush Racing, an auto racing organization focused on Ford vehicles. Goss contributed to Tommy Kendall's IMSA GTS Championship in 1993, and in 1995 he served as a crew chief for the "Nobody's Fool" team consisting of Paul Newman, Tommy Kendall and Mark Martin. This auto-racing trio competed in, and successfully won, the 24 Hours of Daytona that year.[5]

Near the end of 1995, Randy started building truck frames for the NASCAR Truck Series at Roush Racing in Liberty, North Carolina. In 1996, Goss began his career as a Crew Chief for the Roush Racing group in the truck racing series, focusing on the Ford F-150. In 1998 as Crew Chief for Greg Biffle they won the Rookie of the Year honors in the NASCAR Truck Series. His team won a record nine wins in 1999, and in 2000 he won the NASCAR Truck Championship as Crew Chief. Five wins in 2001 led to another Rookie of the Year win, this time with five wins in the NASCAR Busch Championship. In 2002, they repeated this winning season, taking the Busch Championship for a second year. In 2003, Goss will be Biffle's Crew Chief for the NASCAR Winston Cup Series.[6] Randy and his wife, Vicky, live in Mooresville, North Carolina.

Eddie Lawson

In 1976, Eddie Lawson won both the Saturday Novice Final and nearly won again on Sunday, coming from seventh place and nearly passing Randy Mamola at the finish line. Lawson was only 18 years of age. At the 1978 professional short track races at Sturgis, he placed third behind lifelong friend Wayne Rainey. Both instances were only a vague indication of a young rider who would become one of the most outstanding motorcycle road racers of all time.

Born in 1958, Eddie Lawson grew up around motorcycles. His father and his grandfather were both involved in racing, and Eddie began his career on 80cc Yamahas in the desert at age seven. By the time he was

12, he was competing in dirt-track events and began road racing at about the same time.[1] Lawson earned his Expert license in 1978 — the third year he competed in Sturgis. As his career progressed, he discovered that he was winning more road races and losing more dirt-track races. The outcome was inevitable. By 1979 his focus became the pavements of road racing, riding 1000cc Kawasaki Superbikes.[1]

Lawson went on to win the AMA 250cc Grand Prix Series in 1980 and 1981, and the AMA Superbike Series in 1981 and 1982. In 1983, he became a member of the Yamaha team in the pursuit of the 500cc World Championship. Before leaving for the international circuit, Lawson donned his steel shoe one last time and took sixth place in the TT AMA Grand National in the Houston Astrodome. He won at Daytona in 1986 and came off the international circuit in 1993 to ride at Daytona for another championship. Lawson dabbled with automobile racing at Indianapolis in the 1990's but was unable to find a sponsor who could afford top-grade competitive equipment.[2]

Elected AMA Pro Athlete of the Year in 1984, Lawson chalked up 31 500 cc Grand Prix victories before his retirement, including World Road Racing Championships in 1984, 1986, 1988, and 1989.[3]

August 8-14, 1977

On August 3 – five days before the rally opened – the *Sturgis Tribune* reported an influx of riders and printed a special tabloid insert for the locals, which was later placed on sale for the rally visitors. The tabloid included the usual hype about expected numbers (20,000), the big name racers, the Gypsy Tours, and the seven-day schedule. In reference to the rally, Gunner Early, the proprietor of Gunner's Lounge and President of the Black Hills Motor Classic, stated: "I think it is one of the greatest attractions in the State of South Dakota because we have drawn enthusiasts from all 50 states, Mexico, every province in Canada and many foreign countries."[1]

The *Tribune* also reported that much of the discussion at the Monday, August 1 City Council meeting was focused on serious problems regarding camping at the City Park. It seems that the park was to be leased to a local man named John Eddy, and there was confusion regarding his license. City Attorney Russell Molstad informed

Eddy that he would have to apply for a special license and the Council assured him that the lease was in order and that they would surely honor the tentative agreement with one adjustment regarding the "Old Park" section, which was now to be included for camping.* Eddy reassured the council that he would reserve the "Old Park" section for "families and elderly people" in the interest of preventing problems. Eddy also assured the council that he was planning to install additional portable shower facilities.[2] Apparently the problems at City Park during the 1976 rally had driven the City Council to lease the park to Eddy, who would obviously inherit most of the headaches and be responsible for the clean-up process.[3]

The usual list of registered racers was posted, and the *Tribune* made special notice of two women, Margo King of Germantown, Maryland and Debbie Saenz of Tumwater, Washington, who were entered in the Novice class. It was also reported that Ricky Campbell — the current track lap record holder (25.27 seconds) from Milford, Ohio — was returning.

A new feature of the rally format in 1977 was the addition of a second professional short track race, thus using both Friday and Saturday evenings for the event. The Sunday pre-race feature was to include a program by Woody Carson, who would demonstrate some classic bikes from his antique motorcycle collection, and the traditional parade of Motor Maids. The first official race of the "Classic" was a youth mini-bike short-track race for youngsters between the ages of seven and fifteen at 8pm on Tuesday.[4] Racer registration included 52 Novice, 31 Junior (Amateur) and 20 Expert racers who would compete in the Pacific Coast Regional Championship Half Mile on Sunday afternoon.[5]

By Wednesday August 10, initial racing results on an "improved surface" of the short track were reported for the Tuesday evening youth mini-bike races. Troy Sauers of Larchwood, Iowa took first place in the 0-65 cc class, and Don Larive took first in both the 86-105 cc and the Schoolboy Class events. The 7-11 year old class for 66-85cc mini-bikes was won by Todd Giking of Rapid City and the 12-15 year old event was taken by David Durcell of Zimmerman, Minnesota. The Tuesday Gypsy Tours included only 384 riders total for both the Southern and Northern routes. This was somewhat less than in 1976, and rainy conditions on Wednesday drove the numbers down even further. One additional setback, and of great concern to all of the race

---

* It would be interesting to know, in our present age of litigation, where any actual liability was to have been assessed in 1977. Was the leasing a ploy on the part of the City Council to avoid potential law suits, and if so, could they actually avoid such responsibilities? On the other hand, one has to wonder about the amount of insurance Mr. Eddy purchased to cover his culpability to tort liability. In the long run, however, it would not matter. By 1983, the City Park was closed during the rally, and camping visitors were relegated to private facilities in the surrounding area.

Leather everywhere. (Author Photo)

officials, was that Gunner Early, President of the overall event, had suffered a heart attack and was in the Sturgis hospital.[6]

The Tribune went on to report that over 100 racers had participated in the motocross event on Monday. This race, although not part of the official "Classic" program, provided a $1,000 purse and drew a large crowd of spectators. Winners included Al Johnson of Rapid City in Enduro Class, Dave Kahler of Rapid City at 125cc, Archie Simonsen of Grand Forks, North Dakota at 250cc, and Keith Parmelly of Casper, Wyoming in the Open Class.[7]

Races

The grandstand crowd was filled with tension and excitement as they watched the top three riders compete for the championship, changing lead several times throughout the race. In the end, Keith Ulicki of Kenosha, Wisconsin won Sunday's Pacific Coast Regional Championship Half-Mile Race. Second and third place were taken by Vern

Johnson of Albuquerque, New Mexico and Vince Mead of Ashville, North Carolina. The finish was very close and was won by a margin of two to three bike lengths! All three racers rode XR750 Harley Davidsons.[8]

In the Junior (Amateur) Division, the winner was a young 19-year old racer, Ricky Graham. From Pacific Grove, California, Graham went on to distinguish himself in the world of AMA racing and was crowned National Champion in 1982, 1984, and 1993. He was inducted into the AMA Hall of Fame in 1998.[9]

Wayne Rainey, the Novice Champion at half-mile on both Saturday and Sunday, was noted as the most consistent winner of the 1977 rally. He also won both the Friday and Saturday Short Track Novice events. Rainey was inducted into the AMA Hall of Fame in 1999 and apparently switched from dirt-track to road racing in the year following his wins at Sturgis. He was the 500cc World Road Racing Champion in both 1990 and 1992 and was also the AMA Superbike Champion in 1987.[10]

In the combined Junior (Amateur) and Expert Short Track final on Saturday, the winner was Jim Rawls of Euliss, Texas, followed by Jim Mertens, of Sonoma, California and Mike Green of Hurst, Texas.[11]

Marlene Patton of Albany, Indiana was crowned Queen of the 37th Annual Black Hills Motor Classic during pre-race ceremonies on Sunday. The oldest rider award was given to John Schneider of Cheyenne, Wyoming, who was 78. Charlie St. Clair and Debbie Deflice won the distance trophy. Both riders had traveled over 2300 miles, coming from Laconia, New Hampshire.[12]

1977 Pacific Coast Regional Half-Mile Champion: Keith Ulicki

Keith Ulicki was born into a motorcycle family in Kenosha, Wisconsin on March 17, 1951 and his father owned Uke's Harley Davidson of Kenosha but never owned a car. In fact, according to Keith, his father hated cars. The entire Ulicki family was involved with the Harley Davidson Company in one way or another. One of his uncles was a research and development engineer at the factory, and another uncle owned the Harley Davidson dealership in Waukesha. Both of Keith's brothers worked for Harley Davidson in Milwaukee. Needless to say, Keith grew up around Harley Davidson motorcycles and was riding as a passenger soon after birth. He began riding solo at age nine and was entering competitions by the time he was 14.

Keith's first competitions were in local area scrambles, hill-climbs and ice racing. He began dirt track racing in 1969 and applied for his Novice license from the AMA at the age of 18. He won early races at Beaver Dam, Elkhorn, and Sturgeon Bay, all in Wisconsin. Moving swiftly through the Junior class, Keith received his Expert license at age 20.

His first race at Sturgis was in 1969 as a Novice. Ulicki competed at the Black Hills Motor Classic only twice, including the 1969 event and again in 1977 when he took the Pacific Coast Regional Half-Mile Championship. His professional racing career spanned a total of 16 years until retiring from professional racing in 1985 at the age of 34. He then returned to manage the family business. During his career, Keith's best races were the half-mile and the mile. His best finishes in the Grand National Series competition included a fifth place in the half-mile at Columbus, Ohio, and another fifth place in the mile at Du Quoin, Illinois.

Ulicki's fondest memory of his 1977 victory at Sturgis has to do with the strange journey he took in getting there. On a Friday night, the week before the 1977 racing weekend at Sturgis, he decided to enter the Grand National TT at Peoria, Illinois. With only $90 in his pocket, he felt sure he could afford the trip and have enough money for the entry fee. He knew that the promoters at Peoria would pay him a minimum of $50 just for qualifying at the race, and he was confident that he would be able to do so, leaving him with enough money to get home to Kenosha. Because of his limited funds, he had no plans to go anywhere else.

But when he got to Peoria, the race was rained out. Instead of returning flat broke, several of his racing buddies convinced him to accompany them to a race on a sprint car track at Knoxville, Iowa. Ulicki and his friends went to Iowa, and he took fourth place, which gave him enough cash to continue on and compete in a race at Horton, Kansas. At Horton, he took a third on the first day and won the main event on the second day, earning still more money. From Horton, he and his friends went to race in Denver. Ulicki won his heat race purse and was doing well in the feature race before he crashed. It was Friday night prior to the Saturday half-mile at Sturgis. They packed up his bike, drove all night getting to Sturgis, and when Ulicki got there early Saturday morning, he worked on repairing his motorcycle. He took a third in the Saturday main feature and finished first on Sunday. He returned to Kenosha with over $1,300 after paying trip expenses.

Keith Ulicki presently owns and operates Uke's Harley Davidson. His daughter, Brenda Ulicki, manages Uke's Buelle. Brenda also grew up on Harleys, making her first solo ride at age 7. She is an expert in all areas of HD history and lore, as well as contemporary HD technical and developmental elements. The Ulickis live in Kenosha but seldom visit the Sturgis Rally because it is one of the dealership's busiest times of the year.

1977 Junior Champion: Rick Graham

Rick Graham went on to become one of the most outstanding racers in the AMA racing program. His experiences at Sturgis began in 1975 when he placed third in the Professional Short Track Final. He went on to be crowned AMA Grand National Champion in 1982, 1984, and 1993. Graham's career included a total of 39 Grand National victories, seven Harley Davidson Sportster Performance wins, and he was named the AMA's Athlete of the Year in 1993. Riding for Honda that same year, Graham won 12 Grand National races and, in doing so, tallied a six race winning streak — both feats constitute a record that will probably never be broken.

Born in 1958 at Carmel, California into a racing family, Graham began his professional career at age 19, the year he won at Sturgis. His 1982 Grand National title was a close race in points, separated from Jay Springsteen by only a two-point margin. In the mid-1980s, Graham joined

Honda's dirt-track team, which included Bubba Shobert — a former friend and a seriously intense competitor.

His final race, the Del Mar Mile, completed a 20 year professional racing career. Tragically, Rick Graham died in a house fire in 1998. He was inducted into the AMA Hall of Fame the same year.[1]

August 7-13, 1978

An interesting milestone for the 1978 rally, and especially for the Gypsy Tours, was the year's earlier premiere of *Close Encounters of a Third Kind*, a blockbuster feature directed by Steven Spielberg that related the appearance of UFOs around the world and humanity's various reactions to them. The movie's climax takes place at nearby Devils Tower and closes with final scenes of actor Richard Dreyfuss joining the alien crew. Because Devils Tower played so heavily into the last half of the movie, riders coming to Sturgis in 1978 were anxious to include this National Monument in their rally touring experience. Consequently, the Northern Hills Gypsy Tour, which used Devils Tower as the mid-day stop over, was expected to be booked to capacity, and thousands of motorcyclists would be adding this Wyoming loop to their seven-day itinerary. While the Gypsy Tour numbers failed to pan out to expectations, the Sturgis Tribune noted that more and more people were touring on their own.[1]

A second major marker for the 1978 Classic was the number of highway deaths – a total of six – attributed to accidents involving rally visitors. Two deaths resulted from accidents in Boulder Canyon (US Highway 14-A) between Sturgis and Deadwood when riders lost control of their motorcycles. Three more came from motorcycle-vehicle collisions, and the final death resulted from a loss of control along Interstate 90 east of Mitchell during a torrential downpour.

A third facet of the 1978 Classic was decreased pressure on law enforcement because there was little to no trouble. Sheriff John Egger and Sturgis Police Chief Tom Havelaar were already on vacation by August 16 following the rally, and deputies and patrolman alike expressed relief and satisfaction regarding visitor behavior. Sturgis Assistant Chief Ron Munoz described the 1978 rally as "one of the quietest". Munoz reported that he and other law enforcement officials were confident that the quiet nature of the rally was due to the high profile presented by the nearly 50 out of town

On the road to Devils Tower, 1978. (Author Photo)

professional officers from around the state who worked Main Street and various other areas in the city during the week.[2]

Despite a fairly quiet week, there was the usual fair share of curious and interesting behavior. Of particular note, a "gang" of 60 to 100 motorcyclists camping at the VFW park south of town had advised other riders to camp elsewhere but policed themselves very well.[3] Another interesting item dealt with cattle rustling! Following a report from a passing tourist, a Meade County Sheriff's spotter plane observed a number of bikers trying to load cattle into a U-Haul truck on Bureau of Land Management property next to I-90 south of Sturgis. When Meade County Sheriff's deputies responded to the alarm, several of the bikers fled, but the deputies were able to apprehend two men who had stayed with the truck. The two were arrested and charged with attempted theft. Following advice from the States Attorney, the charge was reduced to "traveling off the designated roadway." The two men pled guilty to the reduced charge, paid a total of $744 in fines and were released.[4] The *Black Hills Press* also reported the dynamiting of a portable toilet in the privately owned Boulder Canyon Campground. The campground owners stated that they would not be open for camping in future years.[5]

A fourth important element introduced in 1978 was evidence of enhanced community involvement in the "Classic". On Monday August 7, the Methodist Church women began serving a breakfast for the motorcyclists. By the end of the rally they reported that they had served an average of 50 breakfasts per day for the total week.[6]

Julius Kegel, who had received the award for "Oldest Rider" many times, was again present in 1978. Kegel reported that 1978 was his 29th Classic and that he began riding motorcycles in 1910. A lifelong BMW dealer, Kegel was apparently so important to the BMW people that the Grand Opening of a new BMW automobile plant in Kentucky had been postponed until he returned from the rally. Kegel also indicated, that since the price of restaurant food and motels had gotten to be so expensive, he had chosen to camp on this trip. According to his logs, he had ridden over 300,000 miles on BMW motorcycles.[7]

The rally's schedule of events was a carbon copy of the 1977 program. One unofficial addition was the National Convention of "A Brotherhood Against Totalitarian Enactments" (ABATE), a group focused on combating national regulations about helmets and noise control. Local optimism about the group's visit centered around the additional "several thousand" riders that would be coming to Sturgis. Also, motocross races, again not included in the official program, would be held on Monday August 5

Watching the Sturgis half-mile races from the grandstand, 1978. (Author Photo)

in Spearfish, on Sunday August 13 in Sturgis at the Jackpine Gypsies Course (during the afternoon half-mile championship), and again on Monday August 14 in Rapid City.[8]

Races

The racing program began on Tuesday evening at the newly named "J.C. Pappy Hoel Short Track" with the "Youth Mini-Bike" event. Todd Gikling of Rapid City won two races, including the 66-85cc class for ages 7-11 and the 0-105cc class for ages 7-14. In the 0-65cc class, the winner was Troy Sauers of Larchwood, Iowa, and the 85-105cc class for 12-14 year-olds was won by David Durelle of Zimmerman, Minnesota. To the delight of Pappy Hoel, all of the winners rode Yamahas![9]

The Friday afternoon hill climb included winners in five classes:

Size	Place Winner	Hometown	Cycle
100cc	Ms. Dee Masengill	Dawson, IA	Suzuki
125cc	Clay Alexander	Gillette, WY	Yamaha
175cc	Ms. Maris Masengill	Dawson, IA	Bultaco
250cc	Larry Broen	Rapid City, SD	Yamaha
371-500cc	Joe Aberle	Lead, SD	Yamaha[10]

In the Saturday evening Professional Short Track event, the winner of the Junior event was Wayne Rainey of Norwalk, California, the 1977 Champion and future AMA Hall of Fame inductee. The Expert class short track championship went to Michael Green from Hurst, Texas, followed by Terry Poovey, of Garland, Texas and Eddie Lawson, of Ontario, California in second and third place respectively.[11] Lawson went on to become the 500cc World Road Racing Champion in 1984, 1986, 1988, and 1989. In 1982 he was crowned as the AMA Superbike Champion, and in 1984 he was chosen as the AMA Professional Athlete of the Year.[12]

In the Sunday running of the Pacific Regional Championship Half-Mile, the Novice and Junior classes broke down as follows:

Novice

Place	Name	Hometown	Cycle
First	David Jones	Oklahoma City, OK	Yamaha
Second	Jeff Haney	Seaside, CA	Yamaha
Third	Dylan Niehart	Fontana, CA	Yamaha

Junior

Place	Name	Hometown	Cycle
First	Wayne Rainey	Norwalk, CA	Yamaha
Second	Richard DeLacy	Vallejo, CA	Yamaha
Third	Ronald Jones	Oklahoma City, OK	Harley Davidson[13]

Terry Poovey of Garland, Texas took the Expert championship final and was followed by Phil McDonald of Wichita, Kansas in second place and Frank Ward III from Grant's Pass, Oregon in third. All three rode the new Harley Davidison racer.[14] Poovey is still actively competing in National AMA events.

Miss South Dakota USA, Nadene Oppoid, was the presiding Queen of the Sunday racing program. She was featured in the opening ceremonies and presented trophies to the race winners and the various riding awards to visiting fans.[15]

Different Opinions

Despite a quiet year in general, two regional editorials aired some important issues for the local reading public. In the first, Editor Bob Lee of the *Sturgis Tribune* scolded the Classic Committee for exaggerating the count at the rally, suggesting that the press coverage it effected on the national level would entice more "gangs of rowdies" to attend in ensuing years. He then apologized to present visitors, stating that most of them were "decent law abiding citizens who are a credit to their own communities" and that more "rowdies" actually travel by car than by motorcycle.[16]

The second editorial was not as kind. Reflecting at midweek of the rally, Richard Creed, the editor of *Rushmore Ads News*, dealt with the disproportional growth of the crowds and community reactions to the event. Describing Sturgis and Northern Black Hills residents as generally rural people who knew and understood the values of almost everyone in the area, Creed suggested that evolving American culture on display at the rally was reaffirming local beliefs about the country's downward moral slide. He went on to say that locals, not used to the anonymous lifestyle familiar to the urban and suburban visitors, were becoming uncomfortable with persons who were acting as, "strangers wiping their feet on the carpet of their values."[17]

Responding to actions, behaviors and comments of these main streamed visitors, some of the locals were beginning to feel that some of the idle comments and irresponsible behaviors were quite insulting to their rural way of life. Long gone were the days when visiting cyclists camped in Clarence and Pearl Hoel's back yard and ate Pearl's scrambled eggs for breakfast, coupled with the interaction of a gathering where everybody knew everybody else. Culture shock was clearly beginning to effect everyone. According to Creed, "Incidents of public nudity, obscene signs visible to the general public, street gossip that emphasized the outrageous behavior of a few individuals, have added to a general uneasiness about the event. The clash of a conservative culture with that of a free-wheeling lifestyle cannot be overlooked".[18]

Another major concern in Creed's editorial was focused on Sturgis' ability to provide enough amusement for the mass influx of persons, and in closing admonished the visitors:

> So where does that leave you, the biker, who have been lured to the middle of America by the siren song of party, party, party. It leaves you with the fate of the Black Hills Motor Classic Rally and Races in your hands. Remember, it's the last of its kind, and the reasons why it is. Remember it the next time you feel the urge to flip someone off, or ask some young lady to display her natural gifts to the world. Remember it the next time you feel rowdy from a few brews and want to gain the center stage of Main Street. Remember it when you feel like impressing the natives with your new pipes at two in the a.m. Remember it . . . and think on it.[19]

1978 Pacific Coast Regional Half-Mile Champion: Terry Poovey

Terry Poovey was born on September 16, 1958 in Dallas, Texas. Poovey's older brother was active in motorcycle racing, and Terry started riding motorcycles at age 9 on a 50cc Honda. He turned professional in 1975 and was 19 years old when he won the 1978 championship at Sturgis. His Grand National Series record of 11 wins began in 1976, prior to his trip to Sturgis, with a short track victory at Talladega, Alabama. In 1979, Poovey won two Grand National half-miles at Columbus, Ohio and Meadowlands, Pennsylvania. He won the mile at Indianapolis in 1980, repeating the win in 1981 to end up sixth in the point standings.

Poovey has finished in the top 10 in the Grand National series a total of eight times, beginning in 1981. He improved this position in 1982 with a fourth place, behind Ricky Graham, Jay Springsteen and Randy Goss. It was his best finish. In 1983 Poovey won the short track national

Terry Poovey, 1978 Pacific Coast Regional Half-Mile Champion. (Courtesy of Terry Poovey)

at Houston, Texas and took half-miles at Harrington, Delaware and Louisville, Kentucky in 1984 and '85. He was fifth in 1988, sixth in 1989, seventh in 1987 and placed eighth a total of three times in 1984, 1990, and 2000. Poovey currently carries national number 18, which was awarded to him in 2001 season. At 43, Poovey is still racing on the National AMA Circuit.

His best venue was short track, placing second at Daytona in 1994, 1998, and 2000. He won the season opener short track event at Daytona in 1997. His second best venue was the mile, placing fourth in 1995 at Sacramento; sixth in Du Quoin, Illinois in 1996 and fifth at the 1999 Springfield Grand National mile in May.[1]

In 1978 at Sturgis, Poovey's Harley Davidson broke down early on Saturday, so he borrowed a Triumph from Sonny Burres to compete later that day. Tex Buelle, the famous tuner and bike builder from Texas and developer of the Buelle motorcycle, repaired Poovey's Harley on Saturday night, and Poovey rode it to victory on Sunday afternoon. According to Poovey, his best memory of Sturgis involves winning a lot of money from Harry Lily playing Black Jack in the motel room. He presently lives with his wife, Kathey, and his daughter, Katey, in Garland, Texas.

Wayne Rainey

Wayne Rainey was born in 1960 in the Los Angeles area into a family of racers and began riding a 50cc Honda mini-bike at age 6. By the time he was nine, he was an active participant in the Southern California youth racing scene. Rainey became an Expert at age 19 after racing two years as a Junior. Because his 17th birthday wasn't until October, Rainey was 16 years old when he first raced at Sturgis in August 1977.

His first years as a professional were severely limited by the lack of top grade racing equipment, but in 1981, he was noticed by Kawasaki and began to receive factory support. It was at this point in his racing career that he realized his talents were better served on the pavement. By 1982, he had turned almost totally to road racing on Kawasaki Superbikes. His first national victory was June 10, 1982 at Louden, Connecticut.

When Kawasaki pulled out of the Superbike venue, Rainey lost his ride. For a brief time in 1985, he rode Yamahas in the 250cc Grand Prix championships, and in 1986 he became part of the Honda factory team, winning his second Superbike title in 1987. He rode his last dirt-track event in the Sacramento Mile AMA Grand National in October of 1987, taking fourth place.[1]

In 1988 he returned to Yamaha racing in the 500cc class and earned his World Championship victory in Great Britain. Rainey went on to win three consecutive World Championship 500cc Grand Prix for Yamaha. His racing career ended in September 1993 at the Italian Grand Prix. He is a good friend of life-long competitor Eddie Lawson, and both of them enjoy racing go-carts.[2]

August 6-12, 1979

The 1979 Black Hills Motor Classic marked yet another dramatic year in the evolution of the rally. From growing commercialization and money-making opportunities to law enforcement and public tension, the rally was affecting everyone involved. While the rally format remained largely unchanged from the previous years, the story of the rally, as expressed in the local media, was more about who was making a quick buck and who was upset about it. Racing, which had been at the core of the rally for nearly 40 years, was gradually being relegated to the back of everyone's mind.

Growing Pains

Expanding crowds and the evolution of increased camping and vendor sites were evidence of the serious growing pains that were beginning to affect the city's ability to maintain organizational integrity of the rally. Managing the City Park, along with the competition for camping and vending space, was truly impacting city government to a greater degree each year.

In an interview with the *Sturgis Tribune*, LeRoy Biesheuvel of the Jackpine Gypsies was asked if the races would ever be "put to a stop by irate residents". Biesheuvel replied, "I would hope not. I think that the only thing that would stop them would be we got too big." When pressed by the paper to define "too big", Biesheuvel responded with "a total greater than 30,000."[1] Little did he know what the rally would evolve into.

Despite Biesheuvel's sentiments, many local residents were expressing more and more tension about the rally. The *Sturgis Tribune* poignantly summarized a police department response to news media reports about terminating the rally: "This year's Motorcycle Classic may be the last if there is any violence whatsoever." Chief of Police Thomas Havelaar told the Tribune those calling the police and City Council members to complain were being referred to the Black Hills Motor Classic Board. Meade County States Attorney William Coacher echoed this response, indicating that it was "not his decision to discontinue it." Chief Havelaar went on to state that "The City has the responsibility of law enforcement and set up for the Classic, but it is independently run." Expressing confidence in the projected plan for law enforcement during the event, he also indicated that he was "…not anticipating a bad year." States Attorney Coacher suggested that ending the rally at the suggestion of a few local residents would be like closing down the South Dakota State Fair in Huron because local residents complained about it. "You have to look at the impact on the community," he said. "There is some inconvenience and a few problems, but the merchants don't think it justifies taking away those dollars".[2]

Meade County Sheriff John Eggers also inferred the effects of increasing rally attendance on a recent ban about camping at area Bureau of Land Management (BLM) recreation sites by. Eggers reported that the BLM had given him authority to ban overnight camping in the recreation areas, but persons could camp on BLM land away from the recreational sites if they secured the proper permits to do so.

Chief Havelaar reported that additional "outside professional" policemen had been hired to patrol during the rally, and that three rather than two blocks would be reserved on Main Street for motorcycle parking. He also explained that the State's Mobile Radio van was being sent from Pierre to centralize radio communication during the Classic.[3]

Making a Buck

At the Park Board meeting on Tuesday July 24, it was suggested that Public Works Director James Gammel and Park Coordinator Clancy Walsh be provided with a police escort to deliver nearly $4,000 per day to the bank – if they so desired. It was also reported that the entire west side of the area in front of the City Auditorium had been rented and that the two lots to the east were still available for rent at $1,000 each. Apparently the amount of money being generated by the rally was becoming significant. By Wednesday, August 8, camping fee receipts for sites in the City Park had exceeded $17,000. This was equal to the amount collected for the total week in 1978.[4]

By August 1, "Cycle Shirts" of Birmingham, Alabama – one of the largest vendors to date – was in town and preparing for the 1979 Classic. The company purchased T-shirts in southern mills and then silk-screened related designs for resale at motorcycle meets nation wide. Cycle Shirts had begun by selling shirts to college fraternities and sororities and had moved into motorcycle rally sales when the college market began to wane. In 1979, they were purchasing shirts for 25 cents each at the cotton mill and selling them from March through August each year for about $2.00 each. According to Manager Virginia Lillard, their first year at Sturgis was 1974, and they sold their vanload of shirts in about two days. They had been returning to Sturgis, expanding their offerings each year. Lillard said that her business volume in Sturgis had equaled sales at Daytona by 1978, and that she felt that the number of visitors to the Classic was entirely due to "nice people, accommodating locals, good food and nice rooms." During the 1978 rally, she reported a sale to Robert Blake, the star of the hit TV series "Baretta".[5]

Rally-goers enjoy an open-air bar in nearby Deadwood, late 1970s. (Author Photo)

At registration headquarters in the City Auditorium, several new groups had secured booths and were taking registrations, including the International Retread Motorcycle Association, Women's International Motorcycle Association, Help'n Hands and the Christian Motorcycle Association.[6]

This 39th Classic also saw an expansion of the "open homes" phenomena. More and more Sturgis residents were providing sleeping space for visitors. One couple, Richard and Norma Skavang, entertained 18 riders in 1979 by renting rooms in their house and outbuildings and allowing others to pitch their tents in the backyard. The Skavangs indicated that they would take as many as space would allow and that the riders did not seem to mind waiting in line to use the bathroom. This was the sixth year the Skavangs had opened their home to visitors.[7]

Another phenomenon was the increasing number of churches and groups providing breakfast to the visitors. The First Presbyterian Church had begun serving a breakfast of pancakes, sausage and eggs in 1976. According to Marcia Johnston and Eileen Hodges, co-chairman of the breakfast, the food was served between 7:00 and 11:00am and included more than 3,200 meals over the course of the seven-day event. Profits in the range of $4,000 to $5,000 were used for mission work and providing summer camp fees for needy youngsters. Another group, the "Retired Senior Volunteer Program", indicated that they were in their fourth year of serving breakfast, offering an all-you-can-eat menu. Grace Lutheran and the Methodist Church had only just started their breakfast program in 1979. The Lutherans used the Yamaha Sport Cycle Shop and the Methodist Church used the church basement. More than 30 volunteers from each church were involved in the weeklong process.[8]

By Saturday, a major flap concerning the City's fee for "Transient Merchants" emerged in the *Black Hills Press*. It seems that the City Council had raised the fee from $100 to $500 on July 2. According to Mayor Mike Brandt,

> We have had the problem of people coming in and putting up stands with inferior products and we have no control over the things they are selling. The basic idea of the license is to have control. Plus these people are taking a lot of money out of Sturgis. By requiring the transient merchants license we are giving the local merchant some advantage and are encouraging him to participate in selling goods. We are trying to keep the dollars in town . . . that's what it's all about."[9]

Mayor Brandt also defended the fee as a means of offsetting increased costs for facilities and law enforcement, which was costing the city as much as $85,000 per year. The transient vendors were obviously alarmed by the steep increase. One vendor indicated that it had taken them until Friday to net $500, thereby limiting their entire profit margin to just the two days of the weekend. Another vendor, sensing the difference between the Black Hills Motor Classic Group and the Jackpine Gypsies Club, indicated that he would not mind the fee if the money went to the Gypsies. Some extremely irate vendors indicated that they were considering legal action on the basis of excessive fees and fair application. Some of the larger vendors, including Cycle Shirts, said they were considering year-round rental or even purchasing a local store and or parking lot property.[10]

News

By August 1, 11 Experts, 31 Juniors and 18 Novice racers had registered for the week of racing and a chance to vie for a purse that exceeded $10,000 in prize money. The prize for winning the feature race on Sunday was $4,000, and the Professional Short Track purse had grown to $2,500.[11]

Boyd Newton from Decatur, Nebraska, was the first reported fatality of the 1979 Classic. Newton died after his cycle left the road on Highway 14A (Boulder Canyon) on Monday.

Speaking at Tuesday's Rotary Club luncheon, Joe Doyle, President of the Jackpine Gypsies said that the club had recommended that the State Patrol establish a road-block checkpoint somewhere along Highway 14A in Boulder Canyon. He indicated that all six fatalities in the 1978 rally were alcohol-related, and that the State Department of Transportation had not responded to the club's suggestion. In addition, he indicated that he and other Gypsy members were less concerned about motorcycle gangs than those individuals who were trying "to impress the gangs." "They're the dangerous ones." he said.[12]

Bob Lee, the editor of the *Sturgis Tribune*, again expressed a positive view of the 1979 rally in his editorial, centering on the ever-present challenge of estimating the yearly number of visitors:

> We won't hazard a guess on whether the turnout for this year's Classic is larger or smaller than last year. There's really no way of knowing — for certain. Only a percentage of the cyclists attracted here by the annual event bother to register. Then too, at no single time are all the cyclists in the community. They're constantly on the move and those coming into town usually meet those leaving it for visits to neighboring communities, or traveling to campsites between them.[13]

By Tuesday noon, August 7, riders were represented from all but nine of the 50 states and four Canadian Provinces. Judy Iverson, one of the officials working at the City Auditorium registration site, indicated that, since only about one fifth of the visitors actually registered, officials were optimistic that all 50 states would be represented by the end of the week.

Although numbers for the Northern and Southern Gypsy Tours were down some-what, Gypsy officials predicted that more riders would participate on Wednesday, the second day of touring. The Northern Tour was still drawing the larger crowd in 1979, still coasting on public curiosity about nearby Devils Tower, which had been featured in the previous year's blockbuster movie, *Close Encounters of the Third Kind*.

The *Sturgis Tribune* also announced that the South Dakota Division of Highway Safety would be shooting a 15-minute videotape about the rally for tourism purposes. Rally officials were pleased about the publicity potential of this positive portrayal of motorcycle riding in the Black Hills.[14]

On an additional positive note, the final death toll for the 1979 rally included only two motorcycle-related fatalities. It would be a record low for many coming years.

International Publicity

While Classic officials did not seek international publicity, representatives from around the world were in attendance in 1979. A Frenchman and his girlfriend were in town doing a news-photo feature for *Motojournal* – a Paris newspaper. This photojournalist, Jean-Pierre LeClerc and his friend Yolande Quelleuc, had flown to California where they purchased a new Honda motorcycle and rode it to Sturgis. After Sturgis, they

Main Street Sturgis, 1979. (Author Photo)

planned to travel on to New York, sell the motorcycle and return to France.[23] A German rider, Michael Fritz Huse, was a second international visitor bent on publicizing the rally. Huse said that no guidebook of motorcycle touring in the United States existed in Germany, and he intended to publish such a guide when he returned to West Berlin. He was busy interviewing people and taking photographs, planning to feature Sturgis in this guidebook.[15]

A third international presence at the 1979 Classic included an English family on summer vacation. David and Maureen Jones and their two children Kim and Richard had driven to the rally by car. Mrs. Jones had visited the Black Hills in 1978 on a university tour. When she returned to their home in Dorset, England, she told the rest of the family about the motorcycles and the Sturgis Rally. Since her 14-year-old son Richard was so interested in motorcycles and seeing the rally, they had decided to include Sturgis in their 1979 family vacation tour of the United States. Beyond being impressed with the beauty of Mt. Rushmore and the Black Hills, they were especially complimentary about the friendly and helpful people in Sturgis.[16]

Races

Yamaha motorcycles claimed 52 of the 75 places awarded in the Thursday short track racing program. Rain had postponed the Tuesday night youth racing program, and gusty winds on Wednesday precluded the evening amateur short track preliminaries. Both of these races had to be rescheduled for Thursday. As a result, the Thursday night Amateur Short Track trials were packed, and the five classes of racing were not finished until midnight! The winners included:

Size	Place Winner	Hometown
100cc	Todd Gifling	Rapid City, SD
125cc	Denis Bernal	Rapid City, SD
175cc	Buzz Arndt	Brookley, MN
250cc	Jay Beach	Huron, SD
500cc	Jay Beach	Huron, SD[17]

In Friday's Amateur Hill Climb, Bultacos ridden by the McGraw Brothers of Plattsmouth, Nebraska, dominated three of the six classes. Gailen McGraw took the 126-200cc class and his brother George took both the 201-250cc and the 251-300cc classes. Donald Juhlin from Mankato, Minnesota took the 500cc and the 501-575cc classes on a Honda. The smaller classes, under 100cc and 101-125cc, were taken by Dave Gottschalk of Minsurn, Iowa and Paul Ferris from Murray, Nebraska. Both of these riders used Suzukis.[18]

The Friday-evening professional short track race Novice winner was James Filice of San Jose, California. Filice was threatened throughout the race by Brett Miller of Columbus, Ohio and Jay Beach of Huron, South Dakota.[19]

Junior and Expert Short Track Finals were held on Saturday evening after the preliminary half-mile event at the fairgrounds. The Saturday Novice winner was again James Filice, who went on to distinguish himself as a motorcycle racer. The national 250cc Road Race Champion in 1991 and 1993, Flice also won 22 national road races during his career. He was inducted into the AMA Hall of Fame in 2000.[20] Saturday's Junior winner was David Jones of Oklahoma City with Don Shobert of Lubbock, Texas, taking second place in a hot contest with Gene Church of Turnesburg, North Carolina. Shobert took second by the length of his front wheel. In the Saturday half-mile race, Phil McDonald from Sapula, Oklahoma, won the Expert Feature Race on his Harley Davidson. Sonny Burres of Gresham, Oregon, the 1973 winner at Sturgis, placed second.[21] The Junior Short Track winner was Mickey Fay of Federal Way, Washington. Fay's time trial was so good that he was also allowed to race in the Expert heats and finals. He went on to capture the Expert final as well, making him a double winner in the 1979 Short Track Championships.[22]

On Sunday, in the U.S. Pacific Regional Championship half-mile championships, Filice repeated his Saturday win, making him a triple winner in the Novice Division. Second and third place went to Brett Miller of Columbus, Ohio and Scott Adams of Bethany, Oklahoma. In the Junior Division, the winner was David Jones who also duplicated his Saturday feature race first. Bob Crabbe of Levittown, Pennsylvania, followed him in second with Don Shobert taking third.[23]

The Expert Final and Championship winner was Cliff Keener of Golden, Colorado. The *Sturgis Tribune* credited Keener's win to a second start. Since someone jumped the gun in the first start, a red flag went up and the restart placed Keener in a better position in the front line. Second and third were taken by Frank Ward from Grants Pass, Oregon and Phil McDonald, the Saturday feature race winner.[24]

1979 Pacific Coast Regional Half-Mile Champion: Clifford Keener

Clifford "Corky" Keener was born on October 2, 1945 in Flint, Michigan and became interested in motorcycles at the age of 12. His first

Corky Keener, Pacific Coast Regional Half-Mile Champion at Sturgis, 1979 (Courtesy of Corky Keener)

bike was a Cushman scooter, which he rode until purchasing a 150cc BSA at age 14. He later got a 175cc BSA and competed in his first race at Findlay, Ohio. Keener filed for his AMA Novice license in 1973 at age 18, and by 1975 he had earned his Expert rating. His professional career began with racing in the Chicago area, especially at the old Santa Fe speedway.[1]

Corky Keener's noteworthy career had essentially peaked prior to winning the Pacific Coast Regional Championship at Sturgis in 1979. His Grand National Series (GNS) career spanned three years, beginning in 1974 and ending in 1976. In 1974, Keener was ranked seventh in the nation in point standings. During that year he won two GNS half-mile events, the 10-mile at Louisville, Kentucky and another 10-mile at Terre Haute, Indiana. In 1975 he won the 35-mile Grand National Mile at Syracuse, New York and the 10-mile half at Toledo, Ohio. These wins and other podium finishes placed Keener fourth in the point standing – the best year of his career. He won the 10-mile half at Harrington, Delaware the following year but failed to make the 1976 GNS top ten.[2]

After this final GNS win, Keener kept racing until he was injured in 1980. He then formally retired from professional competition and went to work full-time for General Motors in Flint. He retired from GM in 1988. Keener lives with his wife, Gail, in Fenton, Michigan, a suburb of Flint. During the '80s, Keener purchased a 150 Cessna and became interested in flying.[3]

August 4-10, 1980

The final meeting of the Black Hills Motor Classic group was held early in 1980 to discuss the organization of the rally, and most of those in attendance were Jackpine Gypsies who held membership in both organizations. Only four non-Gypsy main street merchants were present. Because both groups had become so busy (the Gypsies with their own events including the Gypsy Tours, the hill climb and the short track races and the businessmen unable to leave their stores), they collectively agreed turning over responsibility for the half-mile races to the Chamber of Commerce.[1]

According to the *Black Hills Press*, there were 140 members enrolled in the Gypsy group in 1980, and many provided services to all aspects of the yearly Classic. The gate receipts earned were used to cover liability insurance, hire extra police officers, maintain the short track, motocross and hill climb venues, and pay for AMA race officials. Since all of the work was voluntary, no Gypsy member received any remuneration for their efforts, and any excess cash was always donated to the Scouts, the city ambulance service, the hospital, the police department and the volunteer fireman unit.[2]

The *Black Hill Press* also summarized the status of the Black Hills Motor Classic organization. Still characterized as an "organization of Sturgis businessmen," the 110 members of this group were described as working closely with the Gypsies in promoting the races. Like the riding club, the Classic was non-profit, donating net receipts to similar organizations like the new swimming pool, the street department, the South Dakota National Guard, the Sturgis Ministerial Association, the Meade County Sheriff's Office, The High Plains Heritage Center and the Meade County Senior Citizens group.[3]

It is interesting to note that these two groups, while intimately involved in promoting the rally, were still officially separated after 42 years of reluctant but fruitful cooperation.

By Wednesday, the 40th Classic was being described as "quiet." Attendance projections were optimistic enough to open a third block of motorcycle parking by Monday afternoon. Judy Iverson at rally headquarters in the City Auditorium had already registered visitors from 48 of the 50 states, including riders from Alaska, Hawaii and Puerto Rico. Beyond a large contingent of Canadians, international visitors included riders from West Germany, England, Switzerland and Australia. The City Park was packed with tents by Sunday afternoon, and nearly 1,900 camping passes had been

Motorcycle days

The motorcycle days that come
　　Are the saddest of the year,
With wailing bikes and naked women,
　In the hands of each a beer.

Main Street is lined from end to end
　　With cycles spread galore.
It's impossible to find a space
　.To add a little more.

A moving mass of humanity
　　That walk and ride and run,
Like flies on a dead carcass
　　That's rotting in the sun.

But that is mild to what is seen
　　Down yonder in the park.
Nothing's barred as night comes on
　And it gets a little dark.

The show comes on, clothes come off
　　Like nothing you've seen before.
Oh Pam, you seem so innocent
　　With your little purple door!

So if you've been around the world
　　And seen all other places
You'll never top the show here
　　At the Sturgis cycle races

P.S. (With apologies to Winston Churchill) Never in the history of the country have so few endured so much from so many.

A shared poetic reflection regarding the rally by Donald Philippar of Sturgis, early 1980s.

sold, generating more than $22,000. Some main street vendors had already exceeded their gross 1979 sales figures by Wednesday. Police reports revealed no special problems other than open-container and minor traffic violations. Police Chief Ron Munoz speculated that the calm nature of the crowd was due to many independent, individual riders rather than any organized groups or gangs.[4]

A regular schedule of events was reported, and a purse of $9,700 was available to winners of the various events. For the eighth year in a row, the week would be capped off with the U.S. Pacific Regional Championship on Sunday afternoon.[5]

A motocross race, not included in the Classic schedule of events, was held on Sunday, prior to the official opening of the rally. Organized by a motocross group from Rapid City and held at the Jackpine Gypsy track, this event was unique because out-of-state riders began to dominate. In extremely dusty track conditions, seven of the ten classes were taken by riders from outside South Dakota.[6]

Accordingly to the *Meade County Times-Tribune*, the serious problems Sturgis had been facing with inflation, drought and a depressed agricultural market were actually alleviated by the estimated 40,000 visitors to the 1980 Classic. On the following Monday after the end of the rally, one local bank reported nearly $500,000 in additional deposits. A second bank did not provide an estimated figure but admitted that there was a substantial increase in deposits. The Times-Tribune suggested, conservatively, that estimated deposits in the two Sturgis banks had to be at least $800,000, not to mention those monies deposited in Belle Fourche, Deadwood, Rapid City and Spearfish financial institutions along with those dollars taken out of town by transient vendors.[7]

Wayne Baker, owner of the local supermarket, reported tremendous sales, indicating that the early arrivals had made a distinct difference in his gross income for the week. Baker admitted to being a rally supporter and commented that "ninety-nine percent of the bikers are wonderful people just like the people of Sturgis."[8] Chamber President Brian McKay reported that all three blocks of Main Street were filled to capacity for all seven days. The manager of Phil Town, Nick Hobernight, could only characterize the economic impact as "terrific, terrific, terrific, absolutely outstanding!" According to Hobernight, there were times during the week when 50-70 bikes were waiting to fill up with gasoline. The owner of a local restaurant said he had to leave occasionally because of the constant tension in trying to fill never-ending orders for food.[9] The owner of a local body shop, Al Colton, had decided to open his building to vendors, establishing Mr. Al's – a well-known landmark for contemporary Classic visitors. Colton reported that he had grossed more in space rentals in seven days of the rally than he ever had in a full year of business.[10]

A pause along Spearfish Canyon, early 1980s. (Author Photo)

Despite tremendous increases in business on Main Street, race attendance was definitely down at the featured half-mile track. Eddie Miller, Gypsies Treasurer and responsible for ticket sales, indicated that total receipts were down nearly $5,000. He speculated that this was due to lack of the grandstand, which had burned down in June. The absence of seating precluded the sale of reserved seating and limited ticket sales to general admission. There were also strong indications that more and more of the visitors simply were not interested in the races.[11]

Police Chief Ron Munoz characterized the 1980 rally as being "pretty quiet." The only major problems occurred in the city park, where more than 3,900 persons were registered as campers. He suggested that the rally committee limit the number to

3,000 in future years. With such a large number of tents, many problems arose over space limitations, and territorial disputes were common. The Chief characterized the downtown crowd, although the largest to date, as very calm, due in large part to the continued employment of additional law-enforcement personnel recruited from throughout the state.[12]

The number of pancakes, eggs, sausages, "Whimpy" sandwiches and hot dogs served by the Sturgis religious community in 1980 was unprecedented. Local church volunteers indicated that the number of meals served had doubled from the previous year's totals. The Meade County Senior Citizens Center also set a new record, serving more than 2,800 breakfasts over six days of the event.[13]

Races

Friday afternoon's Amateur hill climb was well attended as over 1,200 paying spectators watched dozens of riders compete in six classes of hill climbing motorcycles. The winners by class included:

Size	Place Winner	Hometown	Cycle
0 - 100cc	Timmy Derby	Lead, SD	Yamaha
125 - 174cc	Lonnie Hall	Rapid City, SD	Harley Davidson
175 - 250cc	Dan Deubler	Sioux Falls, SD	Bultaco
251 - 372cc	Rod Kelm	Forsyth, MT	(not listed)
373 - 500cc	Don Juhlin	Mankato, MN	Honda
501 - 750cc	Don Juhlin	Mankato, MN	Honda[14]

Friday night's Novice short track heats, scratch heats, and time trials were dominated by two California racers. Bill Scott from Red Bluff took first and Mike Garrison of Tulare placed second. Both of these California riders rode Yamahas.[15]

The classic Sturgis half-mile events were held on Saturday and Sunday. Saturday's Novice final was taken by David Durelle. Jeff Johnson and Mike Garrison placed second and third respectively and fourth place was taken by Bill Scott. Garrison and Scott had been winners in the Friday night short track event. Richard Arnalz of Stockton, California won Saturday's Junior final on a Harley Davidson in a challenging duel with Todd Glesick, who placed second on his BSA. In the Expert final, Frank Wood of Grants Pass, Oregon overcame second place winner Chubby Armour, a traditional competitor at Sturgis.[16]

The Saturday night Expert short track races were delayed until 10:30pm because of rain. The first three places were taken by Honda, Yamaha and Kawaski riders respectively. First went to Mickey Fay of Puyallup, Washington; second to Jim Filice of San Jose, California; and third to Daniel Atkinson of Boise, Idaho.[17]

In the Sunday Pacific Coast Regional finals, Durelle repeated his Saturday Novice win, besting Mike Garrison and Mark Rooks. In the Junior class, the winner was Jim Filice with second and third places taken by Steve Cort and Daniel Atkinson. In the Expert Championship final, the winner was Mike Minnig on an XR750 Harley Davidson. Minnig was challenged throughout the race by Jeff Haney of team Honda, who took second place on his 500cc Honda single. Haney was able to pass Minnig in the turns, but always lost first position in the straights. These two riders provided the fans with one of the closest Championship finals in many years.[18]

Motorcycle drag racing, a new event not officially part of the Black Hills Motor Classic, was held in Belle Fourche on Friday night and Saturday. Promoted by the Dragbike Bikernationals Group, these races drew a crowd of over 3,000 spectators on Saturday. There were 87 entries and the two major marques present included Harley Davidson and Kawasaki. The promoters were disappointed by a low number of street bike participants. Apparently stock bike "dragsters" preferred to peel out in Sturgis, rather than compete in Belle Fourche. Pete Hill of Granville, North Carolina was the "Top Fuel" class winner, completing the quarter mile strip in 9.44 seconds and reaching a top speed of 146.32 miles per hour. The *Times-Tribune* indicated that Dragbike officials were planning to meet with the Black Hills Motor Classic group in the interest of including motorcycle drag racing as an official event in future rallies, which was ultimately realized in later years.[19]

Neil Hultman

Born on February 19, 1929, Neil Hultman grew up in the Holabird and Highmore, South Dakota areas. When he was 18 years old, he moved to Sturgis and began a career working at Ft. Meade as a laboratory technician. When he was 19, Neil purchased an Indian Chief from Clarence Hoel and used it as his only vehicle, riding it year-round. About the same time, Neil joined the Jackpine Gypsies Motorcycle Club and has been an active participant, promoter, and contributor to the club, the rally, and the community ever since. He has attended and worked tirelessly at every Black Hills Motor Classic, with the exception of 1952, when he was serving in the United States Army and stationed in Korea. His friend, Bob Moore, characterizes Neil Hultman as "the cement that has kept everything together through good times and bad."

Hultman has served in practically every office of the Jackpine Gypsy Board of Directors and Jackpine Gypsy Club. He has also served in almost every capacity in regard to actual rally and racing activities. He acted as Club President and Vice President, and for many years, he served as the AMA Race Manager, AMA Referee, AMA Race Clerk, corner flagman, Hill Climb coordinator, Club Secretary-Treasurer, Road Captain, Assistant Road Captain, Timer, Tour Captain, and Lineman.

In 1954, while serving as a referee for the very first time, Hultman became involved in a tense decision-making process. Larry Stone, an expert rider, foolishly attempted to upset the nationally-ranked racer Joe Leonard (Sturgis Champion in 1953 and 1957) by hooking his left leg coming out of a turn in the back stretch during a heat race. Charlie West (future champion at Sturgis in 1956), who was serving as Leonard's mechanic, came out of the pits waving a large wrench. Joe Leonard, having recovered from this altercation, lapped the track and neatly hooked Stone, sending him high and out of the race. As referee, Hultman could have disqualified all of these racers. But he avoided a fight in the pits thanks to a suggestion from Announcer Jim Tagaris, who was also an AMA representative at the time. Tagaris suggested that Neil threaten to pull their AMA cards, leaving them unable to race at Springfield on the upcoming Labor Day weekend. Peace prevailed, and the protest was settled.

During his early years in the Jackpine Gypsies Motorcycle Club, Neil was involved in all aspects of motorcycle activity. He competed in hill climbs, enduros, "bare tire" events, "chain" events, scrambles, and trials racing. In the mid 1950s, Neil competed and won the Brandon, Manitoba hill climb in the 500cc class. Neil also held a Class C competition card for hill climbing and held a membership in the AMA Congress for one year in the 1950's. In his book, *Life's Bits and Pieces*, Pappy Hoel tells a story about Neil riding in a trials event when a plank that was laid across a creek broke. Hultman and his bike fell into the muck and mire. According to Hoel, he "laughed until he realized that Neil was riding one of his bikes!"[1]

In 1985, Neil was named Rally Coordinator for the Chamber of Commerce, when a new committee was formed of the Jackpine Gypsies and the Black Hills Motor Classic membership. Since the funds allocated to this committee were extremely limited, money was raised through logo sales, which in turn funded Neil's position as Rally Coordinator and prize money for the half-mile races at the fairgrounds each year.

Neil Hultman in his AMA referee uniform. (Courtesy of Neil Hultman)

Neil Hultman served quietly in the development of the White Plate Flat Trackers Association, the National Motorcycle Museum, and has been integrally involved in four different attempts to establish the Sturgis Motorcycle Museum and Hall of Fame.

Selfless to a fault, Neil Hultman, like Pearl Hoel, served Pappy Hoel tirelessly through his support and labor, always there to assist in making each Black Hills Motor Classic a success. His quiet demeanor, friendly attitude, and unassuming manner in planning, organizing, promulgating, and administering the motorcycle rally in Sturgis, South Dakota have often gone unnoticed in the press and in public displays at rally-related activities. The de-facto inheritor of Pappy Hoel's leadership in Sturgis, this unassuming gentleman has devoted 55 years of his life to making the Black Hills Motor Classic a success, and he deserves a great deal of recognition.

Neil retired in December of 1984 from Ft. Meade VA Hospital, where he had been a lab technician for 37 years. He lives with his lovely wife Ramona in Boulder Canyon, about 5 miles west of Sturgis. He is still actively involved in all aspects of the rally, especially in regard to the re-establishment of the Sturgis Motorcycle Museum and Motorcycle Hall of Fame. He has kept many of his motorcycles, including a '55 Indian, an '83 Yamaha Venture and a 500cc BSA. He is presently restoring a 1930 Indian Chief.

Chapter Eleven:
Contemporary Classics

And so we arrive at a major turning point in the Black Hills Motor Classic. The year 1981 marked a definite change in the Sturgis experience. Small evolutionary changes in the rally had begun to emerge in the late 1970s, and these elements began working in concert to affect changes in the overall tone of the rally over the last 23 years. Interest in the "Races", so important to early visitors, began to deteriorate as the crowds of visitors continued to grow. As Bobby Hill so aptly stated in his description of the contemporary motorcycling world, "In the 1950s and 1960s, anyone who rode a motorcycle followed the racing and knew the names of all of the important racers. It's not like that any more."[1]

The diversification of activities was a direct response to the larger and larger crowds of visitors. On-site diversions expanded into shopping for motorcycle accessories or leather clothing, seeking out musical entertainment, and feasting on "Western" food like buffalo sausage, buffalo burgers and Indian tacos. One particular aspect of change includes the traveling experiences riders have in coming to and from Sturgis. There are scores of visitors who ride thousands of miles on touring motorcycles in getting to Sturgis, then spend three hours walking Main Street, only to continue on with their tour. When the City Park was closed to camping in 1982, the door was opened for the establishment of huge, privately-owned campgrounds that actually became self-contained mini-rallies.

As the number of visitors continued to increase, dirt-track racing began to take a back seat. Old guard racing fans were still loyal, but many visitors came and left without paying any attention to the competition. In the mid 1980s, drag racing was added to the competition format, but this venue attracted a totally new group of motorcycle aficionados.

The limited number of vendors available to the visitors in the '70s was expanded to include huge numbers of out-of-town, non-resident commercial interests. Their presence overwhelmed many of the locals. People in Sturgis were jealously torn between the income they could generate renting space and the realization that most of the potential profits were leaving town. As the vendors began to require more and more space, Main Street merchants began leasing their store-fronts and then later their entire store sales areas. As time passed, some of the merchants simply closed their doors, selling or leasing their buildings to corporations from all 50 states.

The difficulties in managing the rally, including overall organization, crowd control, law enforcement, and response to influences like the South Dakota Governor's office and State Department of Tourism, continued to multiply. Surprisingly, adequate adjustments were made along the way, and potential problems were anticipated and derailed in year-long planning sessions.

In his recent book, *100 Years of Harley Davidson*, Willy Davidson describes the rally's evolution quite succinctly. "In 1978," according to Davidson, "I traveled to Sturgis for the first time. It was much less corporate and commercial than it is now."[2] After describing the pleasure, camaraderie, and the scenery in getting to Sturgis, Davidson goes on to characterize the rally of today and poses the big question on every newcomer's mind: Is it really possible for more than a quarter of a million riders to be in the same place at the same time?[3]

Davidson goes on to describe bikes parked handlebar to handlebar on six blocks of Main Street:

> *...license plates a patchwork quilt of colors representing every state. The shops are filled with leather and other vendors and each alleyway is packed with stalls selling every conceivable motorcycle-related product, from T-shirts, belt buckles, and sunglasses, to leather belts, saddle bags, chrome parts and decals. You smell the smoky aroma of frying buffalo meat sausages and onions coming from the food sheds.*[4]

Visitors

As the attendance continued to climb, recreational venues other than dirt track racing emerged. There were massive changes in the general characteristics of the visitors. By 1980, more and more of the new visitors were recreational riders who were involved in touring the country in larger, fully dressed Harley Davidsons, Honda Goldwings and RT BMWs. Many of these riders were persons who, like the author, began riding after the age of 30. As a result, they were generally ignorant of the various forms of motorcycle competition and focused their experiences on cross-country touring, staying in motels or camping in plush campgrounds. Since the new generation of touring motorcycles were mechanically dependable and trouble free, touring concerns centered around after-market accessories like CB radios, saddle bags, and huge trunk carriers designed to tote a variety of "worldly" goods on each trip. Some even began pulling trailers, while the less daring would trailer their motorcycles to the rally each year behind huge expensive four-wheel drive pickups. All of these efforts, focused on ease, convenience, and image, were greatly different from the nature of early rally visitors. As Joe Leonard put it, "Gone are the days when I would wash my skivvies and T-shirt in some pond or creek, and then drape them over the handlebars to dry out!"[5]

Another significant factor that emerged was the arrival of outlaw gangs. Early problems in the mid-1970s continued into the 1980s. Another phenomenon was the proliferation of gang "wannabes" dressed in gang member togs and acting accordingly. It is probably safe to say that the old racing crowd did not totally approve of these new visitors, and at times, the feelings were, most likely, quite mutual. Nostalgia on the part of early visitors about the family nature of early rallies emerged regularly in the 1980s and 90s with efforts to recapture the flavor of the "good old days".

Throughout its evolution, however, the rally has always drawn a variety of persons to Sturgis, and all have come for different reasons and in response to different drives. In 1923, sociologist W.I. Thomas formulated a theory entitled the *Four Wishes* that identified four needs or wishes possessed by every human being.[6] They include:

Security: Every human wishes to feel secure. This security includes self, society, politics and economics. Some persons have a greater wish for security, while others are more willing to cast caution to the wind.

Response: Everyone wishes for a close relationship with another person, a friend to talk with, to enjoy company with, and also a friend that will share one's highs and lows. Again, some people need to have many friends, and others need only one or two.

Recognition: Everyone wishes for a recognizable image. Some will go to great lengths in developing a flamboyant persona, while others seek recognition via subdued demeanor in dress and other outward behaviors.

New Experience: Everyone needs adventure. To some the adventure is involved with life threatening behavior, and to others adventure is more subdued. Each position along this continuum, in its own way, gains its impetus from experience with the new or the unknown.[7]

Thomas proposed that every human possesses all four of these wishes, yet each person does so with different proportions of desire. For example, some persons, like cyclists visiting Sturgis, may have a high need for response. These persons enjoy the motorcy-

Main Street Sturgis, 1996. (SD Tourism Photo)

cling venue, because of the friendship and common interests. They enjoy the experiences they have in interacting with their riding friends. These riders generally come to Sturgis with a best pal or a small group of riders and experience the week as it relates to the group atmosphere generated by their personal motorcycling family. When one reflects on the characteristics of the pre-1980 visitors, it's fairly safe to conclude that the majority of these early visitors embraced Response as their dominant wish or need. Other motorcyclists come to Sturgis purely for Recognition. These riders are there to see and be seen by the others. Although these riders may be part of a support group or club, their major motivation is to show off their new bike, their flashy clothing or lack thereof. Other Recognition elements may include knowledge of motorcycle trivia, racing facts, or the latest engineering/design break-through. In some cases the wish for Recognition is based solely on their ability to drink large amounts of beer. The reader should, however, remember that these riders often still embrace a Response wish for belonging, especially in regard to their personal identity group.

Gang members and gang member wannabes tend to see Recognition as their predominant wish. Many of the post-1980 visitors wear gang related clothing and enjoy being perceived by the "normal" types as members of a motorcycle gang. If a rally visitor spends any time visiting with members of this group, the visitor soon realizes that some of the gang members, and particularly the wannabes, are doctors, law-yers, CPAs, teachers and even wealthy businessmen. To them, the Sturgis rally is nothing more than real life *"Fantasy Island"*. Many of them enjoy playing a role each year during rally week. Women who enjoy wearing see-through clothing or nothing at all are typically included in the Recognition wish group. Parading down Main Street in various states of dress or undress seems to be, for them, a real trip.

Some visitors come for adventure or New Experience. This experience might include the trip to and from the rally as well as those experiences generated in touring the Black Hills, seeing the huge variety of motorcycles, listening to the engines, shop-ping for motorcycle paraphernalia, getting a tattoo, and maybe even watching the races.

Although the general public probably views motorcyclists as ignoring Security in regard to the real dangers involved in this activity, it has been the author's experience that most riders have a definite wish for this element in riding. Security, beyond the physical danger aspects of a crash, can also be recognized in the application of safe riding techniques, the use of protective clothing and helmets, and being sure that tires and engines are in good order.

So for riders and non-riders alike, everyone who visits Sturgis seems to find a place that addresses their wishes or needs.

Commercialization

As Willie Davidson inferred, the Classic assumed a very commercial and corporate image in the 1980s. While the efforts of local organizers in the early days were geared towards a non-profit state of mind, the influx of vendors added a new challenge to local ideas about the rally, heavily affecting the downtown area.

This evolutionary shift became another headache for the Sturgis Chamber of Commerce. Not only did the Chamber members have to deal with the actual ven-dors, but they also found themselves reinterpreting the change in attitude of the lo-cals. Main Street storeowners were overwhelmed by the rent the vendors were willing to pay for the use of their buildings for a couple of weeks. Rental prices continued to increase yearly until several of the vendors offered to buy the buildings at astronomical prices. This was, and continues to be, a challenge for the city of Sturgis.

Denny Kannenberg, a racer from the Minneapolis area who competed in Sturgis in the 60s and serves as the current president of the White Plate Flat Trackers Associa-tion, says he was the first person to rent commercial vendor space at the Classic. Kannenberg, who owns "Sport Wheels" – a recycled motorcycle parts and accessories business in Jordan, Minnesota, hit upon the idea of renting space to vendors. He approached the Jackpine Gypsy organizers, who in turn contacted the city fathers, about renting the National Guard Armory for the 1974 rally. To draw people in, Kannenberg trucked 60 show bikes to Sturgis and set them up in the center of the armory floor. He then divided the perimeter of the hall into booth space, which he filled with some of his own used motorcycles, accessories and parts, and then rented out the rest of the space to vendors. This went so well that the idea caught on, and the number of vendors has been expanding every year.[8]

By 1985, there were over 450 "registered" vendors in Sturgis proper, according to Kannenberg. These vendors were renting space from private individuals, church groups, merchants and other entities. In the years that followed, every conceivable space was rented and vendors began setting up at business establishments along State Highways 79 and 34 to the east of Sturgis, as well as at every Interstate exit between Rapid City and Sturgis. By 1998, nearly 1,000 vendors were licensed in the City of Sturgis. They included 88 tattoo establishments, 92 in leather sales, 94 food stalls, and 169 T-shirt booths. The largest group, in excess of 400, comprised parts and accessories vendors.[9] As the number of vendors increased, dissatisfaction with the "Transient Merchants License" fee evolved into the sale of Main Street commercial buildings to out-of-state owners. Locals, concerned about the loss of shopping for basic essentials, blamed the rally for taking over their hometown stores. Many of these critics failed to realize, however, that their own shopping patterns had changed, along with the residents of thousands of other small towns across the nation. Because of the relatively traffic-free 30 miles of Interstate 90 that separate Sturgis from Rapid City, almost everyone was beginning to shop in "Rapid", and most of the Sturgis merchants were struggling to stay in business. As a consequence, the national pattern of shopping in bigger towns replete with malls, entertainment, other recreational opportunities and health care facilities had emerged in Sturgis. But many of the local citizens began to attribute this natural loss of local shopping to the Classic.

Racing

A declining interest in dirt track racing on oval tracks was not, however, limited to Sturgis. According to the AMA's Ed Youngblood in his recent biography of Dick Mann, the problem was a national trend evolving out of several dimensions that affected the national dirt track racing scene. For example, in the mid-1970's, over 40,000 spectators would fill the Houston Astrodome to watch short-track and TT races. By the end of the '80s and into the early '90s, most grandstands would be only 40 to 60 percent full. Even National Championship races "were drawing crowds not much larger than a high school football game."[10]

Television programming also had a major influence on dirt-track racing. The motorcycle programs of choice became road racing and motocross. Televised coverage of flat track racing proved to be extremely difficult because the actual racing is punctuated with long pauses of track preparation. Flat track, when televised, generally utilizes a taped format because the long pauses between competitions can be edited out.[11]

A third element has to do with rules changes. Since early class "C" racing machines did not have brakes, racers had to slow their bikes in the corners by broad sliding. A rules change that allowed brakes, along with the development of sticky rubber tires, changed dirt track racing in a major way. In contemporary dirt-track racing, the corner grooves are paved in rubber detritus by the end of practice and time trials. Consequently, the racers now merely brake going into the corner, ride the groove and then attempt to pass on the straights, making for a less exciting show. Youngblood quotes one racer who sarcastically stated, "The only reason we use oval tracks any more is so the riders will go by the grandstand, because there certainly isn't any racing going on in the turns."[12]

A fourth threat to public exposure and interest in flat track racing was the explosion of motocross on the American motorcycle-racing scene. Motocross was intro-

Main Street Sturgis, 1997. (SD Tourism Photo)

duced from Europe in the late 1960s. In 1965 the AMA was involved in 156 dirt track events and only 15 motocross races. By 1985, the AMA was sanctioning over 1,100 motocross races and only 191 dirt track events. In the 1950s and '60s, every young racer wanted to be a dirt-tracker. By the 1980s young riders could not afford to compete in the dirt-track events because they had been taken over by factory-sponsored riding teams and only the best of the best riders were chosen. To use a baseball metaphor – the farm system had dried up. The young riders who could not afford to race on the flat tracks turned to moto-cross meets on local courses using inexpensive, race-ready motorcycles, forever expanding this form of racing activity.[13]

Governance

In the 1980s and beyond, the rally organizers still consisted of the two local camps— the business owners (the Black Hills Motor Classic) and the local riders (the Jackpine Gyspies). Local and state law enforcement officials, along with the South Dakota Department of Tourism, gradually emerged as additional entities. Even the Governor's office began to take a major interest in this revenue-generating phenomenon. Everyone was, and continues to be, torn by mounting confusion as the numbers kept growing and growing. Local townspeople who disliked the noise and confusion continued to assail the city government about ending the rally without the simple knowledge that these city officials were never legally in charge. Because of the incorporation of the Black Hills Motor Classic in 1938, the local officials were responsible for supporting this local non-profit enterprise. Many of the local citizens still do not realize that city government could not, legally, close down the Classic anymore than they could close down the local McDonald's franchise or any of the other businesses in Sturgis. Local, county, and state law enforcement bodies continued to do an excellent job of keeping the peace, thanks due in large part to their ability to analyze and anticipate problems through yearly planning and re-organization meetings. The rally survives today because of law enforcment's dedicated efforts and the excellent choices made in adjusting policy formats and enforcement procedures.

While local business owners who made up the Black Hills Motor Classic began to focus on commercial opportunities by renting space to vendors, they also became involved in merchandizing activities of their own during the short and lucrative seven to ten day marketplace. Consequently these business owners found less and less time to devote to the rally, and the work of the rally began to fall largely on local racing enthusiasts, including the Jackpine Gypsies. Neil Hultman, a local rally leader, organizer, and member of the Jackpine Gypsies since 1947, was actively involved in pro-

The sea of bikes on Main Street Sturgis, late 1990s. (SD Tourism Photo)

motional activities in Sturgis since his first year as a Gypsy. In attempting to describe the evolution of the rally, he stated:

> ...the Black Hills Motor Classic became a victim of its own success. The work required to continue each year called for more volunteers and the business owners were too busy to really get involved selling tickets and fulfilling the many duties necessary for the rally's success, so most of the planning became the responsibility of the Jackpine Gypsies Motorcycle Club. This continued until 1985 when the Gypsies asked the Sturgis Chamber of Commerce to take on the half-mile races and some of the other duties necessary for the following year. This was necessary as the Jackpine Gypsies were, and the club was and still is, dependent on volunteer help.[14]

Until 1989, the several groups involved in promoting the Classic had been bound together by a common thread – Clarence "Pappy" Hoel. Although Pappy began to take a back seat in regard to formal and actual leadership, his vision and advice were crucial in maintaining and supporting communication between the various groups involved. His death on February 1, 1989 created a vacuum in the rally community.

Perhaps Hoel did not realize the important role he played in binding everything together. His humility was evidenced by this statement from Neil Hultman, his de-facto heir:

> *Mr. J.C. Hoel told me more than once he was almost embarrassed by the recognition and honors bestowed him for starting one of the most successful and internationally recognized motorcycle rallies. In the same breath he would credit all the help from the Jackpine Gypsies Motorcycle club members over the many years and the commitment of the members of Black Hills Motor Classic.*[15]

Within a year of Hoel's passing, everyone at the local level began to realize that the coalition of local groups in Sturgis could no longer do an adequate job of organizing and managing the event. The Chamber of Commerce, which had been charged with the task in 1985, created the Black Hills Motor Classic Committee to provide structure. Neil Hultman was hired to coordinate fund-raising activities and organize the event. By the summer of 1989, however, all of the members of this new Black Hills Motor Classic Committee had resigned, forcing the Sturgis Chamber of Commerce to hire an outside group to manage the rally. Incorporated under the title "Sturgis Rally and Races", the group managed the Classic until 1995. At that point, Champion, a professional management group from North Carolina, assumed management of the rally. Under Champion, the last half-mile races were held in 1997. While the half-mile races were reinstated in 2002, it remains to be seen if racing, the original core element of the Black Hills Motor Classic, will survive in the 21st Century.

End Notes

Chapter One

Sturgis

1. Sneve Virginia D., Ed. (1973) <u>South Dakota Geographic Names</u> Brevet Press, Sioux Falls SD p. 599

2. South Dakota Place Names (1941) South Dakota WPA Writer's Project University of South Dakota, Vermillion, SD

The Black Hills

1. Amiotte, L. (2002) Personal Communication, February 11.

2. "What is the AMA?" ama.cycle.org/whatis/history/html. P. 3

Pappy Hoel

1. Hoel, P. (2002). Personal Interview. Sturgis, South Dakota. April 29.

2. "Classics 'Granddaddy explains how it all started." Sturgis Tribune(Special Edition). August 1, 1979. P. 7.

3. Hoel, J. C. (1982) Life's Bits & Pieces. Self Published. Sturgis South Dakota.

4. Hoel, P. (2002). Personal Interview. Sturgis,South Dakota. April 29.

5. Hoel, J. C. (1945). "Memories of the Jackpine Gypsies in Sturgis South Dakota." Indian Motorcycle News. July-August, P. 5.

6. Hoel, J. C. (1982) Life's Bits & Pieces. Self Published. Sturgis South Dakota.

7. Hoel, P. (2002). Personal Interview. Sturgis, South Dakota. April 29.

8. Vodden, D. (2002). Personal Interview. Eldon, Missouri. June 27.

9. Hoel, J. C. (1982) Life's Bits & Pieces. Self Published. Sturgis South Dakota.

10. IBID.

11. Hoel, J. (2002). Personal Interview. Sturgis, South Dakota. April 30.

12. Hoel, J. C. (1982) Life's Bits & Pieces. Self Published. Sturgis South Dakota.

13. IBID.

14. IBID.

Pearl Hoel

1. Rogerson, K.L. (1999) "Pearl Hoel". <u>Gypsy Times</u>. V. 1 N. 3 August, 1999.

Don Vodden

1. Vodden, D. (2002). Personal Interview. Eldon, MO. June 27.

2. IBID.

3. IBID.

4. IBID.

5. IBID

Chapter Two

1937

1. "Motorcyclists To Hold Field Meet Here August 1" Sturgis Tribune, July 15, 1937, V. 8, N. 9, p. 1

2. "Cyclist Fatally Injured, Boulder Canyon" Sturgis Tribune, July 22, 1937, V. 8, N. 10

1938

1. "Everything Ready For The Big Race!" Sturgis Tribune, June 29, 1938, V. 9, N. 37, p. 1.

2. Vodden, D. (2002). Personal Interview. Eldon, MO June 11.

3. IBID.

4. Hultman, N. (2002). Personal Interview. April 28.

5. "Big Motorcyle Race Meet Scheduled" Sturgis Tribune, July 6, 1938, V.9, N. 32, p. 1.

6. IBID.

7. Hoel, J. C. (1982) Life's Bits and Pieces. Self Published, Sturgis, SD p.35.

8. Vodden, D. (2002). Personal Interview. Eldon MO. June 11.

9. "First Annual Cycle Race A Hummer" Sturgis Tribune, August 17, 1938, V. 9, N. 38, p. 1.

10. Hoel, J. C. (1982) Life's Bits and Pieces. Self Published. Sturgis, SD p. 35.

11. IBID, p. 87.

Johnny Spiegelhoff

1. Scheets, J. (2002). Personal communication. (telephone) July 21.

2. IBID.

3. Hoel, P. (2002). Personal communication. April 29.

4. Deckert, H. (2002). Personal communication. May 17.

5. Nelson, A. (2002). Personal communication. June 4.

6. Vodden, D. (2002). Personal interview. Eldon, MO. June 11.

7. IBID

8. "First Annual Cycle Race a Hummer" Sturgis Tribune. August 17, 1938. V. N.

9. Nelson, A (2002). Personal communication. June 4.

10. IBID

1939

1. "Speed Classic Gets Major Interest Of Community" Sturgis Tribune, July 13, 1939, V. 10, N. 33, p. 1.

2. IBID. p. 8.

3. IBID.

4. Rapid City Journal (1994). Thunder in the Hills. Rapid City Journal and the Billings Gazette. Rapid City, SD p.7.

5. "Office Opened For Speed Event" Sturgis Tribune, July 27, 1939, V. 10, N. 35, p. 1.

6. "Sturgis Cycle Club Is Host To August Convention" Sturgis Tribune, July 13, 1939, V. 10, N. 33, p. 3.

7. IBID.

8. "Kiddies Parade To Be A Feature of Motorcycle Classic Parade This Year" Sturgis Tribune, July 27, 1939, V. 10, N. 34, p. 1.

9. "Motorcycle Riders To Come From As Far As California" Sturgis Tribune, August 3, 1939, V. 10, No. 35, p. 1.

10. "Sturgis Has Welcome Flags Out; Set For Races" Sturgis Tribune, V. 10, N. 37, pp. 1, 8.

11. "Gypsy Tour Of Black Hills Is Made Friday By 55 Motorcyclists" Sturgis Tribune, August 17, 1939, V. 10, N. 38, p. 6.

12. IBID.

13. Vodden, D. (2002) Personal Interview. Eldon, MO June 11.

American Motorcyclists Association

1. "What is the AMA?" ama.cycle.org/whatis/history/html. P.1

2. IBID. P.2

3. IBID. P.3

1940

1. "First Advertising For Speed Classic This Week." Sturgis Tribune. July 18, 1940. V. 11, N. 34, P.2.

2. "Motorcycle Passes To Be Given To County Graduates." Sturgis Tribune. July 25, 1940. V. 11, N. 35, P. 1.

3. IBID

4. "Endurance Run Planned For Motorcyclists." Sturgis Tribune. July 25,1940. V. 11, N. 34. P.1.

5. "Shorty Cochran Wins 210 Mile Motorcycle Run" Sturgis Tribune, Thursday, August 1, 1940, V. 11, N. 36. p. 8

6. "Entries Pour In For Speed Classic" Sturgis Tribune, August 8, 1940, V. 11, N. 37, p. 8

7. "Speed Classic Is Ready For Crowds." Sturgis Tribune. August 15, 1940. V. 11, N 38. P. 1.

8. Hoel, J. (2002). Personal Interview. Sturgis, SD. April 28.

9. "Gypsy Tour A Success." Sturgis Tribune. August 22, 1940. V. 11, N. 39, p. 5.

10. Hoel, J. (2002). Personal Interview. Sturgis, SD April 29.

11. "Gypsy Tour A Success." Sturgis Tribune. August 22, 1940. V. 11, N. 39, P. 5.

12. "NELSON WINS STURGIS CHAMPIONSHIP; 4 CYCLISTS NIP TRACK RECORD IN TIME TRIALS." Rapid City Journal. August 22,1940. P. 8.

13. "Nelson Takes Black Hills Classic Championship." Sturgis Tribune. August 22, 1940. V.11, N. 39, P. 1.

1941

1. "Chief Of Cavalry Visits Ft. Meade." Sturgis Tribune. July 17, 1941. V. 12, N. 34, p. 1.

2. "Meade County Registrants Get Serial Numbers." Sturgis Tribune. July 17, 1941. V. 12, N. 34, P. 1.

3. " Patriotic Ceremony to Open Motorcycle Races August 2-3." Sturgis Tribune. July 17, 1941. V 12, N 34, P. 1.

4. IBID

5. "Gypsy Tour Plans Completed With Date Set For August 1." Sturgis Tribune, July 24, 1941, V. 12, N. 35, p. 1.

6. IBID.

7. IBID.

8. "Racers Arriving For Motor Classic." Sturgis Tribune. July 13, l941, V. 12, N. 36, p. 1.

9. "Stark Still Holds Track Record Time Of 30.38 Established Last Year." Sturgis Tribune. August 7, 1941, V. 12, N. 37, p. 1.

10. IBID

Chapter 3

Motorcycle Production

1. Indian Motorcycle Memories (1998) "An Interview with Jerry Hatfield." Wgby.org/localprograms/indian/page/hatfield

2. Thorp, D. (1998) The Soldier that Never was; Indian Military Model 841 motorcycle.com/mcmuseum/i841

Chapter 4

1946

1. "Motorcycle Classic, First Since War Will Be Staged August 10-11," Sturgis Tribune. July 25, 1946. V. 17, N. 33, p. 1.

2. IBID.

3. "Gypsy Tour Feature Of Motorcycle Class, Will Cover 150 Miles of Hills." Sturgis Tribune. August 1, 1946. V. 17, N. 34, p. 1.

4. "Top Riders Will Take Part In Motorcycle Classic First Since 1941." Sturgis Tribune. August 8, 1946. V. 17, N. 35, p. 1

Spiegelhoff, National Career

1. "Spiegelhoff Roars to Victory" Indian Motorcycle News. November-December, 1946. V 13, N 6, p. 8.

2. IBID.

3. "Speigelhoff is Daytona Champ" Indian Motorcycle News. March-April, 1947. V. 14, N. 2, p. 14.

4. Kretz, E. Jr. (2002). Personal communication. (telephone) July 24.

5. Deckert, H. (2002). Personal communication. May 17.

AMA Competition

1. "What is the AMA?"ama-cycle.org/whatis/history/hotml. P.5

2. IBID.

3. IBID.

4. IBID.

1947

1. "Large Field Of Entries Expected For Motor Races." Sturgis Tribune. July 24, 1947. V. 18, N. 33, p. 1.

2. IBID.

3. "Motorcycle Classic Opens Saturday, Top Flight Race Riders Are Entered." Sturgis Tribune. August 7, 1947. V. 18, N. 35, p. 1.

4. "Hundreds Of Motorcycles Take Part In Tour, Races Thrill Packed Saturday." Sturgis Tribune. August 14, l947. V 18, N. 36, p. 1.

5. James, B. (2002). Personal Communication (Email). August 18.

Bill Tuman

1. Tuman, B. (2002). Personal Interview. Davenport, Iowa, September 30.

2. IBID.

3. "Bill Tuman" (1990). National Motorcycle Museum Hall of Fame. www.nationalmcmuseum.com.

4. IBID.

5. Tuman, B. (2002). Personal Interview. Davenport, Iowa, September 30.

6. IBID

7. "Bill Tuman" (1990). National Motorcycle Museum Hall of Fame. (Add 3 above)

White Plate Flat Trackers Association

1. Hoel, J. C. (1982). Life's Bits and Pieces. Self Published. Sturgis, SD pp.67-77

2. White Plate Flat Trackers Association. dirttrackerpro.com/mydtp.php3?member=WPFTA

Floyd Emde

1. "Hundred of Motorcycles Take Part in Tour, Races Thrill Packed Saturday." Sturgis Tribune. August 14, 1947. V. 18, N. 35, p. 1.

2. "Floyd Emde, AMA Hall of Fame Member." ama-cycle.org/forms/museum/hofbiopage.asp?

3. IBID.

1948

1. "Jackpine Gypsy Tour Scheduled For Friday, Motorcycle Classics Saturday." Sturgis Tribune. August 12, 1948. V. 19, N. 36, p. 1.

2. IBID. p. 6.

3. "Races Draw Capacity Crowd, Several Records Smashed In Two Day Event." Sturgis Tribune. August 19, 1948. V 19, N.37, p. 1.

4. IBID.

5. IBID. p. 5.

6. IBID.

7. "Letters to the Editor" Sturgis Tribune. August 19, 1948. V. 19, N. 37, P. 1.

Chuck Basney

1. Lee, T. (2002). Personal interview (Telephone). August 12.

2. IBID.

3. IBID.

4. Hultman, N. (2002). Personal interview. Pierre, South Dakota, April 28.

5. Phillips, B. (2002). Personal interview (Telephone). August 14.

Indian Motorcycles

1. Hatfield, J. (1999) "An Interview with Jerry Hatfield" Indian Motorcycle Memories. wgby.org/localprograms/indian/pages/hatfield.

2. IBID p. 1

3. Indian-Digest Indian Motorcycle History. ng.netgate/carl/indintro.html

4. Hatfield, J. (1999) "An Interview with Jerry Hatfield" Indian Motorcycle Memories. wgby.org/localprograms/indian/pages/hatfield.

5. IBID

6. IBID

7. IBID.

8. "Kiwi Indian Motorcycles". The Factory History of Indian Motorcycles. kiwi-indian.com/history.htm

9. "Motorcycle Hall of Fame Museum" ama-cycle.org/museum/halloffame/tuman.html

Babe Tancrede

1. "Babe Tancrede, AMA Hall of Fame Member." ama-cycle.org/forms/museum/HOFbiopage.asp?

2. I BID.

3. I BID.

1949

1. "Plan Contests On Main Street On Night Of Gypsy Tour" Sturgis Tribune, July 21, 1949, V. 20, N. 33, p. 1

2. IBID

3. "Gypsy Tour Scheduled For Friday Next Week, Motorcycle Races Open Saturday" Sturgis Tribune, August 4, 1949, V. 20, N. 35, p. 1

4. "Black Hills Classic Opens This Saturday, Top Racers Will Compete" Sturgis Tribune, August 11, 1949, V. 20, N. 36, p. 1

5. "Ohio Man Wins Top Spot At Races, Amateur Breaks Track Record" Sturgis Tribune, August 18, 1949, V. 20, N 37, p. 1

6. "Ohio Man Wins Top Spot At Races, Amateur Breaks Track Record" Sturgis Tribune, August 18, 1949, V. 20, N. 37, p. 1

7. IBID

8. IBID p. 10

9. IBID p. 12

Dick Klamfoth

Based entirely on personal interview.

Manx Norton

1. Motorcycle Hall of Fame Museum; The Classics. cycle.org/museum/2000/classified.html p. 1

2. Dick Klamfoth AMA Hall of Fame Member amadirectlink.com/halloffame/members/klamfoth p. 1

Dick O'Leary

Based on Personal Interview, August 23.

1950

1. Hoel, J. (2002) Personal Interview. June 17.

2. "Motorcycles Will Churn the Rocks of Time at Bear Butte." Sturgis Tribune. July 6, 1950. V. 22, N. 31, p. 1.

3. Hoel, J. (2002) Personal Interview. Sturgis, SD. June 17.

4. Pearl Hoel.(2002). Personal interview. Sturgis, SD. April 29.

5. "Black Hills Gypsy Tour, Program." Sturgis Tribune,. August 10, 1950. V 22, N. 36, p. 1.

6. "Black Hills Gypsy Tour, Program. " Sturgis Tribune. August 10, 1950. V22, N36, P.1.

7. "Motorcycle Races Saturday and Sunday, Tour Friday" Sturgis Tribune. August 10, 1950, V. 22, N. 36, P. 2.

8. "New Track Record Set at Races" Sturgis Tribune, August 17, 1950, V. 22, N. 37, p. 1

9. IBID.

10. Chet Dykgraaf ama-cycle.org/museum/halloffame/html

Chester Dykgraaf

1. Chet Dykgraaf Motorcycle Hall of Fame. ama-cycle.org/museum/halloffame/members/dykgraaf.

2. "Chester Chet Dykgraaf; 1990 Inductee - Competition Category." National Motorcycle Museum and Hall of Fame. nationalmcmuseum.com/hof/1999/cdykgraaf.

3. Chet Dykgraaf Motorcycle Hall of Fame. ama-cycle.org/museum/halloffame/members/dykgraaf.

4. Andrews, B. (2002). "Catching Up With Chet Dykgraaf." Feature Archive amadirectlink.com/features/dykgraaf

5. Chet Dykgraaf Motorcycle Hall of Fame. ama-cycle.org/museum/halloffame/members/dykgraaf.

Early Racers

1. Hoel J.C. (1982). Life's Bits & Pieces. Self Published. Sturgis, South Dakota. Pp35-38

2. Hoel, J. (2002). Personal Communication. June 28.

3. Hoel, J. C. (1982). Life's Bits & Pieces. Self Published. Sturgis, South Dakota.

4. Hultman, N. (2002). Personal Interview. Pierre, South Dakota. April 28.

Chapter Five

1951

1. "Country's Top Riders To Be In Sturgis For Annual Event, Gypsy Tour of Scenic Spots, This Weekend." Sturgis Tribune. August 9, 1951. V. 23, N. 36, p. 1.

2. "Two Hundred Sixty Riders Register For Gypsy Tour, Classics Queen Chosen." Sturgis Tribune. August 16, 1951. V. 23, N. 37, p. 6.

3. "Country's Top Riders To Be In Sturgis For Annual Event, Gypsy Tour Of Scenic Spots, This Weekend." Sturgis Tribune. August 9, 1951. V. 23, N. 36, p. 1.

4. IBID.

5. Garret-Davis, J. (2001). "Dakota Images; Josef Meier" South Dakota History. Vol. 31, N.1, Spring p. 90.

6. "Two Hundred Sixty Riders Register For Gypsy Tour, Classics Queen Chosen." Sturgis Tribune. August 16, 1951. V. 23, N. 37, p. 6.

7.   IBID

8.   Hoel, J. (2002). Personal Communication(Email). July 15.

9.   "Bill Tuman Sets New Record On Fast Track At Motorcycle Races Here Sunday!" Sturgis Tribune. August 16, 1951. V. 23, N. 37, p. 1.

10. Kretz, E. (2002). Personal Interview. August 16.

11. "Two Hundred Sixty Riders Register For Gypsy Tour, Classics Queen Chosen." Sturgis Tribune. August 16, 1951. V. 23, N. 37, p. 6.

12. "Bill Tuman Sets New Record On Fast Track At Motorcycle Races Here Sunday!" Sturgis Tribune. August 16, 1951. V.23, N.37, p. 8.

Bill Tuman

1.   Tuman, B. (2002). Personal Interview. Davenport, Iowa. September 30.

2.   "Bill Tuman" amadirectlink.com/museum/halloffamer/ members/tuman.

3.   Tuman, B. (2002). Personal Interview. Davenport, Iowa. September 30.

4.   IBID.

5.   "Bill Tuman" amadirectlink.com/museum/halloffamer/ members/tuman.

6.   Tuman, B. (2002). Personal Interview. Davenport, Iowa. September 30

7.   "Bill Tuman" amadirectlink.com/museum/halloffamer/ members/tuman.

1952

1.   "Sturgis Will Host Five Mile National Championship Motorcycle Race". Sturgis Tribune. July 24, 1952. V.24, N. 34, p. 1.

2.   "Motor Maids Of America To Hold Convention With Motorcycle Races." Sturgis Tribune. July 31, 1952. V. 24, N. 35, p. 1.

3.   IBID.

4.   Dot Robinson. amadirectlink.com/museum/halloffame/ members/robinson

5.   "Sturgis Will Host Five Mile National Championship Motorcycle Race". Sturgis Tribune. July 24, 1952. V.24, N. 34, p. 1.

6.   "Cyclists From All Over America Will Take Part In Gypsy Tour This Week". Sturgis Tribune. August 7, 1952. V. 24, N. 36, p. 1.

7.   "Betty Dimmit, Bell Garden, California, Queen Of The 1952 Motor Classics(sic)". Sturgis Tribune. August 14, 1952. V. 24, N. 36, p. 1.

8.   "Estimated Crowd of 7500 See Brashear Win Five Mile National Sunday Afternoon". Sturgis Tribune. August 14, 1952. V. 24, N. 36, p. 1.

9.   IBID.

Everett Brashear

1.   Brashear, E. (2003). Personal Communication. January 12.

2.   Whittinghill, R. (2002) "Low Profile: Everett Brashear" Vintage Vignettes. ahrma.org/vignette.html. May 8, p.2.

3.   Hultmann, N. (2002) Personal Interview. Pierre, SD April 28.

4.   Whittinghill, R. (2002) "Low Profile: Everett Brashear" Vintage Vignettes. ahrma.org/vignette.html. May 8, p.3.

5.   AMA Motorcycle Hall of Fame Member" ama-cycle.org/museum/halloffame/members/brashear/p. 2.

6.   Brashear, E. (2003). Personal Communication. January 12.

7.   AMA Motorcycle Hall of Fame Member" ama-cycle.org/museum/halloffame/members/brashear/p.3.

8.   Brashear, E. (2003). Personal Communication January 12.

Harley Davidson

1.   Harley Davidson Motorcycles.tower.org/museum/ harley_davidson.html. P.1

2.   Harley Davidson History. flash.net/*mcclndon/ history.html. P. 1

3.   Harley Davidson Motorcycles.tower.org/museum/ harley_davidson.html. P. 2.

4.   Harley Davidson History. flash.net/*mcclndon/ history.html. P. 1

5.   IBID

6.   IBID

7.   IBID

8.   "Mark Brelsford's 1972 Harley Davidson XR750" Motorcycle Hall of Fame; The Classics. ama-cycle.org/ musuem/1999/classep.html

1953

1.   Hultmann, N. (2002) Personal Interview. Sturgis, SD April 28, 2002

2.   "Tuman Takes 200 Mile National At Dodge City" Sturgis Tribune, July 9, 1953, V. 25, N. 32, p. 1

3.   "Gypsy Tour Will Open Motor Classics; Hundreds of Riders Will Visit Hills Attractions" Sturgis Tribune, July 30, 1953, V. 25, N. 35, p. 1

4.   "Shirley Couch, Sidney, Nebraska, Chosen As The Gypsy Tour And Race Queen" Sturgis Tribune, August 13, 1953, V. 25, N. 37, p. 1

5.   "Large Crowd See Leonard Take Five Mile National Championship Race" Sturgis Tribune, August 13, 1953, V 25, N. 37, p. 1

Joe Leonard

1.   Joe Leonard - AMA Motorcycle Hall of Fame Member. Amadirectlink.com/museum/halloffame/members/ leonard.

2. Leonard, J. (2002) Personal Interview. November 15.

3. Mann, D. and Scalzo, J. (1972) Motorcycle Ace; The Dick Mann Story.

4. Hultman, N. (2002) Personal Interview. Pierre, South Dakota, April 28.

5. Hoel, J. (2002) Personal Interview. Sturgis, South Dakota, April 30.

Rigors of Racing

1. Mann, D. (1998) "Reflections on a Racers Life." American Motorcyclist, January.

2. IBID.

3. IBID.

4. Youngblood, E. (2002) Mann of His Time Whitehorse Press. North Conway, NH. pp 43-44.

5. IBID p. 41.

6. IBID pp 45-46.

7. Hultman, N. (2002) Personal Interview. Pierre, South Dakota. April 28.

8. Youngblood, E. (2002) Mann of His Time Whitehorse Press. North Conway, NH. p. 47.

1954

1. Hultmann, N. (2002) Personal Interview. Sturgis, SD April 28.

2. "Bill Hunn, Linotyper At Tribune Injured". Sturgis Tribune. July 22,1954.V26, No. 34 P.1.

3. "Top Motorcycle Racers Will Compete In Five Mile National". Sturgis Tribune. August 5, 1954. V 26, No. 36, P. 1.

4. Hoel, J. (2002). Personal Communication June 15.

5. "Top Motorcycle Racers Will Compete In Five Mile National". Sturgis Tribune. August 5, 1954. V. 26, N. 36, P. 1.

6. www.ama-cycle.org/museum/halloffame/html.

7. IBID.

8. Hoel, J. (2002) Personal Communication. June 15.

9. "Motorcycle Polo Game To Be Played Saturday Evening". Sturgis Tribune. August 12, 1954. V 26, No. 37, P. 1.

10. "Packed Crowd See Albert Gunter, California Win Five Mile National". Sturgis Tribune. August 19. 1954. V 26. No. 38, P. 1.

11. Hoel, J. C. (1954). "Gunter Outrides 'Em All At Sturgis". American Motorcycling. V. 8, N. 9, P. 10.

12. Hoel, J. (2002). Personal Interview. Sturgis, SD. April 30

Albert Gunter

1. Keen, N. (2002) Personal Interview September 8.

2. Mann, D. with Scalzo, J. (1972) Motorcycle Ace: The Dick Mann Story. Henry Regnery: Chicago. P. 29.

3. I BID

4. Keen, N. (2002) Personal Correspondence. October 8

5. Mann, D. with Scalzo, J. (1972) Motorcycle Ace: The Dick Mann Story. Henry Regnery: Chicago. P. 32.

6. Youngblood, E. (2002). Mann of His Time. Whitehorse Press. North Conway, NH. P. 37.

7. Mann, D. (2002) Personal Interview September 8.

8. Grand National Series History (1979). American Motorcyclist. January/February. pp. 29-34.

9. Keen, N. (2002). Personal Correspondence. October 8.

Birmingham Small Arms Company

1. Youngblood, E. (2002). Mann of His Time. Whitehouse Press. North Conway, NH. pp. 22-23.

2. Klamfoth, D. (2002) Personal Interview. Sturgis, South Dakota, August 12.

3. Youngblood, E. (2002). Mann of His Time. Whitehouse Press. North Conway, NH. pp. 22-23.

4. Klamfoth, D. (2002) Personal Interview. Sturgis, South Dakota, August 12.

5. Wilson, H. (1993). The Ultimate Motorcycle Book. Dorling Kindersley, NY. pp. 68-69.

6. IBID.

7. IBID.

1955

1. "Entries Coming In for Motor Classic; Carnival Downtown Street". Sturgis Tribune. July 28, 1955. V 27, No.35, P. 1.

2. Motorcycle Hall of Fame, ama-cycle.org/museum/halloffame/html.

3. "Entries Coming In for Motor Classic; Carnival Downtown Street." Sturgis Tribune. July 28, 1955. V. 27, N 35, P.1

4. Cannon, J. (1955). "Hills Motorcycle Riders Active throughout Year." Rapid City Journal. August 7, 1955. P. 9.

5. IBID.

6. IBID.

7. "Black Hills Gypsy Tour Will Open Big Four Days Motor Classic Event.". Sturgis Tribune.

8. "Don Tindall, Oregon Wins Six Mile National On Wet Track Sunday" Sturgis Tribune. August 18, 1955, V 27, No. 38, P. 1

9. IBID.

Don Tindall

Based entirely on a personal interview with Don Tindall (December 7, 2002).

Bobby Hill

1.   Bobby Hill - AMA Motorcycle Hall of Fame Member amadirectlink.com/museum/halloffame/members/hill.

2.   Hill, B. (2002) Personal Interview Davenport, Iowa. August 31.

3.   IBID.

4.   IBID.

5.   IBID.

6.   Bobby Hill - AMA Motorcycle Hall of Fame Member amadirectlink.com/museum/halloffame/members/hill.

7.   Hill, B. (2002). Personal Interview. Davenport, Iowa. August 31.

8.   IBID.

Chapter Six

1956

1.   "30.3 Miles Of Interstate 90 Approved In Meade County". Sturgis Tribune. July 26, 1956, V 28, No. 35, P. 1

2.   "Public Invited To Cycle Program". Sturgis Tribune. August 9, 1956, V 28, No. 37, P. 1

3.   IBID

4.   "Large Crowd See Charlie West Of California Win Black Hills Motor Classic". Sturgis Tribune August 16, 1955, V 28, No. 38, P. 1

5.   IBID

6.   IBID P. 2

7.   IBID

1957

1.   "Motorcycle Race Meet, And Gypsy Tour Program" Sturgis Tribune. August 1, 1957. V. 29, N. 35 P. 1.

2.   IBID

3.   Hoel, J. C. (1982). Life's Bits and Pieces. Self Published. Sturgis SD p. 36

4.   "Motorcycle Race Meet, And Gypsy Tour Program". Sturgis Tribune. August 1, 1957. V. 29, N.35, P.1

5.   "Omaha Lady Named Queen Of The Classics"(sic). Sturgis Tribune. August 15, 1957. V. 29, N.38, P.1

6.   "California Motorcycle Rider Wins Class A Finals Both Saturday and Sunday". Sturgis Tribune. August 15, 1957. V.29, N.38, P.1

Joe Leonard

1.   Joe Leonard 1998 National Hall of Fame/ inductee.nationalchosen.com/hof/1998/jleanard-c98.html.

2.   "Grand National Series History". American Motorcy-clist (pull-out racing records section). January February, 1979.

3.   IBID.

4.   IBID.

5.   Leonard, J. (2002). Personal Interview. November 22.

6.   Joe Leonard National Hall of Fame/ inductee.nationalchosen.com/hof/jleonard-c98.html.

1958

1.   Hoel, J. C. (1982) Life's Bits and Pieces. Self published. Sturgis, SD.

2.   "Gypsys Sponsor Grass Track Event At Sky Ranch". Sturgis Tribune. July 10, 1958, V 30, N. 33, P. 3.

3.   "Motorcycle Races, Fair, Saturday And Sunday". Sturgis Tribune. August 7, 1958, V 30, N. 37, P. 1.

4.   "Dick Mann of California Top At Motor Classic". Sturgis Tribune. August 14, 1958, V 30, N. 38, P. 1.

5.   Distance amasuperbike.com/dayinfor/distance.htm.

6.   "George Roeder, Hall of Fame Museum." amacycle.org/ forms/museum/hofbiopage.asp?

Dick Mann

1.   Mann, D. (1972). Motorcycle Ace: The Dick Mann Story. Henry Regnery Company, Chicago. P. 7.

2.   IBID

3.   Youngblood, E. (2002). Mann of His Time. White Horse Press. North Conway, NH. P. 34.

4.   I BID. p. 37.

5.   "Dick Mann" AMA Motorcycles Hall of Fame Member. amadirtlink.com/museum/halofffame/membres/mann.

George Roeder

1.   "Grand National Series history." (1979). American Motorcyclist (Pull-Out Racing Records Section). January/February.

2.   "George Roeder, AMA Hall of Fame Member." ama-cycle.org/forms/museum/hofbiopage.asp?

3.   I BID.

4.   I BID.

1959

1.   "City Prepares for Big Turnout of Top Cyclists". Sturgis Tribune. July 28, 1959. V. 31, N. 51, p. 1.

2.   "Annual Motorcycle Races This Weekend Highlight of Black Hills Attraction". Sturgis Tribune. August 4, 1959. V. 31, N. 53, p. 1.

3.   IBID.

4.   IBID p.1 "City Council Wars on Outside Privies".

5.   "Cycling Enthusiasts of All Ages Invade Sturgis for Annual Races". Sturgis Tribune. August 7, 1959. V. 31, N. 32, p.1.

6.   IBID p. 2 "A Different Attraction".

7.   "Cyclists Heading Home After Highly Successful Black Hills Motor Classic". Sturgis Tribune. August 14, 1959. V.31, N. 33, p. 1.

8.   IBID.

9.   IBID.

10.   Dick Dorrestyne amadirectlink.com/museum/
      halloffame/members/dorrestyne

Dick Klamfoth

1.   Dick Klamfoth AMA Hall of Fame Member.
      amadirectlink.com/halloffame/members/klamfoth p.1.

2.   Klamfoth, D. (2002). Personal Interview. Sturgis, South
      Dakota. August 16.

3.   Dick Klamfoth AMA Hall of Fame Member
      amadirectlink.com/halloffame/members/klamfoth.

4.   Klamfoth, D. (2002). Personal Interview. Sturgis, South
      Dakota. August 16.

5.   Flat track year by year results. amaproracing.com/
      archive/oodt.

6.   Klamfoth, D. (2002). Personal Interview. Sturgis, South
      Dakota. August 16.

1960

1.   "Annual Motor Classic Program Taking Shape." Sturgis
      Tribune. August 3, 1960. V. 32, N. 29, P. 1.

2.   Hutlman, N. (2002). Personal interview. Pierre, SD.
      April 28.

3.   "20th Annual Motorcycle Races Saturday-Sunday."
      Sturgis Tribune. August 10, 1960. V. 32, N. 30. P. 1.

4.   IBID.

5.   IBID.

6.   "Highway 24 Becomes State Route 34; Only Non-
      Federal East-West Highway." Sturgis Tribune. August
      10, 1960. V. 32, N. 30, P. 1.

7.   Moore, B. (2002). Personal Interview. Sturgis, SD. May
      1.

8.   Hultman, N. (2002). Personal Interview. Pierre, SD.
      April 28.

9.   "Sturgis Site of National Cycle Races." Rapid City
      Journal. August 5, 1960. N. 24409, p. 14

10.   "More Than 400 Cyclists at Sturgis." Rapid City
      Journal. August 12, 1960. N. 24417, P. 14

11.   Rogers, P. (1960). "Sturgis Races 2nd Day." Rapid City
      Journal. August 14, 1960. N. 24418, P 29

12.   "Sturgis Cycle Event; Michigan Racer Wins Top
      Honors." Rapid City Journal. August 15, 1960. N.
      24419, P 13.

13.   Bart Markel Motorcycle Hall of Fame. ama-cycle.org/
      museum/halloffame/markel.

14.   Gary Nixon Motorcycle Hall Of Fame. ama-cycle.org/
      museum/halloffame/nixon.

Bart Markel

1.   Bart Markel, Hall of Fame Member. amacycle.org/
      museum/halloffame/members/markel.

2.   Markel, B. (2003). Personal Interview. January 4.

3.   "Grand National Series History". American
      Motorcyclist (Special Pull-out Section). January-
      February 1979.

4.   Markel, B. (2002). Personal Correspondence.
      December 27.

5.   "Grand National Series History." American Motorcyclist
      (Special Pull-out section). January-February.

6.   IBID.

7.   Bart Markel, Hallof Fame Member. ama-cycle.org/
      museum/halloffame/members/markel

Chapter Seven

1961

1.   "21st Annual Motorcycle Races Successful Event".
      Sturgis Tribune. August 16, 1961. V.33, N.31, P. 1.

2.   IBID.

3.   IBID.

4.   IBID. P. 6.

5.   Motorcycle Hall of Fame Museum. ama-cycle.org/
      museum/halloffame/html.

6.   "21st Annual Motorcycle Races Successful Event".
      Sturgis Tribune. August 16, 1961. V. 33, N.31, P. 6.

Gary Nixon

1.   Gary Nixon. nationalmcmuseum.com/HOF/
      1996ember.

2.   Gary Nixon. AMA National Motorcycle Hall of Fame
      Member. ama- cycle.org/museum/halloffame/members/
      nixon.

3.   IBID.

4.   Youngblood, E. (2002). Mann of His Time. Whitehouse
      Press. North Conway, NH.

5.   Gary Nixon. nationalmcmuseum.com/HOF/1996.

6.   Gary Nixon. AMA Motorcycle Hall of Fame Member.
      ama- cycle.org/museum/halloffame/members/nixon.

1962

1.   "Krazy Days, Parade and Free Baseball Tickets".
      Sturgis Tribune. July 17, 1962. V. 34, N. 27 P. 1.

2.   "$2700 Purse Divided Among Top Cyclists". Sturgis
      Tribune. August 15, 1962. V. 34. N. 31, P. 1.

3.   IBID.

4.   AMA Hall of Fame. amadirectlink.com/museum/
      halloffame/members.

5.   "$2700 Purse Divided Among Top Cyclists". Sturgis
      Tribune. August 15, 1962. V. 34, N. 31, P. 1.

Neil Keen

1.   Keen, N. (2002). Personal Communication. October 6.

2.   IBID.

3. IBID.

4. IBID.

5. IBID.

6. Mann, D. (2002). Personal Communication. September 17.

7. Keen, N. (2003). Personal Communication. January 14.

8. Keen, N. (2002). Personal Communication. October 6.

9. IBID.

Ronnie Rall

1. Ronnie Rall, AMA Hall of Fame Member. ama-cycle.org/forms/museum/hofbiopage.asp?

2. IBID.

3. "$2700 Purse Divided Among Top Cyclists." Sturgis Tribune. August 15, 1962. V.34, N. 31, P. 1.

4. Estep, D. (2003). Personal Communication. January 21.

5. IBID.

6. IBID.

7. "Grand National Series History." (1979). American Motorcyclist (Pull-Out Racing Records Section). January/February.

8. Ronnie Rall, AMA Hall of Fame Member. ama-cycle.org/forms/museum/hofbiopage.asp?

9. IBID.

10. IBID.

Sammy Tanner

Totally based on a personal Interview with Sammy Tanner.

1963

1. "Motorcycle Classic Honors Old Timers" Sturgis Tribune July 31, 1963. V. 35, N. 29, P. 1.

2. Hoel, J.C (1973). "Bits and Pieces of My Life." Road Rider. July, 1973. V. 8, N. 7, P. 27.

3. "Motorcycle Enthusiasts Converge City for Annual Motor Classic" Sturgis Tribune. August 7, 1963. V. 35, N. 30, P. 1.

4. AGA, M.C. (1963). "Sturgis Hosts Record-Breaking Crowds at Annual Motorcycle Event." Rushmore Ads. August 14, 1963. P. 4.

5. IBID.

6. IBID.

7. AGA, M.C. (1963). "Cycle Event in Final Day; Californians Lead the Way." Rapid City Journal. August 11, 1963. N. 25496, P. 15.

8. AGA, M.C. (1963). "Sturgis Hosts Record-Breaking Crowds at Annual Motorcycle Event." Rushmore Ads. August 14, 1963. P 4.

9. IBID.

Bob Moore

1. Hall of Fame Induction Breakfast (2002). Program, Sturgis Motorcycle Museum and Hall of Fame Inc. August 7, 2002.

2. Hultmann, N. (2002) Personal interview. April 28, 2002.

The Assault at Bear Butte

1. Hoel, J.C. (1982) Life's Bits and Pieces Self Published, Sturgis SD pp. 59-63

1964

1. "National Top Cyclists Descend on Sturgis For Annual Races Saturday, Sunday" Sturgis Tribune August 12, 1964 v. 36 n. 31, p. 1.

2. IBID.

3. "Illinois Rider Takes Top Money In Annual Races Here" Sturgis Tribune August 19, 1964 v. 36 n. 32 p. 1.

Babe DeMay

1. Tuman, B. (2002). Personal Communication. (Email). December 8.

2. Everythig else based on interviews with Babe DeMay.

1965

1. "Annual Black Hills Motor Classic Gets Underway" Sturgis Tribune, August 11, 1965 v. 37 n. 30 p. 1.

2. IBID.

3. IBID. p. 2.

4. IBID.

5. "This Year's Classic Really Successful' Too" Sturgis Tribune, August 18, 1965 v. 37 n. 31 p. 1.

6. "This Years Classic Really Successful' Too" Sturgis Tribune. August 18, 1965. v. 37 n.31 p. 6.

7. "Highly Successful" (Editorial) Sturgis Tribune August 18, 1965 v. 37 n. 31 p. 2.

Babe DeMay

1. Keen, N. (2002). Personal Correspondence. October 6.

2. Hoel, J. (2002) Personal Interview. Sturgis, SD March 25.

Phil Town

1. "Phil Town Opened For Business" Sturgis Tribune July 7, 1965. V. 32, v. 26, p. 1

Chapter Eight

Motor Maids

1. "History of Women's Motorcycling Organization Told To Rotarians". Sturgis Tribune. July 6, 1966. V. 33, N. 20, P. 1.

2.   IBID.

3.   "Women Cyclists Converge Here For Convention".
     Sturgis Tribune. July 6, 1966. V. 33, N. 20, P. 1

4.   IBID.

5.   IBID P. 2

6.   "Welcome Motormaids" Sturgis Tribune. July 6, 1966.
     V. 33, N. 20, P.

1966

1.   "Reward Offered For Motorcycle Clubhouse Vandals."
     Sturgis Tribune. July 13, 1966. V.38, N.21, p. 1.

2.   Hultman, N. (2002) Personal Interview. Sturgis, SD
     March 26.

3.   "Extended Motor Classic Gets Underway Here; Devil's
     Tower Tour Kicks Off Five-Day Event." Sturgis Tribune.
     August 10, 1966. V. 38, N. 25, p. 1-2A

4.   I BID.

5.   IBID.

6.   IBID.

7.   IBID.

8.   "Big Crowds See Classic Final." Sturgis Tribune. August
     17, 1966 V. 38, N. 26, p. 1.

Dick Mann's National Career Part One

1.   Grand National Series History. (1979). The American
     Motorcyclist. January-February.

2.   I BID.

3.   I BID.

4.   Dick Mann-AMA Motorcycle Hall of Fame Member.
     Amadirectlink.com/museum/halloffame/number/mann.

5.   I BID.

1967

1.   "Record Number of Cyclists Expected "Sturgis Tribune.
     August 2, 1967. V. 39, N. 24, P. 1.

2.   IBID.

3.   IBID.

4.   IBID.

5.   "Gypsy Tour Kicks Off Annual Classic." Sturgis Tribune.
     August 9, 1967. V. 39, N. 25, P. 1.

6.   "1000 Cyclists Pump Estimated $150,000 into Local
     Economy During Five-Day Classic". Sturgis Tribune.
     August 16, 1967. V. 39, N. 26, P. 1.

7.   IBID.

8.   IBID.

9.   IBID.

10. IBID.

1968

1.   "Volunteers Needed For Classic". Sturgis Tribune. July
     31, 1968. V.40, N.24, P. 1.

2.   "Sturgis Becomes Cycle City Again". Sturgis Tribune.
     Aug. 7, 1968. V.40, N.25, P.1.

3.   IBID.

4.   "Capacity Crowd Watches Classic Wind-Up". Sturgis
     Tribune. August 14, 1968. V. 40, N.26, P.1.

5.   IBID

6.   IBID.

Dick Mann's National Career Part Two

1.   Youngblood, E. (2002). Mann of His Time. Whitehorse
     Press. New Conroy, NH. P. 153.

2.   IBID. P. 154.

3.   IBID. P. 155.

4.   IBID. P. 222

1969

1.   "Sturgis Welcomes You to the 29th Annual Motorcycle
     Rally Races." Sturgis Tribune. August 6, 1969. V. 41, N.
     25, P. 6.

2.   "No Trouble Here During Classic." Sturgis Tribune.
     August 13, 1969. V. 41, N. 26, P. 1.

3.   IBID.

4.   IBID.

5.   "Keen Repeats as Top Purse Winner at Races." Sturgis
     Tribune. August 13, 1969. V. 41, N.26, P. 1.

6.   IBID.

7.   IBID.

8.   IBID.

Jack Hoel

1.   Hoel, C. (1982). Life's Bits and Pieces. Self Published,
     Sturgis SD. P. 91.

2.   IBID, P. 96.

3.   IBID, P 98.

4.   Hoel, J. (2002). Personal Interview. Sturgis, SD April
     28.

5.   IBID.

6.   Brown, R. (1996). The Encyclopedia of Motorcycles.
     Smithmark Publishers Inc. London, UK.

7.   Hoel, J. (2002). Personal Interview. Sturgis, SD April
     28.

1970

1.   "Classic Gets Underway." Sturgis Tribune. August 5,
     1970. V. 42, N.25, P.1.

2.   "Keen Takes Main Event, Top Money." Sturgis Tribune.
     August 12, 1970. V. 42. N. 26, P. 1.

3. IBID.

4. "Classic Gets Underway." Sturgis Tribune. August 5, 1970. V. 42. N. 25. P. 2.

5. IBID.

6. IBID.

7. "Keen Takes Main Event, Top Money." Sturgis Tribune. August 12, 1970. V. 42, N. 26, P. 1.

8. "Classic Fan Recalls Old Welcome Sign." Sturgis Tribune. August 12, 1970. V. 42. N.26, P. 2.

9. "Keen Takes Main Event, Top Money." Sturgis Tribune. August 12, 1970. V. 42, N. 26, P. 1.

10. IBID.

11. IBID.

1971

1. "More Than 2000 Expected for Classic." Sturgis Tribune. July 28, 1971. V.42, p.1.

2. Hultmann, N. (2002) Personal Interview. Pierre, SD. April 28.

3. "More Than 2000 Expected for Classic." Sturgis Tribune. July 28, 1971. V.42, p. 1.

4. "Park Board Preparing for Cyclists." Sturgis Tribune. August 4, 1971. V. 42, p.1.

5. "Cycle City Comes Alive Again." Sturgis Tribune. August 11, 1971. V. 42, P. 2.

6. "Recent Classic 'Best Ever'." Sturgis Tribune. August 18, 1971. V. 42, p. 1.

7. IBID.

8. "Alaska Honeymooners Were Trophy Winners Here." Sturgis Tribune. August 18, 1971. V. 42, p. 2.

9. "Recent Classic 'Best Ever.'" Sturgis Tribune. August 18, 1971. V. 42, p. 1.

10. IBID.

11. IBID.

12. Motorcycle Hall of Fame Museum. www/ama-cycle.org/museum/halloffame.html.

13. "Recent Classic 'Best Ever'." Sturgis Tribune. August 18, 1971. V. 42, p. 1.

14. "Rain Lessens Fire Danger." Sturgis Tribune. August 18, 1971. V. 42, p. 1.

1972

1. "Sturgis becomes Cycle City again". Sturgis Tribune. August 9, 1972. V.43, N. 31, P. 1.

2. IBID.

3. IBID.

4. "Exciting Pro Races conclude classic". Sturgis Tribune. August 16, 1972. V.43 N. 32, P. B-1.

5. IBID.

6. IBID.

Harley Davidson XR750

1. Motorcycle Hall of Fame Museum - The Classics. ama-cycle.org/museum/2000/classapr.html.

2. Motorcycle Hall of Fame Museum - The Classics. ama-cycle.org/museum/1999/classapr.html.

1973

1. "Pacific Coast Regional Championship Races Slated for Motorcycle Classic." Sturgis Tribune. August 1, 1973. V. 43, N.29, p.1

2. IBID.

3. IBID.

4. "World's Oldest Cyclist Attends Rally Days." Sturgis Tribune. August 8, 1973. V. 43, N. 30, p.1.

5. "Mayor Proclaims Motorcycle Days." Sturgis Tribune. August 8, 1973. V. 43, N. 30, p.1.

6. "Lions Club Boasts Sight Conservation." Sturgis Tribune (Photo Caption). August 8, 1973, V. 43, N. 30, p. 6.

7. "A Classic Story — Races Draw Big Again." Sturgis Tribune. August 15, 1973. V. 43, N. 31, pp. B 4-5

8. IBID.

9. IBID.

Sonny Burres

Totally based on an interview manuscript provided to the author by D. Hagen.

1974

1. Hultman, N. (2002). Personal Interview. Pierre, SD. April 28.

2. Hays, G. (1974) "The Black Hills Rally." Rider. V. 1, N.2, Fall.

3. "Classic Action Swings to Short Track Races' Hordes of Motorcyclists Invade 'Cycle City' Again." Sturgis Tribune. August 7, 1974. V. 44, N. 30, p.1.

4. IBID.

5. IBID.

6. "Nationally-Ranked Racers to Compete Here For Pacific Coast Regional Championships." Sturgis Tribune. August 7, 1974. V. 44, N. 30, p. 1

7. "Big Crowd Views Classic Windup." Sturgis Tribune. August 14, 1974. V. 44, N. 31, p. B-1

1975

1. "Short Track Races Hold Spotlight." Sturgis Tribune. August 6, 1975. V. 36. N. 30. P. B-1.

2. IBID. P. 1.

3. IBID.

4. IBID.

5. "Ohioan Gets New Track Record; Texas Racer Paces Expert Field in Cycle Competition Windup." Sturgis Tribune. August 13, 1975. V. 36. N. 31. P. B-1.

6. IBID.

7. Motorcycle Hall of Fame Museum ama-cycle.org/museum/halloffame/html.

8. "Ohioan Gets New Track Record; Texas Racer Paces Expert Field in Cycle Competition Windup." Sturgis Tribune. August 13, 1975. V. 36. N. 31. P. B-1.

9. Motorcycle Hall of Fame Museum ama-cycle.org/museum/halloffame/html.

10. "Short Track Races Hold Spotlight." Sturgis Tribune. August 6, 1975. V. 36. N. 30. P. B-2.

Mike Kidd

1. Kidd, M. (2002). Personal Correspondence. December 10.

2. IBID.

3. IBID.

4. IBID.

5. "Grand National Series History." American Motorcyclist (Pull Out Racing Records Section). January-February 1979.

6. Kidd, M. (2002). Personal Correspondence. December 10.

1976

1. "Record Number of Cyclists Having a 'Hail of a Time' Here." Sturgis Tribune. August 11, 1976. V. 37, N. 41. P. 1-2.

2. "18,000 Cyclists Expected for Classic." Sturgis Tribune. July 28, 1976. V. 37, N. 39, P. 1.

3. "Governor, Skydivers to Be Featured During Motor Classic Event." Sturgis Tribune. August 4, 1976. V. 37, N. 40, P 1.

4. "Motocross Opens 36th Rally, Races." Rushmore News. August 11, 1976. V. 41, N. 3, P 1.

5. "Record Number of Cyclists Having a 'Hail of a Time' Here." Sturgis Tribune. August 11, 1976. V. 37, N. 41. P. 1-2.

6. "Motocross Opens 36th Rally, Races." Rushmore News, August 11 1976. V.41, N. 3, P. 1.

7. IBID.

8. IBID.

9. "Another Record Crowd." Sturgis Tribune. (Editorial) August 11, 1976. V. 37, N. 41, P. 2.

10. Hultman, R. and Kniffen, A. (2002). Personal communication. July 10.

11. Motorcycle Hall of Fame. ama-cycle.org/museum/halloffame/html.

12. "Races Are Close in 'Expert' Class of Classic Finals." Sturgis Tribune. August 18, 1976. V. 37, N. 42, P. B-1.

13. IBID.

14. IBID.

15. "City Council Takes No Action on Plea to Halt Annual Motor Classic." Sturgis Tribune. August 18, 1976. V. 37, N. 42, P. 1.

16. "From Our Readers: COMMENT." Sturgis Tribune. August 18, 1976. V. 37, N. 42, P 2.

17. "Let's Not Panic." Sturgis Tribune. August 18, 1976. V. 37, N. 42, P. B-1.

Randy Goss

1. Wood, B. (1999). "Legends of the Mile". American Motorcyclist. January. P. 27.

2. amaproracing.com/archive/00dt/FTYRXYR/GRNATYR/YR.HTM.

3. IBID.

4. IBID.

5. Randy Goss. Nascar.com/drivers/ccps/rgoss00.

6. Goss, V. (2002). Personal Correspondence. December 30.

Lawson

1. American Motorcycle Hall of Fame: Eddie Lawson. ama-cycle. org/museum/halloffame/members/lawson/index.asp

2. IBID

3. IBID

1977

1. "Black Hills Classic Officials Expect Attendance This Year Will Be 'Bigger Than Ever'." Sturgis Tribune. August 3, 1977. V. 38, N. 40, P. 3 (Insert).

2. "Recreation, Camping Issues Confront City." Sturgis Tribune. August 3, 1977. V. 38, N. 40, P. 1.

3. IBID.

4. "Black Hills Classic Officials Expect Attendance This Year Will Be 'Bigger Than Ever'." Sturgis Tribune. August 3, 1977. V. 38, N. 40, P. 3 (Insert).

5. IBID.

6. "Annual Motor Classic Here Off To a Wet Start." Sturgis Tribune. August 10, 1977. V. 38, N. 41, P. 1.

7. IBID. P.2.

8. "Professionals Wrap Up Classic With Sunday Championship Event." Sturgis Tribune. August 17, 1977. V. 38, N. 42, P. 1.

9. "Ricky Graham-AMA Motorcycle Hall of Fame Member." ama-cycle.org/museum/halloffame/members/graham.

10. ama-cycle.org/museum/halloffame.html.

11. Professionals Wrap Up Classic With Sunday Championship Event." Sturgis Tribune. August 17, 1977. V. 38, N. 42, P. 1.

12. IBID. P. A-2

Keith Ulicki

All based on Personal Interview

Rick Graham

1. "Ricky Graham-AMA Hall of Fame Member." ama-cycle.org/museum/halloffame/members/graham.

1978

1. "Annual Classic Underway; Racing Now in Spot Light." Sturgis Tribune. August 9, 1978. V. 40, N. 40, P. 1.

2. "Six Cyclists Killed in State Accidents." Rushmore Ads News. August 16, 1978. P. 1.

3. "Hectic Classic Week Ends on Sad Note; Death Toll Up." Sturgis Tribune. August 16, 1978. V. 40, N. 41, P. 1.

4. "Cyclists Fined Heavily on Alternate Charge; Off Designated Road." Black Hills Press. August 12, 1978. V. 80, N. 47, P. 1.

5. "Five Road Deaths Mar Annual Motorcycle Rally." Black Hills Press. August 12, 1978. V. 80, N. 47, P. 1.

6. "Cyclists Fined Heavily on Alternate Charge; Off Designated Road." Black Hills Press. August 12, 1978. V. 80, N. 47, P. 2.

7. "87 Year-Old Cyclist Attending 29th Classic; Reports He Doesn't Want to Miss Anything." Sturgis Tribune. August 9, 1978. V. 40, N. 40, P. 1.

8. "Sturgis is 'Cycle City' During 38th Motor Classic." Black Hills Press. August 5, 1978. V. 80, N. 46, P. 2.

9. "Racing Now in Spotlight." Sturgis Tribune. August 9, 1978. V. 40, N. 40, P. 1.

10. "Five Road Deaths Mar Annual Motorcycle Rally." Black Hills Press. August 12, 1978. V. 80, N. 47, P. 1.

11. "Classic Ends With Championship Race; Bikers Return Home." Sturgis Tribune. August 16, 1978. V. 40, N. 41, P. B-1.

12. ama-cycle.org/museum/halloffame/members/html.

13. "Five Road Deaths Mar Annual Motorcycle Rally." Black Hills Press. August 12, 1978. V. 80, N. 47, P. 1.

14. IBID.

15. IBID.

16. "COMMENT: Stop Exaggerating!" (Editorial) Sturgis Tribune. August 9, 1978. V. 40, N. 40, P. A-3.

17. "Sturgis . . . . . Again?" (Editorial) Rushmore Ads News. August 10, 1978.

18. IBID.

19. IBID

Poovey

1. "Flat Track Championship Series" (2001) amaproracing.com/archive/(Zeroes)/FTRIDERS/FTBIOUS/POOVEY

2. Personal Interviews

Wayne Rainey

1. "AMA Motorcycle Hall of Fame: Wayne Rainey." ama-cycle.org/museum/halloffame/members/rainey/index.asp.

2. IBID

1979

1. Theil, B. (1979) "Proposed budget, Motorcycle Classic, possible circus occupy Sturgis Park Board here Tuesday." Sturgis Tribune. July 25,1979. V.41, N. 37, P. 1.

2. Crider, J. (1979) "Police do not expect violent Cycle Classic." Sturgis Tribune. August 1, 1979. V. 41, N. 38, P. 1.

3. IBID.

4. IBID.

5. "Cycle Shirts is back in town; praises people, food and rooms." Sturgis Tribune (Special Rally Edition). August 1, 1979. P. 5.

6. Steward, D. (2002). "Jackpine Gypsies assist Classic; expect 20,000 cyclists this year." Sturgis Tribune (Special Rally Edition). August 1,1979. P. 6.

7. "Sturgisites open their home to some visiting enthusiasts" Meade County Times-Tribune (Special Edition). August 9, 1979. P. 5.

8. "Churches, seniors feed motorcyclists." Meade County Times-Tribune (Special Edition). August 9, 1979. P. 6.

9. Leonard, P. R. (1979) "Transient merchants outraged by City fee." Black Hills Press. August 11, 1979. V. 81, N. 47, P. 1.

10. IBID.

11. "Classic prize money is more than $10,000." Sturgis Tribune (Special Rally Edition). August 1, 1979. P. 6.

12. "Rally sponsors urge bikers to wear helmets." Sturgis Tribune. August 8, 1979. V. 41, N. 39, P. 1-2.

13. "Welcome cyclists." Sturgis Tribune. August 8, 1979. V. 41, N. 39, P. 4.

14. "Registration, road tours only part of headquarters activity." Sturgis Tribune. August 9, 1979. V. 41, N. 40, P. 2.

15. Larmon, L. (1979) "German ships bike to U.S., writes guide book on trip." Sturgis Tribune. August 15, 1979. V. 41, N. 40, P. A-2.

16. "English family plans vacation around Motorcycle Classic." Sturgis Tribune. August 15 , 1979. V. 41, N. 40, P. A-3.

17. Shoemaker, D. (1979). "Beach,Yamaha are big winners in Thursday night Short Track races." Black Hills Press. August 11, 1979. V. 81, N. 47, P.7.

18. Shoemaker, D. (1979). "Nebraskan rides Bultacos for wins in Thursday's Amateur Hill Climb." Black Hills Press. August 11, 1979. V. 81, N. 47, P.8.

19. Jimmy Filice Motorcycle Hall of Fame. ama-cycle.org/museum/halloffame/filice.

20. "Expert driving highlights Saturdays pro half mile." Sturgis Tribune. August 15, 1979. V. 41, N. 40, P. A-4.

21. "Expert driving highlights Saturdays Pro half mile." Sturgis Tribune. August 15, 1979. V. 41, N. 40, P. A-4.

22. "Washington biker takes Jr. Pro short track win." Sturgis Tribune. August 15, 1979. V. 41, N. 40, P. A-5.

23. "Restart helps Colorado biker to win in Classic Pro event." Sturgis Tribune. August 15, 1979. V. 41, N. 40, P. A-5.

24. IBID.

Keener

1. Keener, C. (2002). Personal Interview. December 17.

2. "Grand National Series History."(1979). American Motorcyclist. (Pull-Out Racing Records Section) January/February

3. Keener, C. (2002). Personal Interview. December 17.

1980

1. Hultman, Neil (2002). Personal interview, Pierre, SD, April 28.

2. "Jackpine Gypsies Celebrate 43 Years of Cycle Activity." Black Hills Press. August 2, 1980. p. 5.

3. "Classic Group Sponsors Half Mile Professional Race." Black Hills Press. August 2, 1980. p. 6.

4. Creed, D. (1980) "Quiet Classic Breaking Attendance Records." Meade County times-Tribune. August 6, 1980. V.50, N.30, p.1.

5. IBID.

6. Creed, R. (1980). "Out-of States Are Dominating Sturgis Dust Bowl Motocross." Meade County Times-Tribune. August 6, 1980. V. 50, N. 30, p. B-1.

7. Creed, D. (1980). "Raced Could Have Brought Nearly $1 Million." Meade County Times-Tribune. August 13, 1980. V. 50, N. 31, p. 1.

8. IBID.

9. IBID.

10. IBID. p. 2.

11. "Cyclist Came From Around the World to Main Street and the Park, But Not to the Races." Meade County Times-Tribune. August 13, 1980. V. 50, N. 31, p. 1.

12. IBID.

13. Davis, l. (1980). "Church Groups Cash In." Meade County Times-Tribune. August 13, 1980. V. 50, N. 31, p. 5-A.

14. Creed, R. (1908). "Amateur Hillclimb is Popular Event." Meade County Times-Tribune. August 13, 1980. V. 50, N. 31, p. 8-A.

15. Creed, R. (1980). "Scott Wines Novice Short Track." Meade County Times-Tribune. August 16, 1980. V. 50, N. 31, p. 8-A.

16. Creed, R. (1980). "Stars of the Classic Crown, the Half-Mile Flat Trackers." Meade County Times-Tribune. August 13, 1980. V. 50, N. 31, p. B-1.

17. Creed, R. (1980). "Team Honda Cuts Loose at Expert Short Track." Meade County Times-Tribune. August 13, 1980. V. 50, N. 31, p. B-1.

18. IBID.

19. Creed, R. (1980). "Hill Thunders to Top Fuel Win." Meade County Times-Tribune. August 13, 1980. V. 50, N. 31, p. B-1.

Neil Hultman

Rogerson, K. (2002. Personal Communication. December 16.

Chapter 11

1. Hill, B. (2002). Personal Interview, Davenport, Iowa. September 30.

2. Davidson, W.G. (2002) 100 Years of Harley Davidson. Bullfinch Press: Boston p. 141.

3. IBID, p. 143.

4. IBID.

5. Leonard, J. (2002). Personal Communication. November 12..

6. Thomas, W. I. (1923) The Unadjusted Girl. Little Brown and Co. New York/Boston.

7. IBID.

8. Kannenberg, K. (2002). Personal Communication. Minneapolis, Minnesota. December 6.

9. IBID.

10. Youngblood, E. (2002). Mann of His Time. Whitehouse Press. North Conway, NH. P. 171.

11. IBID. P. 173.

12. IBID. P. 171.

13. IBID. P. 174.

14. Hultman, N. (2002). Personal Communication. November 29.

15. Hultman, N. (2002). Personal Communication. December 21.